Francis Joseph
and the Italians
1849–1859

Francis Joseph

and the Italians

1849–1859

William A. Jenks

University Press of Virginia

Charlottesville

THE UNIVERSITY PRESS OF VIRGINIA
Copyright © 1978 by the Rector and Visitors
of the University of Virginia

First published 1978

Library of Congress Cataloging in Publication Data
Jenks, William Alexander, 1918–
   Francis Joseph and the Italians, 1849–1859

  Bibliography: p. 197
  Includes index.
  1. Austria—Foreign relations—Italy.
2. Italy—Foreign relations—Austria.
3. Austria—History—1848–1867.
4. Italy—History—1849–1870. 5. Franz Joseph I,
Emperor of Austria, 1830–1916. I. Title.
DB49.I7J46   943.6'04   78–5727
ISBN 0–8139–0758–6

Printed in the United States of America

To

Rifa'at A. Abou-el-Haj
J. Bowyer Bell
David D. Bien
Frederic B. M. Hollyday
Robert O. Paxton
Henry A. Turner, Jr.
James A. Vann III

allievi, autori, amici

Contents

Francis Joseph
and the Italians
1849–1859

The Austrian Presence
in Italy, 1815–1848

THE victors who met in Vienna in 1814–15 proposed to contain forever, if possible, the expansionist tendencies of France and to limit the ideology and reformism which French armies and Bonaparte had carried to much of the continent of Europe. Thanks to Metternich's prestige and to the Austrian domination of Lombardy and Tuscany before 1789, the Habsburgs were to be the chief sentinels in Italy against a Gallic resurgence. No one really expected the house of Savoy, rewarded with Genoa for its years of exile, to be capable of more than a token resistance.

The stakes in the peninsula were considerable. The French had planted liberty trees in their early occupations and had diffused rather broad concepts of liberty and equality during the imperial period. The army of the kingdom of Italy had reduced the old Italian preoccupation with municipalism by placing Milanese, Venetians, and Anconans under the same banner. Romans under Napoleon himself and Neapolitans under Murat, if less conscious of their Italianism, directly experienced the end of feudalism, the introduction of new law codes, the reduction of the church's property, and the consequent changes in society. Only Victor Emmanuel I of Piedmont seemed to believe that he could wipe out all that had changed.

Legitimacy also had its limits when the great powers conferred on frontiers. Austria reacquired Venetia as the lesser part of the kingdom of Lombardy-Venetia, and a Habsburg-Lorraine in the person of Ferdinand III returned as grand duke of Tuscany. Another Austrian archduke, son of the Este heiress, became Francis IV of Modena. Marie Louise, daughter of the Austrian emperor, Francis I, took up residence in ducal Parma. Ferdinand IV of Naples, who was but Ferdinand III of Sicily, simplified matters by assuming the title of Ferdinand I of the Two Sicilies. His properties were intact, as were those of another Bourbon, María Luisa of Lucca. More, the Austrians had guaranteed the defense of the more distant Bourbon

state as long as the king did not make changes that would affront
Vienna's principles. The highly respected Pius VII won the plaudits
of his subjects as he made his way back to Rome. The temporal
power was secure, and the powers assigned Austria the task of gar-
risoning the citadels of Ferrara, Piacenza, and Comacchio as a curb
upon those who might be subversive. The disappearance of Venice
and Genoa as independent entities was a reminder that even patri-
cian republicanism had become unfashionable.

The Habsburgs had won more than acceptable marks for their
administration of Lombardy in the eighteenth century. Their officials, however, were not disposed to scrap much that the French
had accomplished after 1797, and Cavaliere Massimo Taparelli
d'Azeglio and Stendhal vied in their praise of Milan's pleasant atmosphere. Austrian law replaced Napoleon's, save for commercial
cases, but the citizen knew he could expect fair and precise treatment in court, if not dispatch. The Josephinian tradition kept the
clergy under control, and those who had invested in confiscated
church lands were recognized as the legal possessors thereof. A new
Monte shouldered the Lombard and Venetian share of the old kingdom's debt, but the world of business soon deduced that a dispro-
portionate share of the new kingdom's income disappeared beyond
the Alps in the unending struggle to offset the imperial deficit. The
imposition of a prohibitive system of tariffs stimulated industrial advance. Those merchants whom it frustrated were somewhat molli-
fied by the abolition of the barrier between Lombardy and Venetia
in 1822. There was less applause when duties were no longer collected on the goods coming from or going to the rest of the
Habsburg monarchy (1825). The ironmaster was in trouble, but the
silk producer would profit.

Taxes and conscription provoked groans as they had under the
previous regime. If few men were taken, the transfer of more than
half of them to lands where Italian was unknown did nothing for
their morale. To garrison the cisalpine territories, Vienna primarily
relied on Germans, Croats, and Magyars. *Divide et impera* was a
policy that usually worked. To soften the impact of financial
assessments, the emperor's councillors permitted the convocation of
two central congregations in the respective capitals of Milan and
Venice. Representing the direct taxpayers and chosen by the em-

peror, they gave advice on the apportionment and administration of funds not fixed by law but decreed by the government. Similar assemblies met in the seventeen provinces and in the communes. No one was left in doubt that the two governors, the commander-in-chief of the military, and the director of police were the chief arbiters of policy. Their disciplined bureaucracy fulfilled their directives with a minimum of the disorder that affected most Italian states, though the custom of referring the most insignificant of decisions to Vienna caused delay. Under such paternalism a network of roads that was one of Europe's best continued to expand, though there was reason to lament the slackness in railway construction.

The Austrian decision to offer a milieu in which noble and bourgeois might pursue their legitimate concerns withstood the challenges of the first wave of postwar revolutionaries. Inspired by the Spanish upheaval of 1820, a coalition of Carbonari, Muratists, and liberals frightened Ferdinand of the Two Sicilies into granting in July 1820 an adaptation of the Spanish constitution of 1812. He thereby violated his treaty with Austria, and Metternich notified the Italian courts that his emperor deemed himself to be the protector of tranquillity in all of the peninsula. The great powers were not impressed and Ercole Cardinal Consalvi, the papal secretary of state, was decisively contrary to an Austrian march across the Patrimony of Saint Peter.

Time and a treaty were on Metternich's side. Tsar Alexander I was shocked by the mutiny of a prized regiment in St. Petersburg, and Louis XVIII of France was uncomfortable that Sicilians and Neapolitans would have greater freedoms than did his subjects. Prussia believed that the treaty which bound Vienna and Naples should be enforced. The English prated of nonintervention, but privately they admitted that Ferdinand's complaint that the constitution had been forced upon him warranted an Austrian expedition. At the Congress of Ljubljana the conservative powers faced no open French and English opposition when they assigned Metternich the duty of restoring the Bourbon absolutism. General Johann Count Frimont breached the Po on February 4, 1821, and his troops were in Naples on March 23.

In Turin less than realistic plotters had decided that Piedmont and Lombardy might be revolutionized while the bulk of the

Austrian forces were busy in the south. In the process they expected to wrest a constitution from Victor Emmanuel I or to replace him with his reputedly pliable heir presumptive once removed, Charles Albert. The night of March 9–10, 1821, the insurrectionists seized the citadel at Alessandria and suborned the garrison. The king wavered, then abdicated without naming as successor his ultra-conservative brother, Charles Felix, who was temporarily away from the capital. Charles Albert served as regent while the only man Europe was likely to recognize as the legitimate king issued from Modena a prohibition of all innovations. To the monarchs and statesmen still assembled at Ljubljana, Charles Felix sent a call for help. The tsar promised 100,000 men if the Austrians could not crush the revolt, a statement which alarmed the English and galled Metternich. On April 9, Habsburg troops occupied Alessandria while loyalists cleared Turin of the small number of conspirators.

How long could Metternich count on the inert masses, on an inflexible prelacy, and on the liberal-conservative division within bureaucracy and military to blunt the force of nationalism in the Italian principalities? At the Congress of Verona in 1822 he revived without success the idea of an Italian league under Austrian auspices, nor did his support of a Modenese plan to establish a central office for police controls escape Tuscan and papal vetoes. Charles Felix secured the retirement of the Austrian forces from Piedmont in 1823, but it was only in 1827 that Francis I of the Two Sicilies decided to allow the imperial regiments to leave his domain. There was evidence that the dissatisfactions which had erupted in Piedmont and Naples were not absent from Vienna's own Italian preserves. Months of careful investigation ended in the arrest of several dozen notables, including Count Federico Confalonieri and Silvio Pellico. Thirteen received death sentences in May 1821, but the Austrian emperor asked for an estimate of Lombard repercussions should he sign the decrees. Apprised of the probability of unfavorable reactions, he commuted the punishment to rigorous imprisonment. The most infamous of the cages was the Spielberg in Moravia, whose harsh regime Pellico would dramatize in *Le mie prigioni* of 1832.

After 1821, incendiary activity was muted for a decade. Metternich deplored the mildness of the Tuscan controls and yet compelled the Two Sicilies to cashier a minister of police whose actions appalled General Frimont and the Austrian ambassador. He kept an eye on Francis IV, whose dreams of winning a more prestigious crown reinforced the chancellor's verdict that Modena was "a bad government, avaricious, intractable." In Piedmont, Charles Felix first forced Charles Albert to expiate his flirtation with liberalism by joining in the French reduction of the Spanish insurgents and then to swear that he would never tamper with the institutions he would inherit. When Emperor Francis visited Genoa in 1825, the Piedmontese ruler communicated to him the text of Charles Albert's promise "to be good." Charles Felix declined, however, to warm to the idea of an Italian league, a concept which Metternich advanced when sure there was no Italian ruler who might advantage himself from such a confederation.

The French revolution of 1830 and the enthronement of Louis Philippe, the son of "Philippe Egalite," was bitter news for Charles Felix of Piedmont, for his outposts in Nice and Savoy could not possibly escape some degree of infection. Vienna ordered Frimont to cross the Ticino should the king face internal or external danger, but the Sardinian government turned aside a direct Austrian request to take over some strongpoints. When disturbances did come in 1831, the imperial generals depended on Metternich to parry French intimations that no great power should impede the establishment of constitutionalism in Italy.

The risings of that year were much like a series of firecrackers. Almost as soon as the cardinals ended a lengthy interregnum by electing Gregory XVI on February 2, Bologna extorted a provisional commission and a civic guard from a legate who quickly decamped. Fearful that these rebels would march on Modena, Francis IV betook himself and his family to Austrian Mantua when Frimont declined to move a man out of Lombardy without a direct order from the emperor. As Modena and Reggio declared the Este rule at an end, Marie Louise found it prudent to quit Parma for Piacenza, and a dozen papal towns ratified the collapse of clerical government.

Metternich was in a rage over Frimont's dilatoriness and over the delivery of a French threat on February 24 to interfere with any power's attempt to intervene in the peninsula. He knew that a decisive number of Austrian troops were required in Galicia while Tsar Nicholas I dealt with the Poles. It was no comfort, either, to hear from Count Franz Hartig, the governor of Lombardy, that Verona, Vicenza, and Padua were not tranquil and that it was inexpedient to diminish forces in the kingdom.

But the rulers of Modena and Parma and the pope requested Austrian bayonets, and Metternich resorted to guile to disarm the French. Allusions to Bonapartist involvement with Italian radicals and a statement that Austria had no reason to mourn Charles X's government were duly assessed by Louis Philippe, a monarch of respectable intellect. By February 26 the French admitted that the emperor had the right to regard the restoration of his daughter and of Francis IV to their thrones as a "family affair." By March 13 the whitecoats were in the ducal capitals and moving on Bologna. A frantic curia begged for a cavalry column to protect Rome, but the citizens did not live up to predictions that they would seize control. By the end of the month, hopes for the "United Italian Provinces" were dead. The Austrians had marched into Bologna and Ancona while the French were still mulling over "nonintervention."

Metternich was aware that incompetence, insensitivity, and pure mulishness were factors in the ephemeral rebellions of 1831. His ambassador to the Holy See collaborated with representatives of the other great powers in formulating a memorandum to guide the papal government toward a limited laicization of the administration and a degree of popular participation in elections. Direct French pressure elicited a relatively generous act of amnesty, and in July the Austrians evacuated Bologna and Ancona. The chancellor simultaneously was concluding a secret and rather ambiguous military alliance with the new Piedmontese ruler, Charles Albert. There would be concerted action in case of an attack by the French or by the enemies of order. No term was set, and the lands guaranteed were defined as those lying "in Italy."

A renewal of agitation in the Legations for civic guards impelled Giuseppe Cardinal Albani, who had full powers there, to ask the Austrians in January 1832 to return to Bologna. The French warned they would retaliate by landing their own expeditionary force, but Feldmarschall Leutnant Josef Count Radetzky, without formal approval from Metternich, took only a week to act on Albani's request.

Within a month the French had disembarked at Ancona and ignored the pope's insistence that they depart. On April 16 a convention legitimized the French presence in the port as long as the Austrians remained at Bologna. All the powers were perturbed by the arbitrary actions of the *Centurioni*, a disreputable militia led by ultraconservatives. Metternich eventually persuaded Tommaso Cardinal Bernetti, the secretary of state, to put the hated irregulars into uniform as "Pontifical Volunteers," but their excesses continued. After long negotiations the chancellor secured a promise that the government would strip the men of their arms and retire them to the status of reservists. Even so, they continued to harass ordinary citizens, and Metternich finally resorted to intrigue to encompass Bernetti's dismissal in January 1836. Two years later, despite signs that Mazzini's "Young Italy" was infiltrating the papal domains, both Austria and France recalled their troops.

Metternich was careful to balance admonition with example in his dealings with the other Italian princes. Under Austrian pressure Francis IV issued a decree of clemency in October 1831, but it was sufficiently qualified to please very few. Marie Louise was happy to be guarded by Austrian troops and to be served by Austrians as advisers in police and financial affairs. The grand duke of Tuscany permitted a volunteer urban guard in 1831 but soon dissolved it in the face of Austrian disapproval. In 1833 the Austrian ambassador to Florence complained of Giampiero Vieusseux's *Antologia*, the most distinguished of Italian periodicals, alleging that its editor permitted odious, if indirect, insinuations against the imperial government. When Vieusseux refused to reject anonymous or initialed articles, the Tuscan administration ordered complete suppression.

Far more devastating to the Austrian image was the publication of Pellico's *Le mie prigioni* in Turin in 1832. Despite strict injunctions against its circulation in Lombardy-Venetia, the indictment of life in the Spielberg was soon a matter of conversation among the cultivated. Charles Albert made something of an example of his censor when Vienna remonstrated and ordered a pro forma confiscation that briefly inhibited the printer. The king was eager to prove that he was living up to his oath to Charles Felix, but he was careful to avoid a commitment to an Italian league, whether hinted at by Metternich or specifically proposed by Ferdinand II of the

Two Sicilies. Not inclined to tolerate competitors in the peninsula, the chancellor was gratified by Sardinia's declination of the Neapolitan suggestion.

In the Austrian domains, Hartig warned that membership in "Young Italy" or failure to report its machinations were justification for trials for high treason. In 1835, nineteen were sentenced to death, but all received prison terms instead. Earlier a general who once had served under the imperial eagles before joining the insurrectionists of 1831 also had been spared the scaffold. Metternich had no taste for political martyrdoms and hoped that the small Italian courts would follow Austrian precept. When the new emperor, Ferdinand I, came to Milan for his coronation in 1838, there was a most liberal amnesty. Refugees might apply for repatriation or for regular emigration permits. Those who returned found a Lombardy that was increasingly prosperous and a Venetia which seemed to languish despite the extension of free port privileges to all of Venice and the granting of naval contracts to the Arsenal there.

They also discovered that the censors allowed the continuation of the *Annali universali di statistica, economia pubblica, storia, viaggi, e commercio*. This journal did not touch political questions, but its coverage of economic questions and of developments in the rest of the world cast a revealing light on Austria's restrictions and indifference. Why did not the Milan-Venice railway line project a connection with Piedmont and Genoa? Why did Vienna imply that the same line was for local traffic rather than part of a grand imperial network? There was less of a consensus for Baron Karl Friedrich Kübeck's dream of uniting all of Italy in a customs union with the Austrian Empire as a counter to Prussia's domination of the Zollverein. Metternich killed the proposal, for he distrusted Italian collaborations that might induce the "wrong" kind of patriotism.

The economic crisis of 1845–47 probably was less severe for Italy than were the famine conditions of 1815–16, but the coincidence of widespread distress with the election of a reputedly liberal cardinal to the papal throne in 1846 posed problems for Metternich. Of less moment was a quarrel with Piedmont over Turin's rather sly attempt to evade a promise of 1751 not to sell salt to Swiss cantons. When protests failed, Austria imposed virtually prohibitive rates on Piedmontese wines, which were quite dependent upon Lombard customers. But Europe's eyes were on Pius IX, the new pope. Would one of the continent's most discredited administrations purge itself of indolence and graft and move to solve the miseries of provinces which were not bountifully endowed to begin with?

Austria and the other powers had been committed since 1831 to the idea of greater lay involvement in papal affairs, particularly in a *Consulta di Stato*. A circular of April 22, 1847, announced that worthy citizens would be summoned to sit on such a body, but increasing signs of press liberties upset Vienna. Political journals began to appear in the pope's domains early in 1847, and the nervous authorities no longer challenged articles on "administration and contemporary history" as long as nothing was written to disparage the regime and its officials. On May 10 the grand duke of Tuscany also relaxed restrictions on periodicals, just after Metternich had warned him that the liberal movement would not be satisfied with mere reform. They were intent upon a federal republic, and an Austrian archduke should be enough of a realist to comprehend he would never be picked by Italians as their sovereign.

In June 1847 Pius IX gladdened the hearts of his Romans by establishing a council of ministers (albeit non-lay) and civic guard and by forcing the resignation of his secretary of state, Pasquale Cardinal Gizzi. This conservative, on his own, had asked Metternich if the emperor would respond to a papal plea for help should matters deteriorate. The chancellor restated his unchanging rule that the pope would have to make a formal request. Making a move before there was evidence of disorders would tag Austria as an enemy of liberty. After trouble broke out, an expedition would require substantial forces, cause bloodshed, and probably invite a French riposte. On July 17, before the actual institution of a civic guard in the provinces and in the midst of rumors that ultras of reactionary or radical disposition were plotting to seize the pope, some 800 Croat infantry and 60 Hungarian cavalry moved into Ferrara to shore up the tiny regular Austrian garrison there. The legate protested, but within a month Radetzky had ordered night patrols and the taking over of strategic points. Gabriele Cardinal Ferretti, the new secretary of state, challenged Metternich's assertion that there was a dangerous subversive movement at work in the Papal States, and the underground press flayed the Austrians for their aggression.

On August 2, the chancellor appealed to the powers to reconfirm the territorial agreements on Italy reached in 1814–15. "Italy is a geographical expression." Republicans were plotting the overthrow of legitimate governments, but his emperor would never relinquish his possessions there. Lord Palmerston replied that Austria should take the lead in encouraging Pius IX to improve his regime. When a misapprehension spawned a report that Austria might attack Piedmont, the English statesman promised Charles Albert full support. More, he reinforced the Mediterranean fleet and sent Gilbert Elliot, second earl of Minto, to the Italian courts as an apostle of reform. Radetzky received constant reinforcements, and there were rumors that Vienna might incite a jacquerie against the landed aristocrats of Lombardy and Venetia. Many believed this had just been done in Galicia, and there were comparable scare-stories of Habsburg encouragement of communism.

It was the city dwellers, however, who were reacting most positively to the news of papal concessions. The first bloody incident, which came in September 1847, indicated that the Milanese artisanate was looking for an altercation. When rain broke up the gaslighted celebration of the institution of Carlo Bartolomeo Romilli as archbishop, the authorities sanctioned a repetition. Tenser than usual, the police resorted to their sabers in breaking up the singing of a hymn which lauded the pope. One citizen died, sixty were hurt. The nobility and the bourgeoisie pointedly ended or diminished their relations with officialdom. One Giovanni Battista Nazzari, representing Bergamo in the central congregation, asked his colleagues to petition the emperor for the kingdom's autonomy. All representative bodies should do more than offer advice, and more citizens should serve in the bureaucracy. There should be less censorship, less power for the police, reduced taxes, and a shorter term of military service. Rather surprisingly, the Milanese congregation dispatched its desiderata to Vienna, and there were signs that the Venetian body would follow suit.

A less patient professor, Giovanni Cantoni, had his own proposal to bring the Austrians to heel. Man might not live without salt, but a patriot might swear off tobacco. If he did, the Austrian treasury would suffer. On the first days of 1848, abstainers hissed or expostulated with those who smoked in the streets. Unwisely, the administrators decided to send out police and gendarmes in plain clothes, cigars alight, to provoke the zealots. Serious clashes on the third day of the new year left a half-dozen dead and fifty wounded. The city's notables protested and raised subscriptions for the stricken families. For the first time since the restoration, Milan was ready to fight for better treatment.

Insurrection,
War, and Peace,
1848–1849

RADETZKY was no stranger to the provocations that ended in the
tobacco riots, and he had reason to worry that his army in the
kingdom might not be able to handle an emergency. Only 34,000
were combat-ready, but they were far better prepared than most of
the imperial troops. Of eight Italian infantry regiments, four were
part of his contingent, proof that the high command unwisely discounted the chances of desertion. Ten thousand soldiers were garrisoned in Milan, for that city was deemed to be more volatile than
Venice.[1]

News from the rest of Italy was increasingly unpleasant for the
veteran commander-in-chief. An insurrection in Palermo on
January 12, though separatist in inspiration, initiated a series of
changes that seemed to undo Metternich's Italian system. In response to defeats in Sicily and demonstrations in Naples, Ferdinand
II conceded a constitution on January 29. Charles Albert, at first
contemptuous of the Bourbon ruler's surrender, yielded to his advisers and to agitation in the streets of Turin by announcing on
February 8 what was to be the basis for the famous *Statuto*. Three
days later Leopold II promised a "national representation," and
great jubilation accompanied the publication of a Tuscan *Statuto*
on February 17. The pope's allocution of February 10 implored a
divine blessing upon Italy but reserved to himself the right to judge
whether or not reforms were opportune. Should he be attacked un-
justly, he counted on being upheld by the entire Catholic world.
From the balcony of the Quirinal he reminded a cheering crowd
that he would not give in to demands contrary to the church's sacred
mission. Italy chose to remember the benediction, not the qualifications, for the pontiff appointed a commission on February 14 to
coordinate existing institutions and to propose modifications compatible with papal authority and the needs of the times.

The revolution in Paris which forced Louis Philippe's abdication
on February 24 and the formation of a republican government coin-

cided with reports of Piedmontese troop concentrations along the Lombard frontier. On February 22, Radetzky had proclaimed martial law, which would apply to civilians and troops alike. Venice heard on March 17 that insurgents had driven Metternich from Vienna and that the emperor had granted a constitution. Demonstrators forced the release of Daniele Manin and other patriots jailed in January, and by March 22 the commander of the garrison, Count Ferdinand Zichy, had surrendered the city to a provisional republican cabinet. The same day, after five days of street fighting which had exhausted his men, Radetzky left Milan in the hands of a moderate junta which decided to invite Charles Albert's armed support. Of the kingdom's important fortress-cities, only Mantua and Verona, as parts of the Quadrilateral, dared not move. There Radetzky was able to concentrate about 50,000 as he awaited the anticipated Piedmontese attack. For the time being there was no chance to restore the rulers of Modena and Parma, who had scurried away from their mutinous subjects.

The Piedmontese ventured beyond Milan in April, but Radetzky defeated them at Santa Lucia on May 6. Too much time had been lost in reconnaissance and debates over strategy. Charles Albert was more concerned over the need to persuade Lombards and Venetians to accept fusion with his state, and the Austrians profited from his decision to rely on positional warfare to reconquer towns north of Venice. In April and the first part of May, Count Hartig issued proclamations from Gorizia and Udine promising the citizens of the kingdom full enjoyment of the Austrian constitution of April 25, with "modifications" consonant with their Italian nationality. There was no apparent response. Appeals for English good offices came to naught when Palmerston concluded that a Habsburg viceroyalty in northern Italy would not satisfy Italian sensibilities. A special emissary, Karl Schnitzer-Meerau, offered to negotiate the surrender of Lombardy in meetings with the Milanese provisional government in June, but the discussion foundered on the issue of Venetia's future. When Radetzky heard that the court, which had fled to Innsbruck in May, was willing to make an armistice with Piedmont, he reacted vigorously. Through Prince Felix zu Schwarzenberg, recently wounded in action, he sent the emperor a plea to discountenance such negotiations. He was confident he could proceed from the Quadrilateral and roll back the enemy, and the prince convinced the imperial councillors and the ministers still in Vienna that such was the case. On July 1, two weeks after Prince Alfred zu Windischgrätz recovered Prague, the cabinet formally declared that the war in Italy would go on.

Three weeks later Radetzky attacked, and by the morning of July 27 he had defeated the Piedmontese in actions near Custoza. It was clear that Austrian superiority in men and artillery would force a truce, but Charles Albert surrendered Milan only on August 5 and agreed to vacate Lombardy, evacuate the duchies, and raise the blockade of Trieste on August 9. The armistice allowed a shift of imperial forces to the Hungarian front and to positions commanding unruly Vienna. Venice meanwhile could be starved and bombarded into submission. Feldzeugmeister Ludwig Baron Welden reoccupied Modena and Parma, but his attempt to hold the key gates to Bologna caused pitched battles with the citizenry and a retirement to the line of the Po. Pius IX on April 29 had denounced the war and separated himself from the forces of Italian nationalism, but Radetzky, wary of French susceptibilities, disclaimed any intention of a unilateral operation to arrest papal disintegration.

Moderate regimes in Turin, Florence, and Rome counted on English and French mediation to rescue the Lombards from the Habsburgs, but the events of the autumn and early winter pointed to quite another conclusion. Pius IX fled Rome for Gaeta in Neapolitan territory on November 25, just as Schwarzenberg was accepting the presidency of a talented council of ministers in Austria. Windischgrätz had vanquished the students and democrats of Vienna at the end of October, and the guardians of the dynasty decided that Ferdinand I, who had promulgated a string of concessions, had to abdicate. On December 2, in gala attire, the court listened to Schwarzenberg's reading of the documents that would send Ferdinand to dignified retirement in Prague and install Archduke Francis Joseph, an apprehensive eighteen-year-old, as the new sovereign.

The young man had first experienced Italy and the Italians when he was fifteen. Accompanied by his brothers, Maximilian and Karl, he was making the trip expected of an heir to the Habsburg domains. At twelve he had added the study of Italian to his lessons in French, Magyar, and Czech, but the formal little speeches he later offered in the languages of his peoples were a distant prospect in 1845. In Verona, the core of the Austrian defenses in Italy, the three archdukes met Radetzky, who entertained his guests with reviews and the launching of a military balloon from the ancient arena.

In bright moonlight they next saw Venice, moving by gondola along the Grand Canal to St. Mark's Square, newly illuminated by gas lamps. Like tourists of all ages, they gaped at the four bronze horses which their grandfather and Metternich had retrieved from the French at Napoleon's downfall. Then to Pola by warship, whence they returned in September to Schönbrunn. An interesting by-product of the trip were the vignettes which Francis Joseph drew for Maximilian's diary. They revealed a whimsical streak which he could ill afford when crushing responsibilities descended upon him three years later. A scene at an osteria included a well-padded priest on a donkey, a weather-beaten female slavey, and a rather tense young country gentleman who seemed upset by the cleric's inquisitive eyes. Another sketch took pity on a horse whose portly rider, shielded by a parasol from the late summer sun, relied on a top-hatted servant to prod the animal up a treacherous incline. An Italian patriot would have railed at the condescension, perhaps at the lack of social insight. Adolescent Habsburg princelings were not prepared to see beyond the local color that had entranced generations of visitors.

In the spring of 1848, while still an archduke, Francis Joseph had quite another view of Italy. He had been appointed governor of Bohemia on April 6, but Windischgrätz, glowering over tumults in Vienna and Prague, persuaded Archduchess Sophie to allow her son to inspect Radetzky's theater of operations. By April 27 the young Hussar officer was writing his mother from Bolzano that there could be no rest "until we cleanse our provinces of the Piedmontese and run up the double-eagle in Turin."

Radetzky kindly but emphatically told his visitor in Verona that all the advantages his army might wrest from the enemy would disappear if Francis Joseph should be captured. Blushing but firm, the later responded that his parents expected him to shrink from no danger. On a reconnaissance, Radetzky pointed to the enemy's strength and to his own desperate need for more troops. On his own, and latter at the Feldmarschall's request, the archduke dashed off letters to his mother, requesting her intercession with the military authorities. When the Piedmontese attacked at Santa Lucia on May 6, he served calmly under fire as ordnance officer to Feldmarschall Leutnant Konstantin Baron D'Aspre. After a cannonball came within a few feet of the dynasty's best hope, D'Aspre ordered him to a rear position in preparation for a counterattack. When the Piedmontese broke off action, the future emperor could not have realized that Radetzky had won the decisive encounter of the Italian campaign. Some days later the emperor and his kin deserted Vienna for Innsbruck, and on June 5 a letter from Archduchess Sophie ordered her son to that more reliable city.[2]

In Italy he had met Schwarzenberg for the first time, and it is not surprising that he was fascinated by the older man's elegance and sophistication. Born in 1800 to one of the greatest families of the aristocracy, the prince was a captain of Uhlans at twenty-two, when he embarked upon a diplomatic career that took him to Russia, Brazil, Portugal, England, and France. A routine six-year assignment to Berlin ended his apprenticeship, and in 1839 he became envoy extraordinary to the courts of Turin and Parma. Turin bored him, and the developing rivalry between Piedmont and the Habsburgs for the future domination of the peninsula sharpened his disdain and his sarcasm. Naples was a pleasant relief when he was transferred in 1844, and his passion for art, music, and classical literature compensated for the pettiness of routine that marked many of his days. Upon the outbreak of disturbances in Naples in 1848, he returned to active duty as a brigadier on the Italian front. It was he, arm in sling, whom Radetzky hurried to Innsbruck in June to fend off talk of an armistice.[3]

Seven months later, Schwarzenberg's strategy as minister-president called for prosecution of the war against Lajos Kossuth and the Magyars and evasion of all English and French mediation that might compromise the restoration of Austrian predominance in Italy. Radetzky's mission was plain. He was to honor the truce until or unless Charles Albert denounced it. Then he was to strike for a quick and decisive victory that would immobilize the revolutionary underground in the kingdom. It was no secret that Paris and London were urging the king of Sardinia to stay his hand. Should he disregard their advice, he would alienate moderates and conservatives throughout Europe.

On March 2, 1849, the Chamber of Deputies in Turin voted, 94–24, to urge their monarch to take up again the crusade to rid Italy of the foreigner. Smarting from criticism of his conduct of the previous campaign and from sneers that he had abandoned the Milanese, Charles Albert grasped at the chance to rehabilitate himself and to assure the succession to his son Victor Emmanuel, duke of Savoy. He could have hoped to achieve little else. Why did the great majority of the parliamentarians wish to chance another round with Austria? Some hoped for an eventual Magyar triumph, despite the rebels' failure to retake Budapest in late February. Others expected Milan and the rest of Lombardy to expel the whitecoats once again while the governments in Rome and Florence dispatched volunteers. A few desperate souls may have assumed that hostilities alone would end the unbearable cost of refitting the army. Almost unanimously the cabinet acceded to the wishes of the king and his legislators and notified the Austrian command on March 12 that war would be renewed in eight days. They were living up to the terms of the armistice, and there was no surety that the delay would benefit Radetzky more than it would the patriots who were assumed to be waiting for a second deliverance.

At noon on March 20, the precise minute allowed, the Austrians attacked from their concentration at Pavia. The evening of the next day they took possession of Mortara, and a prolonged struggle at Novara on March 22 ended in a Piedmontese retreat. Charles Albert sent for terms, and the reply called for occupation of the land between the Ticino and Sesia rivers, the occupation of Alessandria, which was to be personally guaranteed by the duke of Savoy, the withdrawal of the fleet from the Adriatic, and speedy negotiation of a peace treaty. The reference to Victor Emmanuel was pointed enough, and Charles Albert abdicated, perhaps in the hope that the Austrians would be more merciful to the son and the husband of Habsburg archduchesses.

The new king's mother was Maria Theresa, daughter of Ferdinand III of Tuscany, and he had married his first cousin, Maria Adelaide, the child of Archduke Rainer, the viceroy of Lombardy-Venetia, by Maria Elisabetta of Savoy-Carignano. Radetzky had been present at his baptism in 1820 and at his nuptials in 1842, which Schwarzenberg perforce also attended. Victor Emmanuel endured the usual regimen prescribed for heirs to thrones, supplemented by some "Réflexions historiques" composed for him by his father. These maxims insisted that revolution was the great danger and that domination of a state by a foreign potentate was nothing less than divine castigation. When the Austrians occupied all of Ferrara in 1847, the duke of Savoy in crown council vigorously seconded the idea of Piedmontese intervention in behalf of the pope. In the campaign of 1848 he won praise for getting the rearguard out of Santa Lucia in time and jailed a colonel of his own regiment when that officer implied an approval of dissidents in Genoa. Willfulness, a certain degree of anti-intellectualism, fierce pride, and a love for the active life — such were the personal traits which he had manifested down to the disaster of 1849. He sickened over the loss of discipline and the outright cowardice that contributed to Austrian victories, and the bravery of many could not erase from his mind a conviction that the eternally captious lawyers at home were the most guilty of all.[4]

His first duty as king was to sign an armistice, and Radetzky hinted to a Piedmontese emissary that a personal visit from the young monarch might lead to some mitigation of the conditions. Happy to comply, Victor Emmanuel chattered self-consciously to his Austrian escorts of the six fine horses he had lost at Mortara and galloped noisily into a farmyard at Vignale where the Feldmarschall awaited him. The two dismounted to greet each other, and the junior bestowed a kiss upon the elder. The imperturbable Austrian officers noticed with disdain the king's campaign cap, red-ribboned and set rakishly on his small head, the shortness of his stature, and the extraordinary length of his moustache and chin whiskers. Radetzky, a bit stooped and slightly corpulent, emerges in the chromos of the period as a rather stumpy old gentleman. Insignia on collar and cuffs, rather than manner, established his rank.

In an hour's conversation Radetzky yielded to several of the king's urgent pleas. To disarm opposition to a treaty in the Piedmontese parliament, the occupation of Alessandria would be joint for the period of the armistice and there would be no references to the agreements of 1815. In return Victor Emmanuel promised to disband all military corps composed of Lombards, Hungarians, and Poles who were subject to Austria. He permitted Austrian troops in his lands bounded by the Po, the Ticino, and the Sesia until ratification of a peace treaty. The fleet would quit the Adriatic, and the army would return to its peacetime strength. Radetzky required no indemnity, but he was subject to correction on this point by the cabinet in Vienna.[5]

On March 26, the day of the formal signing of the armistice in Novara, Radetzky composed a letter to the ministers in Olmütz to explain his concessions. There was no political sense in undermining the new king's position by seizing Turin, which might provoke the French. Though aware of his own government's need for cash, he argued against trying to make Piedmont pay for "Charles Albert's war." An indemnity would estrange those Piedmontese who realized the enormity of the abdicated ruler's actions. The general situation in Europe demanded a speedy solution of the challenges Austria faced in Italy and should rule out any talk of annexing the lands which his army would occupy.[6]

His missive shocked and chagrined the crown council which met on March 31. Their salvation was Article IX of the convention, which stated that the final treaty would be concluded independently of the terms agreed to at Novara and in accord with the reciprocal self-interests of the two governments. It was decided that Ritter Karl Ludwig von Bruck, minister of commerce and public works, would strive to modify the effects of Radetzky's leniency in negotiations slated for Milan. He was the most incensed of the councillors, he was cognizant of Austria's severe financial pinch, and he had a liberal reputation that might blunt Sardinian protests to France and England that Austria was trying to throttle constitutionalism in the defeated state.[7]

It was decades later that interested persons concocted the legend that Victor Emmanuel refused to surrender constitution or tricolor at Vignale.[8] Rather, he had bargained effectively with a veteran campaigner who was aware of the fact that Austria also had a constitution in addition to a problem of calamitous proportions in Hungary. The king expected groans and imprecations from his deputies when the clauses of the armistice were disclosed, if not the election of a commission to question him on his conduct. In no humor to appease men he deemed intractable, he swore to uphold the *Statuto* on March 29 and next day dissolved his legislature. The great port of Genoa was in revolt, and his ministers could not afford commissions of inquiry which would protest the necessary military solution.

Genoese disaffection originated with the fear that Austrian forces would attempt to hold the city. Many democratic elements also felt that Genoa was better fitted to lead the struggle for Italianism than was retrogressive Turin. When the city council declared itself a committee of public safety, General Alfonso La Marmora moved his division against the rebels. The investment began on April 4, and the bombardment continued until a truce was signed six days later. All save 12 of the leaders were amnestied, and some 450 deserters from the regular army were allowed to take refuge on an American ship. No Sardinian ruler could have countenanced the threat of Genoese secession in 1849, and the ultimate arrangement was decent enough. The short-lived crisis also indicated to Austria that Victor Emmanuel would not suffer the direct challenges of the street or of democratically inclined subjects who already had found him lacking.

Bruck reached Milan on April 5, determined to saddle Piedmont with the costs of the wars. Born into a modest Protestant Prussian bookbinder's family, he was a soldier at seventeen in the last campaigns against Bonaparte. In 1821 he vowed to join the volunteers who went to the aid of the Greek revolutionists, but his money gave out in Trieste and he went into insurance. Thanks to his marriage to a rich girl, he had greater scope for his ambition in the world of business. Credited with the founding of the Bourse and of the Austrian Lloyd in Trieste, he was a natural choice for a cabinet that required the best of Austria's talents to extricate the state from near financial collapse. A commanding figure, with alert eyes and well-formed head, he was the stereotyped blond from the north. At times, to his Piedmontese opponents, he seemed as unbending and truculent as one of Barbarossa's henchmen of long ago. The Sardinian plenipotentiaries were not his match. General Giuseppe Dabormida was a cut above his peers in intelligence and sobriety of temperament, but he had no training as a diplomat. One meeting with Bruck, and he was sick with the thought of his own incapacity. Count Carlo Boncompagni di Mombello, a jurist whose rectitude did not obscure his retiring and provincial nature, would be equally vulnerable to Bruck's threats.

In the first encounter the Austrian negotiator demanded a guarantee of the frontiers of 1815 and Piedmontese assumption of the expenses incurred by his empire's forces in the two wars. To his surprise, the Sardinians responded with a request to purchase part of Parma from the reigning duke. Schwarzenberg had instructed Bruck to ask for an indemnity of 50 million Austrian florins (about 125 million Piedmontese francs). At worst, Austria might accept 20 million florins. Sensing that Victor Emmanuel's treasury was less depleted than expected, Bruck declined to budge on the issue of the old frontiers and raised the indemnity figure set by Schwarzenberg to 200 million Piedmontese francs. As for the king's insistence upon full amnesty for those Lombards, Hungarians, and Poles who were serving under the Piedmontese tricolor at the time of the armistice, he answered that the crown alone granted such clemency in Austria. One could not imagine that such a prerogative would be stated in a mere treaty.[9]

On April 15 the Piedmontese envoys informed Bruck that their king would abdicate and his conservative cabinet would resign before they would negotiate on the basis of the indemnity demanded. He replied that they had three days to secure a counteroffer from Turin. If it did not come very close to the Austrian figure, there would be no sense in further talks.[10] When apprised by Marquis Francesco Sauli, the Piedmontese envoy to London, of the conflicting proposals advanced by each side in Milan, Palmerston was careful to discourage Turin's expectations. Talk of buying out the new duke of Parma, Charles III, would increase Austrian cupidity. It would be better to approach him after he had discovered whether or not his people wanted him. Vienna's financial demands, he admitted, were truly enormous, but he understood why the Austrians refused to include an amnesty in the peace protocol and noted that they had the right to garrison Alessandria conjointly with the Piedmontese until peace was concluded.[11]

To Bruck's astonishment, the ministers in Olmütz repudiated his line of attack. Schwarzenberg alluded to the unfortunate turn of the war in Hungary and the need for a quick peace with Piedmont as Austria tried to grapple with the problems of Tuscany and the Papal Legations. There was to be no denunciation of the armistice, and the maximum indemnity should be no more than 115 million francs, of which 15 million would go to persons who had suffered losses. Schwarzenberg also mobilized Francis Joseph, who wrote Victor Emmanuel's wife, his cousin, that he yearned to embrace her and her family once again. Perfidious counsels had inspired the conflict, and foreign interference should not deaden the mutual confidence that had just been reestablished.[12]

On April 23 the Austrians moved into their zone in Alessandria, and a rather desperate Sardinian cabinet ordered Count Stefano Gallina to proceed to Paris and London to sue for French and English mediation. He discovered that the price of French aid was a base at Genoa, which the king would not hear of and which Palmerston was most reluctant to support. Schwarzenberg advised the French that Austria was disposed to reduce the amount of the indemnity, and he was encouraged by Massimo d'Azeglio's appointment on May 7 as chief minister. After some weeks of skirmishing, the Piedmontese assented to the reopening of discussions on the basis of an indemnity of 70 million francs. The Austrians evacuated Alessandria on June 17, and Dabormida and Boncompagni returned to Milan. Azeglio had furnished them with a list of proposals, two of which he deemed "nonnegotiable." Austria was to concede amnesty to its subjects who were fighting with Piedmont's forces at the time of the armistice and would have to promise to honor the Italian nationality of the inhabitants of Lombardy-Venetia. He also wanted to avoid paying more than 70 million francs.[13]

After days of fruitless bargaining, Bruck recommended on July 5 that his government issue an ultimatum. If the Sardinians refused to accept the major Austrian propositions within four or five days, he would suspend negotiations and return to Vienna. In the presence of the emperor, Schwarzenberg and his colleagues approved the stratagem. Should Turin reject the ultimatum, Austria would denounce the armistice, but, in the carefully chosen words of the Ministerrat's secretary, at a time when the army could be sure of a quick and successful result.[14]

The sincere but unconfident Dabormida and Boncompagni meanwhile asked for an expert who could deal with problems of contraband controls and a commercial treaty. Azeglio dispatched Count Carlo Beraudo di Pralormo, distinguished by his looks, his social graces, and his expertise with Austrians. Between 1821 and 1834 he had represented his country in Vienna, developing a friendship with Metternich and the acquaintance of Schwarzenberg. He had no instructions to give way on amnesty or indemnity, however, and Bruck prevailed upon Radetzky to remind Victor Emmanuel by letter of his solemn promise at Vignale to hasten a definitive peace.

Both men made solid progress in the conference of July 20. Pralormo knew he could drop Azeglio's demand for a mention of the Italian nationality of Lombardy-Venetia in the treaty, and he did so. He also eliminated the earlier insistence on some guarantee of autonomy. Unilaterally he suggested a delineation of his country's frontiers as described in the Final Act of the Congress of Vienna. He accepted the Austrian position on the frontier at Gravellone, left a blank space for a possible Austrian formula for an amnesty, and deferred the final indemnity figure to decisions that neither he nor Bruck ultimately would make. In return for an Austrian abolition of restrictions on the salt and wine trade, he promised a commercial treaty, a convention on contraband, and regulations concerning persons claiming dual citizenship. Bruck responded affirmatively to Pralormo's propositions and advised Vienna not to ask for more than 75 million francs.[15]

The final obstacle was the question of the amnesty. France and England never had appreciated Azeglio's and Victor Emmanuel's determination to send home as many émigrés as possible under cover of an Austrian promise not to prosecute them for treason. Disturbed by Vienna's slowness to respond to Pralormo's concessions, Azeglio wrote to Louis Napoleon directly. "We cannot believe that France, that neighboring and friendly power, would consent to the consummation of our ruin." The queen of Sardinia prepared a letter of entreaty for Francis Joseph. In the end, a tactful note from Pralormo to Schwarzenberg and a shrewd suggestion from Radetzky, plus lingering concern over unpredictable generals in the French army, persuaded the Austrian Ministerrat and the emperor to grant the substance of an act of pardon.

On July 28 the Austrian ministers concluded their consideration of the Piedmontese counterproject and of the strong pleas for an amnesty that came from Milan. Pralormo discreetly asked for a spontaneous action prior to the ratification of the treaty. Radetzky provided the form. Without using the word *amnesty*, he would issue a proclamation inviting compromised Lombards and Venetians to return home within a given period of time. The most dangerous of these individuals, roughly 150 in number, would be excepted.

Schwarzenberg, convinced a few days before that such an amnesty would preclude the just punishment of the most hardened Hungarian and Venetian rebels, now cajoled his colleagues into accepting Radetzky's formula. Alexander Bach, minister of the interior and the unrelenting foe of forgiveness, offered no further resistance. The young emperor, touched by his cousin's letter or by a dim comprehension of the enormous responsibilities he had inherited, wondered if law and rectitude allowed the exclusion of the 150. With Hungary in mind, his minister-president swiftly countered with the arguments that every amnesty had its exceptions, that no one could lament the treatment meted out to men of such notorious actions and opinions. Later in the day, he warned Bruck to impress upon Pralormo Austria's resolution to concede no more for the moment. Once the world situation was more favorable, he hinted, there might be a review of the most flagrant cases of disloyalty.

Pralormo did not protest the number excluded or ask their names. He did insist on some action which would commit Austria to an act of grace before he would sign the treaty. Again Radetzky was the key to a mutually honorable solution. He was to communicate confidentially to Victor Emmanuel the manifesto he would issue after the signing of the peace and before the exchange of ratifications. No one in authority in Turin required a surety greater than Radetzky's. Also, on August 1, Francis Joseph wrote Adèle, as he called his cousin, that she would hear in time what he had been able to do. To forgive everyone would be an injustice to those who had suffered from the principal authors of evil. Time, the great pacifier, should enable him to draw a veil over the past as he witnessed all of his subjects enjoying the benefits of a brighter future.[16]

In response to a last appeal from Victor Emmanuel, Radetzky magnanimously cut the list of the unpardoned to less than 100. Bruck acquiesced in an extension of the amnesty to subjects of Parma and Modena and promised the return of the siege park captured at Peschiera. On August 6, the plenipotentiaries signed the treaty.[17] To recapitulate, Victor Emmanuel accepted the frontiers

set by the Congress of Vienna and surrendered all titles and claims
to lands beyond these frontiers, save for the established right,
through reversion, to the duchy of Piacenza. As a concession to
Piedmontese sensibilities, the dukes of Modena and Parma-Piacenza
would be invited to accede to the treaty.

An indemnity of 75 million francs would extinguish all claims
made by Austria, Modena, Parma, and their citizens against Piedmont. Fifteen million francs were payable in ready cash at the end
of October 1849. Thereafter, there would be ten payments of 6
million each due every two months, with interest at 5 percent levied
on the decreasing principal owed. The contested boundary line near
Pavia was fixed at that channel of the Gravellone canal which
Austria had long preferred. Both states agreed to construct a toll-
free bridge over this canal. They also promised to work out a treaty
of commerce and a convention on persons of dual citizenship and to
reinstate their convention of 1834 against smugglers. Austria also
canceled the Sardinian-Lombard convention of 1751 and revoked
the surtax on wine coming from Piedmont.

Schwarzenberg's motives for granting reasonable terms were
many. He was dismayed by the French capture of Rome in July. The
Hungarians were about to surrender, but the problems of pacifica-
tion were substantial, and the monarchy's prestige demanded some
kind of subtle denigration of what Tsar Nicholas had done to defeat
Kossuth. Habsburg paramountcy in Germany was by no means en-
sured by the king of Prussia's refusal to accept a "crown from the
gutter." In Italy, Bourbons and Habsburgs might retrieve their
scepters, but none, except possibly the king of the Two Sicilies,
could fend off those radicals and republicans known as the party of
movement without foreign aid. Victor Emmanuel was eloquent in
his denunciations of those who had beguiled his father into a disastrous war, but he had kept the *Statuto*. Radetzky seemed willing to
gamble on his conservatism. Schwarzenberg and Francis Joseph
were resentful and wary. Knowledge of Palmerston's distaste for
Austria and of Louis Napoleon's ambition did nothing to reassure
them. Relations with Turin required discreet firmness. There could
be accommodation only if the king and his ministers kept their
hotheads under strict control.

Schwarzenberg
and Azeglio,
1849–1852

SCHWARZENBERG and Azeglio had much in common. Each was an aristocrat, though Azeglio's family was of modest means. Neither was content to while away his life in a fashionable regiment, though both fought with distinction and were wounded in 1848. While Schwarzenberg moved with ease in the world of diplomacy, charming women with his elegance and fine figure, Azeglio persuaded his father to allow him to study art in Rome and its neighboring villages. His gallantry and his disdain for Turin rivaled the prince's, and he decided in 1830 that Milan should be the scene of his contemplated triumphs in literature as well as art. His first marriage, to Alessandro Manzoni's daughter, ended with her death, and a second venture terminated in a separation. Usually in Piedmont after 1843, he gradually turned from painting and novels to politics. Aware of Charles Albert's unpopularity, he extolled the king's fundamental reliability in one Italian town after another. His reward was the ruler's promise that "all will be spent in the Italian cause" at the right moment.

Azeglio won a seat in the Chamber of Deputies in June 1848. When convalescence permitted him to go to Turin in December, he discovered that the king wished him to become president of the council of ministers. Rather cold-bloodedly, he declined. He saw no chance to whip the Austrians in another encounter and preferred that someone else sign the inevitable peace treaty. In Victor Emmanuel's early days, he lapsed into complete cynicism. "The people of Italy are twenty per cent. stupid, rascally, and bold, eighty per cent. stupid, honest, and timid, and such a people has the government it deserves." No one really knows why the new king decided to draft Azeglio on May 5 as the head of his council of ministers or why he accepted. For a few years, however, this unlikely politician would restrain his fiery young monarch and win for his country much of the sympathy which the British and French customarily bestowed upon an underdog in the world of international affairs.[1]

Two insistent problems haunted both men as they strove to pull the kingdom together without suffering another humiliation by Austria. The king's inheritance of a constitutional regime included a press law which gave democratic and nationalistic editors sufficient freedom to antagonize those Austrian ministers who in 1849 still believed in civil rights for the Habsburg domains. Worse, Piedmont was host to thousands of refugees from Lombardy and Venetia who could be neither totally absorbed nor ruthlessly forced across the frontier. The king was not hesitant in denouncing the Lombards when he assumed he had a sympathetic auditor, for they were part of the misadventures of 1848–49 that he sincerely deplored.[2] The poorest of them were migrant laborers, driven by need to find work or frightened into flight by the sound of cannon and marching troops. The richest, often contemptuous of Turin's provincial ways, sometimes subsidized the journals whose jibes imperiled the policy of accommodation with Austria which the king had sworn to maintain.

The vanquished moved first to restore diplomatic relations by naming Marquis Antonio Brignole Sale as plenipotentiary. Notably Catholic and conservative, this veteran of the sessions at Vienna in 1814–15 symbolized Turin's resolve to gratify Francis Joseph and his formidable mentor. On October 12 the latter announced that Count Rudolf Apponyi, thirty-five years of age and an obvious comer in Habsburg diplomatic circles, would handle affairs for Austria in Turin. Son of Metternich's longtime ambassador to Paris and husband to a Russian princess, he would receive all due courtesy and security, but little else, in Piedmont. On occasion an aristocrat spoke of the good old times of Habsburg-Savoy entente, but most of society found it advisable to linger no more than briefly in his company.[3]

The marquis arrived in Vienna on November 21, bearing excuses not likely to amuse Schwarzenberg. Azeglio's instructions argued that the emergence of a French republic, agitation in Rome, and popular passions in the inexperienced parliament in Turin had compelled Charles Albert to declare war. Now, however, the Piedmontese ministry was sure that the country could prosper with constitutional institutions that would interest men of order in public affairs. The cabinet preferred the radicals to compromise themselves by excess rather than to have the king renege on his promises. At the right moment the government would act with courage.[4]

The Austrian minister-president replied by complimenting Victor Emmanuel for his "proclamation of Moncalieri" against the tyranny of parties and the cabinet for its dissolution of an unruly Chamber. By the end of the year, however, Brignole's descriptions of Schwarzenberg's black moods caused Sir Ralph Abercromby, the British plenipotentiary in Turin, to ask Palmerston for a positive assurance to Azeglio that "he will find England ready to support Sardinia against the effects of the unmerited ill humour and disappointed pride of Austrian Statesmen."[5] A variety of problems accounted for the quick deterioration of relations.

Schwarzenberg was full of rancor over the recent hostilities and the problem of the émigrés. Indirectly his government had admitted that Radetzky's first time limit for the return of the amnestied was too brief by moving the date to October 12. Too few appeared, and the authorities seemed to retaliate by rejecting the mass of applications for legal emigration.[6] Dabormida secured an interview with Radetzky in Verona in early December. He wanted a new amnesty for practically all who had failed to avail themselves of the first act of grace. He also requested the restitution of what Abercromby delightfully termed "the remaining moiety of the Sardinian Battering Train detained by the Austrians in Lombardy."[7] Radetzky refused, asserting that such high policy rested with the two cabinets.

On December 21 Schwarzenberg told Brignole that there never had been a question of a new amnesty, nor of a prolongation of the old one. Only the matter of speeding up the refugees' petitions was open to discussion. He would never consent to the restitution of the artillery park. Radetzky was at fault in surrendering the first half of it, for Sardinia forfeited all hope of recovery when the fleet failed to evacuate the Adriatic in the manner prescribed by the armistice.[8]

Schwarzenberg's instructions to Apponyi of December 4 appraised Piedmont as a state which in time of war ranged itself either with France or Austria, depending upon the better chance of success and the larger reward offered. After Novara, Victor Emmanuel could have remedied the defective political institutions he inherited from his father, but he lacked resolution and initiative. By appointing Azeglio, he revealed his intention to pursue the constitutional system to the very end. Apponyi was to give no advice and to stay clear of the parties which disputed the terrain in Piedmont. His language with king and ministry should be frank and simple. In Italy, Austria wanted an entente among all the governments against the dissolvent doctrines of socialism.[9]

A debate in the Chamber of Deputies in January 1850 sent Apponyi to Azeglio for explanations. General Dabormida, fighting moves to reduce the army, spoke of Piedmont's importance in Italy and of the initiative the Piedmontese had taken in the last war. The honor of the tricolor demanded a preparation for a new war that would assure a worthy, indeed an advantageous, outcome for the state and for Italy. Azeglio admitted that the speech had embarrassed the cabinet. The army, however, was the government's weapon against internal factions. This could not be said publicly, and the general had simply proved that a maladroit friend was more dangerous than an enemy. The Sardinian leader reported to Brignole that he told Apponyi, "If I had an army of 700,000 and Radetzky only four men and a corporal, I would not attack Lombardy." Apponyi on the other hand mentioned to Schwarzenberg his inability to repress a smile when Azeglio offered as a pledge of peace his own signature scrawled across the Treaty of Milan.[10]

During the year 1850 Austrian anger over articles in the Piedmontese press twice threatened a rupture in formal relations. Aurelio Bianchi Giovini, a fiery controversialist specifically excluded from the amnesty offered by Austria, created both crises with his muckraking stories in *L'Opinione*, published in Turin. In one article he alleged that Apponyi had demanded the expulsion of a certain number of refugees. In the second he described Baron Franz Metzburg, secretary to the Austrian legation, as the head of a reactionary, Austrian, and Jesuitical conspiracy.

When the cabinet summoned the offending journalist, he promised to turn his attention from the Austrian legation. On March 20, nevertheless, *L'Opinione* carried a sneering attack upon official and nonofficial Austrian agents who intrigued in sacristy and boudoir. In Vienna, Schwarzenberg vowed that he would demand reparation for every insult to the imperial legation and would recall his envoy if not satisfied.[11] Azeglio put in Abercromby's hands Brignole's reports of the prince's ugly humor, for he wanted the minister to ask if England would be disposed to aid Sardinia in case of an Austrian attack. The reply was that England would employ its influence and good offices but not risk the danger of war on Sardinia's account.

For the moment Azeglio should give England an assurance that Sardinia would avoid "every act that could justly give umbrage to Austria." Accordingly, the minister-president promised severe punishment for anyone who subjected Apponyi to insult, though it seemed to him that Austria always was looking for a chance to catch Turin in error as prelude to more demands.[12]

April brought general relaxation and a change in the Piedmontese representation in Vienna. Brignole had taken great exception to the antiecclesiastical bills which Giuseppe Siccardi was sponsoring in the Piedmontese parliament and gave way to Adriano Thaon di Revel, not yet forty. Revel's grandfather had petitioned for Austrian aid against the revolutionists of 1821, and his father had been one of Charles Albert's confidants. After seeing a most polite and friendly Schwarzenberg in Vienna, Revel surmised that, short of general European complications, Sardinia would not run the chance of an invasion.[13]

Bianchi Giovini ruptured the tenuous truce by accusing Austrian generals of thievery and rapine and Archduke Sigismund of graft in *L'Opinione* of July 22 and 24. The Piedmontese press law required the sovereign or the legation of an insulted power to bring suit, but Apponyi, declaring that Austria would no longer accept the excuse that the law paralyzed the prosecution of such journalists, refused to move. Instead, Schwarzenberg warned that his envoy would quit Turin immediately should a single article of the same kind again appear. Why did Piedmont constantly make war on Austria and then go to Paris and London to complain of Austrian hostility? Because Piedmont was the only revolutionary government in Europe, giving hospitality to refugees wherever they were, even in Constantinople and Smyrna.[14]

Azeglio agreed that the latest articles were indefensible, and he decided to expel Bianchi Giovini. Later he talked to Apponyi of the pressures he had to withstand in enforcing the decision, affirming that if the journalist "had not left the country, I would have quit the ministry."[15] His air of propriety did not mean that he had forgotten his suspicions that Austrian agents were helping to foment the opposition to Siccardi's bills. Schwarzenberg, having read reports of such supposed agents in several Piedmontese papers, in turn advised Azeglio to hang any he could find.[16] The latter wrote Revel that he was duly grateful for such an authorization. If the matter came up again, would his plenipotentiary, as a joke, ask the prince if Sardinia could apply the same remedy to someone in the diplomatic corps?[17] Apponyi was respected, even liked; Metzburg was the presumed agent provocateur.

On March 7, 1850, at the height of the first crisis over *L'Opinione*, Radetzky published a decree on the émigrés which even Apponyi described as "rigorous." The property of those who had not returned in the prescribed time limit was subject to sequestration. This also applied to the property of persons who had requested permits for legal emigration and who, whatever the reasons, had been turned down. Those who wished to return to Lombardy or Venetia could petition Radetzky. They had to submit papers proving they had been prevented from accepting the earlier amnesty, and they had to declare they were ready to pledge half of their present and future holdings as a guarantee of good behavior.[18] These restrictions reflected Schwarzenberg's disdain for traitors, Radetzky's anger over the number of officers, once Austrian, who opted for service with Victor Emmanuel, and the Austrian cabinet's determination to keep from Sardinia the income from some of the greatest estates in the kingdom.

During the second tempest over Bianchi Giovini's forays, Schwarzenberg notified Turin that persons who left Austrian territory after the campaign of 1849, after the last repression of Brescia (if they were Brescian), or after the reoccupation of Venice (if they were Venetian) would be accepted at the frontier if expelled as vagabonds by Sardinia. Provincial authorities were to furnish such persons with certificates proving the time of their arrival on Piedmontese soil.[19] The rich, the aristocratic, and the advantaged still had to make personal application for reentry. In September, Bach confirmed Revel's assumption there would be no general amnesty.[20]

The Austrian ministers had their eyes fixed on Germany throughout 1850, and Apponyi watched Azeglio and the military in Turin for signs that constitutional Prussia and constitutional Piedmont might dare challenge Austria on two fronts. It seemed wise to send to Vienna the latest details on the Piedmontese army despite Azeglio's assurance, "What is happening in Germany is designed to make us prudent and reasonable. I hope it will calm our mischief-makers." He declared that he was cured of his old idea of "fusion," of Italian unity. On the eve of the Austrian victory at Olmütz, he reiterated his country's pacific intentions. "Even if Austria retired its last man from Italy and the Lombards begged us to occupy their land, we would not budge. And it is not just we untenured ministers who think so, the king shares these convictions, and he will never swerve from them."[21]

Austro-Sardinian relations at the end of 1850 were what they had been all year long. Azeglio reiterated his country's pacific attitude and his king's determination to consolidate institutions and to resist popular effervescence. The general public was not likely to accept the illusions of the émigrés, for whom they had no sympathy save that demanded by adversity.[22] Revel struggled in vain to soften the prescriptions regulating emigration and reentry. Bach insisted that sequestering was not confiscation. In time wives and children would be able to reclaim their natural inheritance. Revel concluded that Austria had resolved to punish those who lived abroad in opposition and who yet wished to keep their property and their eventual right to return.[23]

In the first months of 1851 rumors of troop concentrations in Lombardy led to a mild "war scare." When questioned, Schwarzenberg denied that the forces had been increased. Some who had been transferred had not even returned. Austria had no intention of forcing Piedmont to get rid of the refugees.[24] In London the Sardinian minister, Emanuele Taparelli d'Azeglio, obtained from Palmerston an assurance that, theoretically speaking, English interests would compel the government to protect Piedmont from an Austrian attack.[25] On March 11 the *Corriere Italiano* of Vienna, known to follow Schwarzenberg's hints, rejected the stories of untoward military activity, and Revel decided that this was proof that no aggression was planned.[26]

Francis Joseph's tour of Lombardy in the autumn aroused attention in the press, which in turn led to recriminations between the two cabinets. In the official gazette published in Milan appeared a sonnet which seemed to label Charles Albert a poltroon and counseled Sardinia to bend the knee to the emperor, "who can change the destinies of all Italy." A supposedly straight news story insisted that Victor Emmanuel's personal emissary to Francis Joseph had presented "a tribute of official homage." Turinese papers protested the insinuations and retaliated with accounts of Francis Joseph's "cowardice under fire" and rumors of recent disorder and confusion in the Austrian maneuvers near Como. Apponyi and Azeglio met for the usual exchange of expostulations, while Revel had to counter Schwarzenberg's lively questioning and renewed threats to recall his envoy. The interview embarrassed Revel, for he protested to his own Foreign Ministry that no other country on the continent would have tolerated such gross attacks on the Austrian emperor.[27]

The Piedmontese cabinet responded by submitting to the Chamber of Deputies a stricter press law. In the future the government would initiate prosecution of journals which committed offenses against foreign sovereigns. Second, jury trial of such cases, which had been mandatory, would end. Regular judges would render verdicts in the future.[28] Later Azeglio would swear to the Chamber that the modifications were not suggested because of foreign representations. This was technically correct, but he knew that Sardinia had to prevent a rapprochement between Louis Napoleon and Schwarzenberg that might put his country in serious danger.[29]

The shadows cast by Bonaparte's accent on "order" at the end of 1851 could not obscure the solid progress which Piedmont and Austria had made in repairing their relations. In October a new commercial treaty reduced the duties on Piedmontese wines appreciably, while Austria received the most-favored-nation status which Turin had accorded France, Belgium, and Great Britain. During negotiations for a revised convention for the repression of smuggling, the Piedmontese protested the existing custom of mixed surveillance. The appearance of Austrian officials, sometimes soldiers, on the Piedmontese banks of Lake Maggiore created too much resentment. The final draft mirrored Piedmontese sensitivities and Austrian realism. Pursuit would end appreciably short of a lakeshore owned by the other signatory and at the edge of those rivers which formed the boundary.[30]

Austrian treatment of the émigrés was a mixture of rigor and concession in 1851. Those who had not availed themselves of the various summonses and still remained abroad lost their Austrian citizenship. They continued to have the right to appeal to the competent authorities for status as legal emigrants. These rules applied to every individual "implicated in the revolutionary movements that took place in Lombardy-Venetia in 1848 and 1849." They could not return to Austrian soil. If they desired restoration of the rights due an Austrian citizen, they would have to follow Austrian procedures for naturalization. Officers who were not on active duty when they "passed over to the enemy" received the status of legal emigrants. Those who actually had deserted the imperial colors would be prosecuted if they dared return. Excepted were those who remained in Piedmontese service in accord with the armistice of Novara and those exiled as a result of Venice's surrender. Any person who arrived in Piedmont before September 30, 1849, would have to prove he was not implicated in the revolutionary movement. As before, vagrants needed a statement from the Piedmontese provincial officials proving entry into Piedmont after September 30, 1849, if they were to be received by Austria.[31]

Louis Napoleon's seizure of dictatorial power in December 1851 inspired Victor Emmanuel to some unusual confidences in his customary New Year's conversation with Apponyi. He expressed satisfaction with the fall of Palmerston, "a dangerous man" who obstructed harmony among the powers. Still an abhorrer of revolutions, he welcomed the change in Paris and promised action on Piedmont's "detestable" press. He claimed he had given orders to banish a certain number of refugees, all of them Lombards. "You know that I despise them as much as you do." Schwarzenberg merely commented that the king's character was "weak and quite unreliable."[32]

The prince's last months were a period of decent relations with Turin. The cabinet forced Bianchi Giovini, whose banishment had been of brief duration, to step down from the editorial board of *L'Opinione* and resorted to severe measures against two intemperate papers in Genoa. The Senate completed action on the treaties on commerce and contraband at the end of January 1852.[33] Only a probably calculated indiscretion committed by Victor Emmanuel disturbed the atmosphere. He and Apponyi were assessing the chances of war, and the Austrian asked what conditions small states might find themselves in after a general war. "Either happy or overwhelmed," was the piqued reply. At the end of the audience the king was protesting that he knew his duties too well to provoke or even to desire war.[34]

Schwarzenberg's last message to Apponyi, dated April 5, the day of his sudden death, was a typical disquisition on Bonaparte's interest in leaving the demagogues hopeful, the great powers apprehensive. Count Karl Ferdinand Buol-Schauenstein took over the conduct of foreign affairs on April 11, and his appointment aroused curiosity, if not joy, in Turin, where he had been minister plenipotentiary, 1844–48.[35] He soon was upbraiding Revel for articles in *L'Opinione* of April 27 and 30, and Azeglio was quick to agree that the complaints were justified. To contain Bianchi Giovini, he persuaded the owners of the paper to announce that a member of the directors' council would pass on and, if necessary, revise everything the journalist submitted. The "desperado" refused to concur and so ceased to be part of the staff.[36]

Azeglio's weariness and boredom were no secret, and in the autumn attention seemed to turn to the king once again. With a show of brusque extravagance, Victor Emmanuel told his entourage that he and his horse were ready for war. More explicitly, he announced to a visiting French officer that the Piedmontese forces were the advance guard of the French army.[37] Apponyi was reporting, however, that a letter from the pope had changed the king's point of view on the strife between church and state, and Buol was delighted. Such a reversal of policy might lead, step by step, to a modification of the political system. Austria would support the king's recapture of the reins of government and do all in its power to facilitate his country's liberation from the preponderating influence of ideologues and revolutionaries. Should the ruler change course, Austria might relieve Piedmont of some of the embarrassments caused by the émigrés. Buol instructed Apponyi not to give this message to Azeglio, who could not be counted upon. The latter had already resigned when Buol composed this directive, and the failure of the conservatives or the king to effect a coup d'état disappointed Apponyi. "Liberal ideas, inseparable in the king's mind from ideas of war and conquest, are too deeply rooted in that weak intelligence to allow one to hope for a complete and lasting return to saner doctrines."[38]

On November 2 Count Camillo Benso di Cavour assumed the task of forming a cabinet, and he instructed Revel to read to Buol a statement which reaffirmed Piedmontese devotion to constitutional principles. In the same dispatch he promised to end any abuse of such principles that would endanger foreign relations. The execution of the "Five" at Mantua in December aroused the usual anti-Austrian outcry in the press, and Dabormida, the minister of foreign affairs, offered Apponyi the same explanations Azeglio had resorted to. The increasingly cynical Austrian was beginning to repeat himself in his reports. The king's propensities for good "never came to anything." Discussion of press attacks "never came to anything."[39]

After more than three years of peace, Austro-Piedmontese relations were cool but proper. It was realized in Vienna that Victor Emmanuel was not likely to emulate Francis Joseph in a repudiation of constitutionalism. Radicalism, on the other hand, had not triumphed in the Chamber of Deputies, and a Bianchi Giovini had been neutralized. The émigrés were little more than tolerated guests, and the Austrian military had no reason to amend their low opinion of the small kingdom's military potential. Schwarzenberg was contemptuous of the land and of its ruler, but his preoccupation with German affairs and his effort to comprehend Louis Napoleon's psyche meant that he had little time to devote to Turin. The Piedmontese appeals for English and French reassurances were annoying, but a few words to the right person in Paris and London undermined such maneuvers. The serious problem was Lombardy. The frontier at the Ticino would not remain inviolate unless the Italians under the Habsburg crown were persuaded, indeed bribed, to believe that membership in a great empire was preferable to the uncertainties of fusion with twice-defeated Piedmont.

The Kingdom of Lombardy-Venetia and Trieste, 1849–1856

Finance and Administration

To AVERT bankruptcy in the aftermath of the revolutions of 1848-49, the Austrian ministers imposed an indemnity on Sardinia and resolved that Lombardy and Venetia would have to endure greater fiscal burdens as partial payment for their disloyalty. On April 22, 1849, the government announced the issuance of treasury bonds in the sum of 70 million Austrian lire, drawing 3½ percent until retired by the income from supplementary taxes which would begin the first day of 1850. Italians within the range of Austrian bayonets who had the wherewithal to participate would find it advisable to do so. In this sense, this loan and later ones were "forced." The first new tax was a 50 percent increase in the land tax, reduced in 1851 to 33 percent. In February 1850 businessmen learned they would pay 25 percent more in fees for contracts and conventions. Estate taxes rose from 1 percent to 8 percent of gross evaluation, while the assessment on sales of mobile and immobile property went from 1½ percent to 3½ percent. The two lands would contribute 170 million Austrian lire a year after 1848 in taxes rather than the 112 million collected in 1847, and it has been estimated that only 70 million of the greater sum were expended for local needs.[1]

The resistance to the treasury bonds had convinced Baron Philipp von Krauss, the minister of finance, that voluntary subscriptions were much to be preferred. Bruck predicted that a "free-will loan" would fail. He wanted a forced loan, sweetened by 5 percent interest and purchasable by equal amounts of cash and treasury bonds. After all, the monarchy would not bear the interest charges; Lombardy and Venetia would.[2] The issue remained in abeyance until April 16, 1850, when the government invited the Lombards and Venetians to underwrite bonds with a face value of 120 million Austrian lire, yielding 5 percent returns.[3] Sales were unimpressive, and in May there was a request from Radetzky to extend the

deadline by ten days. He wanted to turn aside the reproach that this
was a forced loan, "meanwhile to make all preparations to effec-
tuate a compulsory loan."[4] The commission of Italian notables
which was to float the paper was still pleading for more time in October. Business was depressed, the silk production had been disap-
pointing, and there was a dearth of capital. Patience exhausted, the
government announced on November 25 that it would be happy to
accept voluntary purchases of the obligations until January 10,
1851. For the months of December, January, and February,
however, it would compel cash purchases of 5 million a month. In
the end the affluent proprietors and the pious endowments, generally administered by noble and upper bourgeois trustees, had to absorb the loan.[5]

In addition to the stamp tax, the salt and tobacco monopolies,
customs duties, and the lottery tax, Vienna decreed a 5.9 percent increase in the income tax on landed property on April 11, 1851. A
year later another 1.4 percent was added, so that a landholder faced
a 25 percent levy upon his revenue. The patent of 1851 also
demanded 5 percent of all commercial and professional earnings,
salaries, wages, annuities, and interest upon capital.[6] Radetzky had
recommended such imposts as a substitute for the compulsory circulation of 5 and 10 lire notes and to reduce the 50 percent sur-
charge on the land tax to 33 percent.[7] Italian conviction that the
Austrians deliberately discriminated against the well-to-do
aristocrat and businessman had considerable justification, for direct
taxes, aimed largely at land, industry, and the income thereof, accounted for 46 percent of the general increment in fiscal income
after 1848.[8]

The administrative scheme which Bach worked out for the kingdom in October 1849 seemed to make Radetzky quite powerful. As
governor-general he would direct civil and military affairs from
Verona, aided by formally separate sections there. He would control
the higher echelons of the police as well as command the Army of
Italy. He would decide on the imposition of "exceptional conditions," with the proviso that he would notify the minister of the interior of all matters relating to the monarchy's security. He
nominated all officials selected by emperors in the past and personally appointed the rest. It was up to him to decide on the powers

and responsibilities to be delegated to the governors of Lombardy and Venetia, stationed respectively in Milan and Venice. These preliminary decisions retained a court of appeals for the kingdom and envisaged separate representative assemblies once a *Statuto* was decreed.

In reality, the Ministry of Finance in Vienna had complete control of financial matters from the beginning.[9] As time passed, the central agencies increased their control. The Ministry of Justice guided the legal system, the *Allerhöchstes Armee Oberkommando* left to Radetzky little more than the training and discipline of his troops, and the postal authorities developed the system of communications. The Ministry of the Interior corresponded directly with and ultimately controlled the *Direzioni generali* of the police in Milan and Venice, and the lower ranks of the police gradually divorced themselves from the supervision of local officials.[10]

Despite the fears of the conservative courts of Italy, the chance for a *Statuto* for the kingdom ended with Francis Joseph's abolition of the constitution of March 4, 1849, on the last day of 1851. His ordinance of December 31, 1850, established two governorships (Michael Strassoldo for Lombardy, Georg von Toggenburg for Venice) and provided for a delegate who would represent the governors in each of the nine Lombard and seven Venetian provinces. This man, much like a French prefect, was head of the provincial congregation and responsible for the administration of all communes within his province. Aiding the delegates were eighty district commissioners in Lombardy, seventy-nine in Venetia. Stuck with the odious duties of drafting young men and collecting resented taxes, the delegates and district commissioners garnered no affection. Sometimes the provincial congregations challenged their decisions, for these men, who received no pay and usually were of the "respectfully unloyal" strata, were sensitive to local opinion.

In the communes the landed proprietors met in convocation twice a year to approve a budget, fix and apportion taxes, decide on public works, and choose the teacher, physician, and midwife. In the larger cities municipal councils of thirty to sixty members wrestled with the problems of finance, sanitation, water, public instruction, and conscription lists. Representatives of industry and trade picked one-third of these councillors, while the rest had to come from the richest landowners of the municipality. The larger cities and provincial capitals had a podestà, who was nominated by the council, subject to imperial confirmation.

Austria required the passive collaboration of the Italians if the empire was to draw sustenance from Lombardy and Venetia. Through the representative bodies of the communes and the provincial congregations, the monarchy obtained a surprising degree of cooperation. A sociologist of Emile de Laveleye's prominence praised the maturity and equilibrium, even the sense of liberty and order, that emerged from communal deliberations. Stefano Jacini, who by residence and observation knew the Lombard scene well, wrote in 1854 of the success of the communal "constitution" despite the pressures of an exceptional state of affairs. The elementary schools, the medical and charitable services, the supervision of midwifery, and the magnificent system of roads were the glories of the kingdom, preparing the way for what the English called "self-government." In Milan, Venice, even Pavia, the upper classes might absent themselves from the theater and their sons might provoke Austrian officers to duels in a running show of passive resistance, but there was little or no boycott of communal life. The "flight" to local administration was the aristocracy's way of reasserting its influence over society.

The judicial system evoked less enthusiasm because it was so often at odds with the traditions of the past. Austrian law was good, but procedure was often maddening and the magistracy mediocre. The courts of first instance in city and country were supposed to mediate cases whenever possible, but the judges either left this to their employees or made decisions on the basis of written depositions. The provincial tribunals came under fire for procedural confusion and for secret sessions, which flouted public opinion. In criminal cases which had political overtones, the preliminary investigation was a tough inquisition, and the trial was weighted against the defense. In no court was there trial by jury. As Francis Joseph put it, all who knew Lombardy-Venetia counseled against such a concession.[11] A special extraordinary commission sat in Mantua for "infamous" political derelictions.[12]

In 1850 the Austrian ministers split quite markedly over the suspension of the Lombard-Venetian Senate, which had handed down verdicts in Verona, and the transfer of its attributes to the Supreme Court of Justice in the imperial capital. Anton von Schmerling, minister of justice, was determined to uphold the unity of the empire. If the Senate remained, the almost complete isolation of the kingdom would continue, and the Italians would never accustom themselves to the idea that the empire's center of gravity was Vienna. Bruck, Bach, and Krauss denied that it was necessary or advisable to eliminate the Senate. The inhabitants of the kingdom formed a compact mass of 4 million, fundamentally different from the rest of the monarchy in speech, customs and culture. The regime should capitalize on their national sentiment. The empire should be an Italian great power on the other side of the Alps. Why arouse such subjects by depriving them of an institution they valued? A bare majority of the ministers at the end of a second vigorous debate on July 19 requested Francis Joseph to leave the Senate provisionally in Verona.

On July 27 an impatient emperor wanted to know why the decree on the Supreme Court had been postponed. Bach spoke of the unpleasant impression which this would create in the kingdom. Francis Joseph replied that the news would soon leak out anyway. Delay in announcing the transfer of the members of the Senate to Vienna would invite surmises of governmental indecision and weakness. There were no further hesitations. The law of August 7, 1850, did away with the Senate. Its jurists would join the Hungarians and Croats already assigned posts alongside the German Austrians. [13]

The young dynast was disinclined to concern himself with the feelings of former rebels. Schwarzenberg was already an advocate of a highly centralized state, and Bruck would soon surpass him in dilating upon the necessity of subordinating all to Vienna. Why should Italians have a tribunal which would set them above the more reliable Croats? Again, the empire was in an embarrassing financial plight, and the ministers were not predisposed to elaborate a budget which would guarantee the kingdom an equitable share of what was collected in taxes and forced loans. Revolution had largely contributed to the expected deficit, and those responsible were to pay for their actions. If the central congregations had not been restored, the propertied had some opportunity for limited involvement in provincial and communal bodies. Straightforward collaboration might well bring the reinstitution of the congregations in Milan and Venice. First, there would be a regime of justice tempered with rigor, a time of testing the fundamental loyalties of Italians under the Austrian crown.

Conspiracy and Rebellion

On the occasion of Francis Joseph's first birthday as emperor, August 18, 1849, the amnesty for possible returnees was prolonged, and, as seemingly unimportant byplay, one Teresa Olivari, a glove seller whose relations with Austrian officers were the talk of her quarter in Milan, hung from her balcony a black and gold carpet as a token of her political inclinations. The military who watched from a neighboring café laughed and applauded, but some displeased artisans milled about and threatened to rip down the impromptu decoration. Next day jailers in the forbidding Castello flogged fifteen men and two girls who had been arrested in the melee. A very much shocked Western Europe and America heard that the victims had been half-stripped and that Radetzky had ordered the Commune of Milan to pay for the vinegar, the ice, and the rods employed, as well as for the service of the jailers.

Radetzky's service in the kingdom after 1831 and his trying experiences in quelling the nationalistic fervor of 1848–49 left him no illusions about the temperament of many of his charges. On October 25, 1849, he issued a proclamation exhorting the Lombards and Venetians to realize that the monarchy's liberal institutions would assure them the advance of their interests and of their nationality. His motto was forgiveness of past actions. He needed their cooperation and loyalty to promote the welfare of a land which was his second fatherland.[14] A week later he was writing his son-in-law that the Italian territories had never loved the Germans and never would. The people would be submissive, however, for they realized the uselessness of a recourse to force, and that was that.[15]

On the surface it seemed that the year 1850 would be relatively quiet. The Austrians restored the provincial congregations and the universities opened in the autumn. Bianchi Giovini observed that the military moderated the state of siege and that there were fewer acts of cruelty.[16] Underground, however, patriots were selling the bonds which Giuseppe Mazzini's Italian National Committee had printed in London in September. Anyone involved in the operation knew he would be subject to trial for high treason. Mere possession of the certificates was sufficient evidence.

Dr. Alessandro Vandoni, sincerely pro-Austrian, reported to the police in Milan that his subordinate, Dr. Gaetano Ciceri, had such bonds. A month after Ciceri was condemned to ten years' imprisonment, an artisan murdered Vandoni, and Radetzky wrote directly to the emperor for permission to fine the city of Milan if no one turned in the assassin. Schwarzenberg, Bruck, Bach, and Krauss advised against such a fine, which would embitter the general population. In council Francis Joseph thought otherwise. Recent attacks in Rome and Leghorn pointed up the weakness of most Italian governments. Austria should act with energy. Concern for the innocent in Milan was out of place, for all the inhabitants paraded their ill will unceasingly. The response to the monarch's testiness was immediate. The ministers empowered Radetzky to levy a fine on the entire city if, within a limited time, someone did not reveal the identity of the guilty one. To hasten such action, the authorities were to offer a sustantial reward. Schwarzenberg warned Radetzky not to let it be known that the decision came from the emperor or his ministers.[17] The implication was that the governor-general should bear the opprobrium. On July 19, a "full" state of siege was restored, and the French agent in Milan wrote scathingly of the new severity. Radetzky evidenced as before a forgetfulness of the simplest principles of justice and good sense and a tendency to exasperate the people subjected to his authority.[18] The fine was not imposed, for Francis Joseph was planning his first comprehensive visit to the kingdom.

In Venice the citizens gaped at the tons of imperial luggage transferred from ship to railway depot on September 14, 1851, but they offered their ruler no signs of welcome. In Brescia a triumphal arch rather ambiguously declared that "the love of the people is the prop and strength of kings." Strassoldo picked Sunday for the imperial sojourn in Milan in the hope that shopkeepers and artisans would make up for the predictable absentees among the patriciate and intelligentsia. Francis Joseph wrote his mother that the military review under Radetzky in the square before the cathedral was magnificent, the city beautiful but "bad." At least Victor Emmanuel sent a special envoy to convey his salutations.

With obvious relief the emperor initiated great maneuvers on the plain of Somma on September 27. A steady rain turned the land into a quagmire, and the wind ripped apart the great tent where Radetzky had planned a formal dinner for fifty. A supplementary banquet from Milan arrived in time for a late afternoon rendezvous in a solid house, but the rumors which floated from the mock battle on September 28 warmed the hearts of the dissident Italians. Through faulty orders, attributed to the sovereign, the Hussars charged the Bohemians, who replied with bullets. At night the soaked and irritated soldiers pillaged their own supplies. Before dawn on September 29, the disgusted monarch quit the camp. By midnight he was in Venice, by October 1 en route to Vienna.[19]

Undoubtedly he had heard much of the trafficking in Mazzinian bonds and in the *Documenti della guerra santa d'Italia*, printed in Switzerland and venomously anti-Austrian. Agents hung around Alpine hotels and lake-steamer stations or smuggled the pamphlets through forest on horseback. Once in Italy, greater danger of discovery compelled the utilization of wine casks with false bottoms, cheese wagons with capacious wooden forms, and women who could stuff the little books in their undergarments. Priests' breviaries were not always what they seemed, nor were the ubiquitous sacks of charcoal. Without the connivance of certain employees of the royal diligence service and even of the police, distribution would have been much more difficult. Luigi Dottesio had edited the documents and organized the sales campaign. The police picked him up in January 1851, and he suffered the torments of a botched hanging on October 8. The next martyr for the Italian cause was Don Giovanni Grioli, a priest found guilty of suborning troops and of possessing subversive books and Mazzinian bonds. His dignified refusal to save himself by naming accomplices reassured and inspired other conspirators.[20]

The cases of Dottesio and Grioli indicated that clandestine operations probably involved hundreds. A routine search of a suspected counterfeiter in December 1851 turned up some Mazzinian bonds rather than forged bills. He implicated a priest who in turn incriminated Don Enrico Tazzoli, a teacher of theology in Mantua whose attitudes already had warranted Austrian watchfulness. In his dwelling the police found an encoded register, for his conscience had compelled him to keep a record of sales and contributions.

It took the cryptographers of Vienna rather a long time to crack Tazzoli's code, but the solution was on its way to Radetzky on May 24, 1852. A month before, the police had arrested Luigi Castellazzo, a young man who, close to the theologian, knew the key to the register. Few seem to doubt today that Castellazzo soon decided to talk. In fact, too many knew too much, and the Austrians had fearsome dungeons, nauseating food, the weapons of physical violence, and some shrewd practitioners of mental torture to break down the more impressionable of those incarcerated. "Auditor" Alfred Kraus inaugurated an outstanding career "for the emperor" with his brilliant tactics as an inquisitor.

As early as July 20 Bishop Giovanni Corti besought Pius IX to intervene with Francis Joseph so that more priests would not suffer Grioli's fate. The pontiff's reply of August 2 expressed bitterness and scandal over the liberalism of the kingdom's clergy. He hoped there would be no death sentence. Should there be, the bishop was to fulfill the duties prescribed by the church, that is, degrade the convicted from the clerical state. On July 31 Giacomo Cardinal Antonelli, the papal secretary of state, had asked the Austrian minister in Rome to secure imperial clemency should the court decree execution. On August 10 Radetzky informed Rome that there was no way to extend mercy to priests who had been the actual leaders of the secret committees. A week later came the emperor's regrets that he could not pardon such unworthy clergy.[21]

The interrogations dealt with 110 persons, 9 of whom would die. On December 7 Tazzoli; Angelo Scarsellini, a prosperous butcher who had toyed with the idea of kidnapping Francis Joseph; Giovanni Zambelli, a painter; Bernardo de Canal, a writer; and Carlo Poma, a physician, mounted the scaffold near the Belfiore fort of the Mantuan fortifications. The memory of the five bodies swinging in the wintry air was a reproach to every act of reparation the Austrians subsequently were to attempt. The execution of four more in March 1853 only increased the sense of horror.

Realizing that the scenes at Mantua affronted Western feelings and intensified Italian passive resistance, Austria announced on March 19 that the high treason process was at an end. The most guilty had been punished. Others who were implicated or who had confessed to Kraus had begged for mercy. Continuing the investigation would disgrace a large number of families, for many had been seduced. The fifty-seven still not disposed of were freed. Next evening the municipal officials of Milan ordered the city's illumination as a thanksgiving.

A month before that city had been the scene of an amateurish and brief rising against the whitecoats. Economic distress, common to all of Europe in the early 1850s, affected to some degree the porters, carpenters, shoemakers, goldsmiths, and hatters who gathered in modest inns to sing patriotic songs and mutter of rebellion. Upper-class conspirators were aware of the workers' anger over rising prices and the decline in opportunities for full employment. The habitués of Countess Clara Maffei's salon finally decided they would not join a rising from the streets. The well-to-do feared Austrian reprisals against their property in case of failure and were not sanguine about a poor man's provisional government in case of success.

Mazzini heard just enough about the lower-class ferment in Milan to leave London for Lugano on January 2, 1853. Two of his agents were already trying to organize an insurrection in the Lombard capital. Giuseppe Piolti De Bianchi was to handle the "civilian" aspects of the proposed coup, while Eugenio Brizi would be the military commander. From the beginning they disagreed on strategy, but Brizi persuaded the popular leaders to move just before five on Carnival Sunday, February 6, when many soldiers would be on pass and when strange antics in the streets would attract glances rather than questions.

For a few minutes twenty porters immobilized the Austrians in the guardhouse of the royal palace, only to be put to flight by soldiers who rushed from a nearby café with sabers flashing. Brizi was in command of the storming of the Castello, but only thirty volunteers arrived and nothing was done. The Porta Tosa quarter threw up barricades, but all was over in two hours. Ten Austrians had died, fifty-four had been wounded. Some Milanese had rescued injured troopers from inhumane treatment, but Radetzky, like Francis

Joseph, was quite sure that the whole city was "bad" and deserved severe punishment.

The fiasco had many explanations. The upper class would not join in, nor did the Hungarians of the various barracks. The rebels lacked decent rifles and ammunition, and it is probable that this fact kept most of the artisans at home when the hour of movement arrived. Brizi, personally brave, overestimated the courage of others. Mazzini's failure to name a supreme dictator of the operation may also have been a factor, though it is dubious that the popular leaders would always have bowed to Mazzinian precepts and orders. After February 6, 1853, extremely few Italians would have any further confidence in Mazzini and his tactics.[22]

Shaken and embarrassed, Radetzky reinstituted the state of siege and ordered the expulsion of every foreigner whose behavior was not correct. Milan would pay indemnities to the Austrian wounded and life incomes to the families whose breadwinner had been killed. On February 18 a decree sequestered the lands and personal property of émigrés who were living in Piedmont. The governor-general assumed that their money paid for the unending conspiracies. He would end such machinations, even if some of those involved had become Piedmontese citizens.

Austrian overreaction to the insurrection is generally explained in terms of Vienna's growing sense of outrage over Sardinian actions. If the émigrés who had snubbed the rather easy conditions of repatriation were forced to realize that the regime in Turin could not save them from a kind of despoilment, their manners might change. It is likely that before the rising in Milan Radetzky had been inclined to commute the death sentences imposed upon the second batch of prisoners at Mantua. His mortification over the two hours of surprise and skirmish in the streets sealed their fate, though it should be remembered that fifty-seven were released.

Less than two weeks after the outburst in Milan, Francis Joseph barely escaped a double-edged knife wielded by a Magyar journeyman-tailor named János Libényi. Archduke Maximilian called for the building of a cathedral to commemorate the fortunate deliverance from assassination.[23] By April 20 Milanese had contributed over 73,000 Austrian lire for what was to be the Votivkirche in Vienna, and the city was returning to normal. Church bells could ring, several well-known émigrés returned and recovered their properties by signing promises of good behavior, and the military announced they would mitigate the state of siege as of October 1.

Austria substantially modified the regime in the kingdom in 1854. The Piedmontese denunciations of the sequesters had not been without effect in France and England, and indications that a surprising number of émigrés would bow to financial pressure and return with pledges to be orderly also impressed Vienna. Last, the serious crisis in the kingdom's agricultural sector placed in jeopardy Austria's chances of securing absolutely necessary tax support from the Lombards and Venetians. It was unwise to alienate sentiment by constant searches, interrogations, and gallows scenes that outraged the public. During the year there were no political executions and relatively few arrests for subversive activity.[24]

Francis Joseph's marriage to Elizabeth of Bavaria was a proper occasion for sovereign acts of grace. On April 16 the bridegroom-to-be freed or reduced the sentences of 160 who were imprisoned in military fortresses. Soon thereafter he announced that the state of siege in the kingdom would end on May 1, 1854. In the same period Radetzky lifted the sequester on the property of 189 émigrés whose patrimonies were so small that the members of the families they had left behind could not survive without the income.

An imperial wedding was an extraordinary event, but the precarious state of the imperial treasury was quite normal. Turned down by the Rothschilds, the state notified the crown lands it would require 350 million to 500 million florins. Lombardy was to subscribe 40 million, Venetia, 25 million. One communal council after another deliberated on what it could absorb. The Milanese promised 18 million and undoubtedly bore the brunt of the exaction. The final figures indicated that Lombardy lent 37,954,740 florins, while Venetia advanced 24,616,761.[25] Radetzky wrote his daughter that the "quasi-forced free-will loan" had been collected without incident but also without any discernible advantage. The "sword of Demosthenes" still dangled over their heads, and he worried that winter would bring new dancing to thunderous music. Sentiment in the kingdom worsened daily, for everyone preferred a state of siege to civilian bureaucrats.[26]

Francis Joseph and his ministers thought otherwise, for sensitivity to Western opinion and relief over the general calm in Lombardy and Venetia opened the way to further concessions. There was a new code of criminal procedure in the spring of 1855 and an amnesty which released or reduced the sentences of all who had been found guilty by civil courts of lese majesty or of disturbance of public tranquillity. A patent of July 15 reactivated the central congregations after the cabinet struck down two changes recommended by Radetzky. There was no disposition to add the apposite archbishop or his representative to these bodies or to have the emperor appoint the members directly. In both cases Bach's reasoning had been decisive. Episcopal representation would conflict with existing concepts of church-state relations in the kingdom, and it would be impolitic to take away from the communal councils their right to suggest men for the provincial organs. The final draft actually expanded the deliberative and consultative powers assigned these congregations.[27]

A decisive moment in the renewed attempts to establish some base of loyalty to Austria in the kingdom was the meeting of the Ministerrat on November 17, 1855. Francis Joseph had summoned Count Friedrich Thun-Hohenstein to report on a revision of the lines of communication with Vienna, and the visitor had an interesting estimate of the situation in Lombardy and Venetia. He perceived no revolutionary threat, only the educated class's "reticence" in regard to the regime's important social affairs. They dared not tempt the Sardinian press. He would not deny that the Austrian military's attitude toward Italians and the army's tendency to offend Italian sensibilities had done a great deal to nourish the discord. His most important suggestion was to bring the émigrés home, where they could be watched.

Buol agreed that a complete cleansing of the question would do much to calm both lands. Would it not be wise to give the unrepentant a chance to sell their possessions while offering those who wanted to be good citizens every opportunity to return? Bach concurred, and the ruler commanded the preparation of an appropriate decree.[28] In a subsequent discussion the ministers were unanimous that sequestration should end. Should the émigré who could or would not come back be forced to sell his land? Bach, Buol, and Count Leo Thun-Hohenstein, the minister of education, admitted that the legality of the sequestration was questionable, but Bach wanted to compel the nonreturnee to dispose of his property. He wanted no toleration of impudence, no concession that would discredit Austria and enhance Piedmont's standing. Bruck liked the prospect of a public announcement of the end of sequestration, but he had no support.[29]

Bach submitted a compromise early in 1856. The governor-general would have the right to readmit those who applied during 1856 and restore their property if they signed the pledge of good behavior. Those who chose not to return or who knew they would be refused reentry were also to apply during 1856 for a decision on their estates. Some would have to sell, others not. If an émigré made no move to take advantage of the concession offered, the state would liquidate his possessions and deposit the proceeds for the émigré or his heirs. A nonpropertied émigré could petition for a penalty-free return or for status as an emigrant. A confidential report of the decisions reached would be dispatched to the Sardinian government, which in turn would notify the petitioners. Bach's colleagues unanimously approved his project. Their objections to forced sales had been softened by his insistence that the most intransigent, who ignored nearly every overture, deserved some unpleasantness.[30]

By October the greatest part of the land under sequester was "freed," but some sixteen hundred still had done nothing to clarify their rights. Since the imperial couple were planning a splendid progress through the Italian possessions, the ministers wanted an end to the affair. Bruck proposed a general pardon, with no exceptions, to destroy Piedmont's influence with the emigration with one blow. Again, he was alone, for Bach convinced the others that Austria had to have the right to exclude the worst of the undesirables. A united cabinet decided to lift the sequester on October 28. All who had not requested reentry by the end of 1857 would be regarded legally as "emigrants." If they could prove naturalization by a foreign state, Austria would recognize their new citizenship. At Bach's suggestion, there was no time limit on requests for repatriation.[31] On December 2, while Francis Joseph and Elizabeth were in Venice, an imperial rescript ended sequestration and empowered Radetzky to receive petitions for the right to return and for the restoration of Austrian citizenship.

In four years the Austrians had proved they could be implacable with leaders of conspiracy, panicky over a minor uprising in Milan, and eventually intelligent enough to end the state of siege, to restore the central congregations, and to annul the sequestration of émigré property. They had abandoned Metternich's unwritten law that the state should not execute for political crimes, even to the point of hanging degraded priests. Sentiment in England and France, concern over serious economic problems in the kingdom, and the inevitable relaxation of the hysteria which had marked the years of military reconquest all contributed something to the modification of a tough regime. Radetzky's usefulness manifestly was at an end. With his retirement, the emperor might send a viceroy pledged to increasing concessions. Lombardy and Venetia were valuable possessions, a fact realized by ministers and generals alike.

Education and the Press

Elementary schools in the kingdom were the responsibility of the communes, and Jacini had high praise for what was accomplished. Parents were fined if their sons were absent from classes, but the rule was infrequently enforced in the smaller rural areas. At the higher level of *licei* and *ginnasi*, classical studies were paramount, and the curriculum was bare of courses in the history of Milan and Venice, even of the papacy. Schools and colleges under the direction of parish priests and monks did not enjoy a good reputation among the literate and well-fixed. The universities of Padua and Pavia aroused the greatest apprehensions among the Austrians, for students whose parents had properties in Lombardy and in Piedmont often attended the latter and were blamed for propaganda that was difficult to track down. The professors were not particularly distinguished, but few were apologists or spies for the regime. Almost never did the authorities discipline them for the ideas they professed, and these academicians were not loath to plead for students who ran afoul of the police.

The regime was particularly concerned over instruction in philosophy and in politico-legal affairs. When the two universities reopened by governmental order in the autumn of 1850, they were permitted to accept students in these disciplines and in mathematics only if the students were legal residents of the provinces of Pavia and Padua. Students in other provinces had to seek private tutors, though the private teaching of philosophy was forbidden everywhere. Any properly qualified candidate could enroll for theology at Padua or for medicine at either university. Austria realized that university training of some kind was imperative, whatever might be the risks.

The private tutors in politico-legal studies often were men of distinction whose political past prevented their appointment to posts in university or *liceo*. Their classes offered opportunities for freewheeling discussions, and the authorities realized it was impossible to monitor all of the sessions. In a long *mémoire* of August 9, 1852, Strassoldo besought Radetzky to allow all "reliable" Lombards to enroll in law courses at Pavia. The resulting ordinance sanctioned the admission of only those men who could present a certificate of good moral and political conduct and who could enlist a sponsor, acceptable to the government, who would guarantee the student's good behavior. Private instruction was permissible, but only to classes of four and for no longer than six hours a day. The tutors had to demonstrate such exemplary moral, social, and political standards that it was easy to deny licenses to the more provocative. Though students from both public and private sectors would anger Francis Joseph and Maximilian in the last years of Austrian control, it cannot be shown that their instruction played the dominant role in stimulating their increasing readiness to turn to political manifestations. The older Milanese cultural tradition and livelier currents from the liberal states of Europe were probably more influential.[32]

That cultural tradition could not openly challenge the Austrian determination to keep the press under tight control, but in subtle and indirect ways it was quite effective in sustaining native pride. *Il Crepuscolo*, which published its first number in Milan on January 6, 1850, was the most impressive example of the intelligentsia's resolution to treat the most urgent questions arising in literature, science, art, and industry. For some years in every number there was a political article, but Carlo Tenca, the editor, never mentioned Austria or Austrian policy in Italy. It was no wonder that the *Luogotenenza* of Milan wrote to Radetzky on July 24, 1853, that the journal's dangerous tendencies were not to be found in isolated statements, but in its general tone and procedure. Its silences demonstrated an orientation that was completely inadmissible. Anyone who read the issues carefully could discern its muted opposition to imperial policy. With its encomiums it furnished arguments for all who were against the regime. Under cover of literary and art criticism, it nourished the foolish doctrine of national independence. Tenca survived warnings from the authorities until 1857, when they suppressed his political section for his refusal to mention the emperor's visit to the kingdom. Definitely the voice of the bourgeoisie, for he distrusted the workers and socialism, Tenca was one of the constructive forces of the decade.

The press law of September 1, 1852, instituted a licensing system for all internally published books and periodicals. Should the publication evidence hostile tendencies toward state, throne, dynasty, or the organs of the Lombard-Venetian regime, it was due no more than two written warnings. Thereafter the governor could suspend its issuance for up to three months. Only the highest police authority could order a longer suspension or revocation of license, and it will be remembered that Vienna controlled such decisions. The press reacted to such admonitions and suspensions by retreating to purely technical discussions or by reprinting stories which had caused no repercussions in Viennese papers. The *Eco della Borsa* survived in this fashion until 1859, and a warning its editor received in February 1854 is a good example of those matters which aroused official displeasure. According to the bill of complaints, it had depicted as a distinctive characteristic of the age a restless striving for intellectual liberties. It had paid tribute to constitutionalism and republicanism and had implied that governments would have a more solid base if they satisfied the exigencies of the times and did not depend on diplomacy and guns.[33]

The official gazettes of Milan and Venice circulated the texts of decrees and made necessary announcements with the dryness that afflicts all such organs. *La Bilancia*, which never suffered from administrative warnings, was so pro-Habsburg that it stayed alive thanks to subventions rather than subscribers. The government's most interesting experiment with a newspaper that might appeal to reasonable Italians originated in a Ministerrat of December 24,

1849. Schwarzenberg reported that a certain Mauroner wished to start a paper in Vienna in Italian but did not have enough money to meet the *Cautionspflicht* (the depositing of a sum to pay possible fines for infractions of press regulations). Sure that this experienced and reliable journalist's articles would be influential in Italy, the minister-president indicated that the rule would be waived. If Mauroner did not live up to expectations, the government would make him put up the deposit.[34]

The *Corriere Italiano* lasted from 1850 to 1857. Records indicate that it received something less in subsidies in 1852 than the sums bestowed upon the *Wiener Zeitung* and *Die Presse*. A loyal son of Trieste, Alessandro Mauroner respected Italian culture while decrying Mazzini and ultranationalism. When he detected corruption and excessive punishments, he was critical and so earned the dislike of the papal and Neapolitan governments. Radetzky complained that he directly contradicted the purposes of the regime in Lombardy-Venetia, while the Tuscan ministry subscribed to keep check on what was written. The issues that survive have a prevailingly gray tone that Mauroner's circumstances dictated. On occasion he broke away, publishing some verses by Silvio Pellico and praising Cesare Balbo, whose works could not circulate in Radetzky's realm. He pilloried the papal government for its neglect of public education, its impotence in the face of brigandage, and its failure to effect municipal reform. Since the Austrian government held similar views, his paper suffered confiscation only in the papal dominions.

In March 1856 Antonelli asked Michele Viale Prelà, the nuncio in Vienna, to investigate the man responsible for such "vicious" articles, and he received a most interesting reply. Mauroner had called upon the papal envoy when he first published his journal, indicating he would print stories friendly to the church. On the contrary, the paper had been hostile, especially during the quarrel between Rome and Turin over Siccardi's legislation. A third person suggested that Mauroner would appreciate a papal decoration, and Viale had responded that he would have to earn "my recommendation." Nothing had really changed in his columns, however, and little was accomplished by official complaints, because of the guarantees of press freedom. In the nuncio's opinion, Mauroner lived high, needed money, and enjoyed little esteem. There was one way to deal with his journal. It should be kept from papal territory.[35]

In the tense times of the Congress of Paris in 1856, Mauroner was critical of Piedmont's "egoist" and "impractical" policies and declared that only fools and madmen could believe that Austria would abandon Lombardy and Venetia. It is not clear why the *Corriere Italiano* ceased its operations in 1857. Indubitably it had not attracted enough subscribers to merit a proposed move to Trieste. More than likely, Francis Joseph's acquiescence in a new approach to Lombard-Venetian problems eliminated the need for this type of journalism.[36]

Austrian subsidies to sympathetic publishers had as a corollary the strict control of foreign printed materials within the kingdom. Under general police supervision a commission in Milan reviewed all works deemed suspicious by ordinary police censors, with final decision left to the governor-general. It exercised a moderating influence but forbade historical and political works which implied that Italy should be for the Italians. The commission's chief concern was the flood of newspapers from abroad. A tax of 10 centesimi upon all such copies did not deter the reader who already "thought too much," and in August 1851 Vienna decreed an empirewide embargo on certain anti-Austrian journals of Turin and Genoa. Sometimes issues of conservative and clerical Piedmontese periodicals did not get beyond the frontier because they did not adequately live up to their professed principles. At the end of 1851, Radetzky decreed that no private companies could transport publications. All had to come in by post. Swiss journals were often as inflammatory as the Piedmontese, and occasional confiscations of the *New York Tribune for Europe* and the *New York Herald* testified to suspicions of a country that feted Kossuth and named overactive democrats to consular posts.

The system rarely frustrated those who were determined to sample liberal sentiment. If not under "police provisions," a subject could visit Piedmont, Switzerland, and even England. Letters passed without unreasonable delays to friends abroad, and a perusal of what was written indicates that postal interceptions were either few or perfunctory. Should all else fail, there were the smugglers who brought in journals, books, messages, and persons of distinct interest to the police. Austrian rebuttals of foreign criticisms and attacks, officially published, revealed to the perceptive Austria's reputation in the liberal states.

The bourgeois and aristocratic circles who supported *Il Crepuscolo* and glanced disdainfully at the *Corriere Italiano* tended to fear the urban workers and worried over a peasantry that shouted "Viva Radetzky!" in hope of land reform. Some concluded that duty and self-interest demanded an educational campaign, especially among the country folk, through almanacs, simplified historical accounts, and instructive narratives.[37] A generation that shuddered over *Uncle Tom's Cabin* and the miseries of the Russian serfs circulated such materials widely. The attitude of the peasantry to the Austrians in 1859 would depend, however, more upon their canny estimate of what the Austrians had done for them.

Economic Conditions

Only a reasonably prosperous land could absorb the tribute which Austria demanded of Lombardy in the 1850s. Throughout the period, agriculture remained the livelihood of the majority, with many of the peasants turning to industrial employment in the slow months. Obviously, it was the fertile land of the Po valley which enticed so many émigrés into returning. Industry was developing rather slowly, so that Lombard towns escaped some of the horrors of a Manchester. The most striking example of Austrian indifference was the dragged-out pace of railway construction, but the much admired road system and the interlocking net of river, lake, and canal softened the effects of that neglect.

Lombardy was synonymous with silk in the middle of the nineteenth century, and the surpluses of credit built up in London by raw and manufactured silk lubricated much of Milan's export and import business. Peasants tended the silkworms for their landlords or for themselves, and they and their wives and children made up much of a labor force for whom steam-driven machinery was still something of a novelty. In 1853 a terrible disease, pébrine, appeared and killed off enough silkworms to cut production some years to a third of normal. As early as March 1853 a decree permitted the temporary importation of raw silk and its consequent exportation as a finished product duty-free. Imports did not suffice to maintain the industry, which was, as a luxury enterprise, always subject to elastic demand. The town of Como seemed to weather the crisis better than the other centers, but the dislocations which pébrine brought about added to the general picture of depression in the first part of the decade.

Wine was another important product, though it is likely that Lombardy was not self-sufficient. Simultaneously with the sporozoa that attacked the silkworm came the vine mildew that reduced crops seriously by 1855. The incidence of cholera in 1855 and 1856 added to the people's misery, and a longtime dependence on corn, intensified by lack of money for meat or cheese, resulted in a substantial increase in pellagra.

Such disasters were hardly the fault of the Austrian administration, but it would be difficult to argue that Lombardy shared adequately in the unprecedented expansion of the European economy from 1852 to 1856. There was such a threat of famine that duty-free importation of cereals was allowed between 1853 and 1856. In normal times, there was self-sufficiency in grains. Cheese was a profitable export, but it was usually necessary to import cattle, fish, olive oil, fresh fruit and vegetables, and, as mentioned, wine. Silk, in every possible form, ordinarily paid for such imports. When that industry went into decline, the repercussions were general.

The cotton industry expanded during the decade, but it lacked sufficient capital and sources of energy to install power looms. The spinning mills had already claimed most of the waterpower, and Lombardy consequently imported a great deal of raw cotton without providing enough cloth to satisfy home demand. The linen industry was even more modest, though some was exported. Competition from the rest of the empire and the forbidding cost of mechanization inhibited the entrepreneurs. Lack of fuel and of modern furnaces kept metallurgical establishments small and traditional. For political reasons the government severely restricted the Brescian arms industry, which had been one of Lombardy's glories.

In 1851 the empire introduced protectionism in place of the older system of prohibition. The tariff favored Lombardy by permitting the free entry of mulberry leaves, coal, rags (for the small and vulnerable paper industry), and peat. Colonial products paid over 50 percent of their valuation. The poor might eschew coffee and chocolate, but the five or six great importers of raw cotton found it advisable to buy directly in New Orleans rather than through London. The regulations exacted 10 to 30 percent on agricultural items, 40 to 50 percent on iron, and an average of 20 percent on manufactures and semi-finished goods. There were minimal export duties on raw silk and textiles. To harmonize the rates with those of the Zollverein, Austria cut the duty in 1853 on iron and silk manufactures. The export tax on the finest silk ended. For ordinary silks, it was reduced.

Economic historians cannot come to a positive verdict on the effects of protectionism, for they agree that smuggling seriously impaired Austria's dream of a great customs union embracing Italy and Germany. Ira A. Glazier concluded that one-third of the sugar, textiles, and manufactured goods consumed in the kingdom came in as contraband. Bruno Caizzi surmised that smuggling was probably the invisible element that assured Lombardy its monetary equilibrium. Exports always surpassed imports in the official tables. Money went to Vienna for taxes and bonds and to Venetia for raw silk, but Caizzi believed that only the utilization of excess income for contraband saved the land from inflation. One could describe the industrial sector by the phrase, "Silk is king," for that commodity accounted for 77 to 94 percent of all exports between 1851 and 1858. Other manufactures could not meet local demand, the frontier was admirably suited for covert operations, and it was not likely that the customs officials were incorruptible.

Aware of the omnipresence of smuggling and desirous of better relations with the Lombard entrepreneurial class, the empire made some reductions in 1856 that were insufficiently sharp to end contraband. It cost less to bring in cotton and woolen yarns, iron, lead, olive oil, and colonial goods, but entire villages continued to make a living from illegal trafficking. Much came from Switzerland and the smaller towns of Piedmont, but Milan's chief emporiums were Genoa, Venice, and Trieste. It is difficult to believe that the businessmen of these competitive ports wer innocent of involvement in the illicit trade.[38]

Society became more complex in the last ten years of Austrian

rule. In the lands watered by the Po and by an excellent system of irrigation, most of the aristocratic landowners were absentee, leasing
much of their land to tenants who had the status of a rural
bourgeoisie. In turn, these tenants made contracts with peasants
who had free, if dismal, quarters and a bit of land for their own
gardens. Other peasants rented cottages and received pay only for
the days they worked. The most miserable were the itinerant and
part-time laborers, hired only for the busiest times. They were lucky
if they could sleep in stables or under porches. Workers in the rice
fields suffered from intermittent fever, pellagra was a way of life for
those who subsisted on corn bread and polenta, and the open sewers
facilitated the incidence of cholera.

Most of the industrial establishments were in small towns, where
the owners exploited the labor (often women and children) not
utilized throughout the year by landlords and bourgeois tenants. If
the workrooms never were as fetid and crowded as England's, they
were but a relative improvement over the back-breaking toil in the
fields. The extra income was welcome, and some of the peasant-
workers carried on spinning and weaving at home, which was not
always of unquestionable benefit. Peasants on fixed contracts,
especially if they or their families had a chance to help in the textile
industry, were distinctly better off than the most depressed of
Galicia, Hungary, and Croatia. Life for the rest of the kingdom's
peasantry was "very sad," in Stefano Jacini's opinion.

In the hilly regions the greatest complaint centered about the rais-
ing of silkworms. The peasant received only half of those which lived
and had to buy the mulberry leaves from the proprietor. Too, the
latter decided how many would be brought to maturity, even at a
time when a scarcity of mulberry leaves forced up prices. Women
consequently sought employment as spinners, weavers, and reelers,
while their men competed for jobs in construction and road
building. In the mountains most of the farmers were owners of tiny
bits of land, though there was a considerable amount of communal
pasture and woodland for cattle, sheep, and goats. Poverty was the
fate of nearly all, with the possible exception of some who had flocks
of cattle.

The workers of Milan and the larger towns probably enjoyed a
better life. Catering to the affluent and servicing the needs of a sol-

vent and active commercial class, they also might take advantage of the textile mills which appeared in the suburbs. The democratic tendencies of some perturbed the upper classes, as the abortive rising of 1853 in Milan indicated. Radetzky wrote of "communism," and "socialism" was a word of import after the French experience of 1848. Undoubtedly there was a normal quotient of rancor among the "have-nots" against the rich, but strict Austrian prohibitions against collective action and the dispersal of the labor force throughout Lombardy militated against the development of class consciousness.[39]

The Milan rising infuriated Francis Joseph and embarrassed Radetzky, but they and the rest of Austrian officialdom sensed that the real enemy was the aristocracy which had not deigned to return. The sequester, with the strong hint of eventual confiscation, was notice that the traditional pillars of society, when untrustworthy, could expect drastic, even illegal, punishment. It was one thing to strike at émigrés in Turin or even in Paris. The Lombards who foregathered in salons and private homes and who traveled with some frequency to the West posed quite a different problem. Their declinations of invitations to high social functions and their sporadic boycotting of the theater were irritating, but it was realized they were the subject of surveillance and subtle pressure from the exiles. Austria systematically excluded them from the highest posts in the administration and judiciary, but there was an awareness of the positive role they played in communal affairs and of their value as more or less involuntary subscribers to imperial loans. It was clearly better to have them within the confines, and consequently emperor and ministers moved to a liquidation of the issue of sequestration.

The passive resistance of a part of the nobility and their friends among the intelligentsia has long been a favorite theme of patriotic Italian writers. A century and some later one must ask how important their negations were. At Countess Clara Maffei's salon the best minds in Milan discussed literature, art, and economics in the context of Italy's resurrection. In a sense the gatherings were counterpoint to the articles in *Il Crepuscolo*, for Tenca, Emilio Visconti-Venosta, Carlo Cattaneo, and Stefano Jacini were regulars. Giovanni Visconti-Venosta remembered the countess as petite, pleasing rather than beautiful, of elegant manner. Her fervent nationalism colored all of her comments, but she and her friends, save one, resolved to stay clear of the popular rising of February 1853. A more daring hostess was Giulietta Pezzi, who received dedicated Mazzinians in her home and was an accomplice in the sale of Mazzini's bonds. A third coterie, primarily aristocratic, enjoyed the hospitality of Carlo D'Adda and his wife. On occasion Jacini and Emilio and Giovanni Visconti-Venosta appeared in these precincts, where fear of the "Barabba," as the lower-class insurgents of 1853 were called, was more pronounced.[40]

The Mantuan trials and the implications of the Milanese rising gradually turned sentiment toward the house of Savoy, whose chief servant, Cavour, was realizing the moral and material advance which Tenca and his associates evangelized. The Maffei and D'Adda salons were adjuncts of this process, but little more. Those entrapped by the police had other inspirations, and the apparent Austrian disinclination to worry over the tenor of the conversations was realistic. They nabbed the overt plotters. In time they would try, under Maximilian, to enlist the thinkers.

Venice's stalwart resistance of 1848-49 conditioned Austrian policy toward the city for two years after the capitulation. Persons compromised in the revolutionary movement received little pity. The siege had left the city's population hungry and easy prey to disease. Commerce was at a standstill, and General Karl Gorzkowski decreed on August 27, 1849, that the free port was limited to the island of San Giorgio, already overrun with military and naval units. He also had vaguely promised that all save the hopelessly unfaithful could stay in Venetia without fear of reprisals. In reality the victors soon began to purge magistrates, teachers, and lawyers from the state complement and inveigled private firms into dismissing employees who had been identified with the republican government. Often, professionals who were self-employed found themselves stripped of the right to practice. The authorities fired most of the workers at the Arsenal, provoking one into a murderous attack upon an Austrian official.

The communal council decided in early September to send a delegation to Francis Joseph to request the restoration of the free port and "all those other generous sovereign favors" without which the wounds would never heal. Heading the group was Patriarch

Jacopo Monico, and the bill of particulars prompted in-
credulousness among Austrians who believed that rebellion warranted retaliation, at least for a time. In addition to the revival of
the free port, the commune wanted a reduction in financial exac-
tions, recognition of at least two-thirds of the debt run up by the
revolutionary regime, full-time operation of the Arsenal, completion of the port of Malamocco, the substitution of civil for military
government at the earliest possible moment, and a guarantee of
Venice's commanding position above the rest of the Venetian
provinces.

Schwarzenberg was brusque, reminding the petitioners that
30,000 had died because of Venice's "blind defiance." The delegation told the emperor that all of Europe had been enmeshed and
deluded. What had happened in Venice was the work of alien,
rather than of indigenous, seducers. In measured tones Francis
Joseph noted they had been the last to submit to the legitimate
power. They should be the first to obey all the laws, "without which
nations and individuals would come to ruin." Without promising
anything, he adjured them to unite their forces with his to make
Venice flourishing and spotlessly loyal, as of old. Before leaving, the
emissaries also begged that the entire kingdom assume part of the
revolutionary commune's debt, since this had been promised by the
provisional government in Milan and by committees in the Venetian
provinces.

At Bruck's suggestion the patriarch raised the question of the
workers forced to leave the Arsenal. The ecclesiastic asked for
diligent investigation, to separate the truly guilty subversives from
men who had to support their families under every regime. Public
order could not last if the Arsenal shut down. Austria also should
not levy the heavy "war tax" on those Venetians of the provinces who
found themselves in the city during the siege and had to contribute
to the republic.[41]

Before the delegates returned home, Bruck informed the
Ministerrat that he would reject the request for reestablishment of
the free port.[42] Radetzky was not insensitive to the city's economic
woes, and he supported Bruck against Franz von Gyulai, the
minister of war, in allowing the storage of foreign goods on the
island of San Giorgio.[43] At the end of January 1850 he slashed the

supplementary (and punitive) tax from 25 percent to 5 percent, and in March he restored the dole for those dismissed from the Arsenal and left some commissions with its directors.

Such palliatives did little to remedy the city's miseries. Count Niccolo Priuli, one of the few whose advice Schwarzenberg sought, wrote the emperor that he hoped history would not record that a city which emerged from the sea in barbaric times had perished during the century of progress. In September 1850 Francis Joseph received another petition for the restoration of the free port, and a commission did begin to study the means to come to Venice's aid. The official gazette printed realistic descriptions of empty stores and beggars.[44] Toggenburg informed Bach that only a restoration of the free port would bring financial relief and calm the people. Krauss opposed such a move. Customs receipts had gone up since the abolition of the privilege. Its reestablishment would only encourage smuggling. Too, why give the Italians such a break? There were good political reasons against such a grant. Bruck contested these arguments eloquently. The siege of Venice had proved that a ring about the city could eliminate contraband. Austria, with a small coastline, needed to do everything possible to develop Trieste and Venice. An act of grace would instill a sense of sympathy for the emperor and his government. Bach seconded Bruck, pointing to the deadly Genoese competition and to Radetzky's preference for the old arrangement. On March 22 the ministers discussed the relevant patent, which reminded the Venetians that "regrettable acts" had damaged their shipping and commerce.[45]

A few days later, Francis Joseph, Maximilian, and Radetzky gathered in Venice. Verdi's brand-new *Rigoletto* was the gala performance at La Fenice on March 27 for the distinguished visitors, and the audience buzzed with rumors of a free port once again. The *Gazzetta* confirmed the speculation, declaring that the emperor desired his people's happiness when that was practicable. His inspiration was history, not romance, for he wanted to ameliorate life's actual conditions. He was averse to the deceptive appearances of a utopia.[46]

Venice and the provinces of Venetia were no utopia during the 1850s. Lombardy might be a verdant garden, with a burgeoning industry that could soften the rigors of peasant existence. Venetia suffered from the same blights that assaulted Lombard viniculture and sericulture, and the greater extent of mountainous terrain and of marginal fields enhanced the land's struggles with nature. The statistics for the decade exclude the free port's activities, and so the picture of international trade is blurred. Even so, there is little doubt of Venetia's passive balance between 1851 and 1858. Exports dropped by 15 percent, imports rose by 18 percent. There were compensations, for the great quantities of raw silk exported from Verona to Lombardy do not figure in the record. Too, there is a distinct possibility that some of the invisible payments associated with the free port ended up in pockets across the lagoons. Certainly the profits from brokerage, insurance, stevedoring, and ship's services helped balance the free port's constantly increasing deficit. Too, tourists spent money in Europe's most exotic port. Glazier concludes nevertheless that the condition of free port and terra firma was very grave.[47] The ships which entered and left the waters of Venice did not grow in number or tonnage markedly during the decade. In 1852, 4,139 came in with a tonnage of 394,510, while 4,514 entered in 1858 with a tonnage of 405,246. For Giovanni Zalin, this was stagnation, in view of rising maritime activity throughout the world. There was insufficient utilization of men and resources.[48] Gino Luzzatto was somewhat more impressed that the value of the goods that entered in 1859 was almost double that of 1847.[49]

Most Venetians of the terra firma were agriculturists. Probably there was a rough equilibrium between those who left the land and those who returned. Seasonal migration, most marked from the mountainous areas, meant income for temporary masons, chair makers, porters, sausage makers, and road laborers. Nowhere did the nobility possess as much as half of the land, though their estates were characteristic of the plains surrounding Padua and Verona. They might be opulent or needy. The latter were likely to sell to the bourgeoisie, especially the families of Greek and Jewish descent in Venice.[50]

Venetian grain production could not adequately compensate for the plagues which overtook the silk and wine industries. Almost all of the countryside was devoted to mixed cultivation, with never enough animal power to plough and manure the soil. As in Lombardy, the regime tried to encourage the importation of cereals, but prices of grain, sorghum, millet, rape, rice, potatoes, turnips, and apples rose appreciably by 1854-55. Publicists who once blamed landlords and peasants for inertia and apathy were more likely to look askance at the regime's all too limited relief measures. Somehow it seemed to Venetians that Lombardy had an industry which yielded profits and developed skills among the peasantry, while Austria demonstrated no interest in taking steps to encourage or revive similar enterprises in Venetia.[51]

In reality the Lombards had a fuller acquaintance with textiles and waterpower. There was nothing wrong with the north of the Veneto and the province of Padua in regard to agricultural productivity, but Jacini estimated Lombard agrarian income at 425 million lire a year, Venetian at 270 million lire. In general the Lombards had better land. Venice was still turning out more than 2 million kilograms of glassware about 1850, but there was not enough capital, skilled labor, or power to initiate the early stages of industrialism. The competition of the non-Italian crown lands and of the Zollverein surely had much to do with Venetia's continuing agrarianism. Lack of experience and resources were just as pivotal, however. Veronese craftsmen had once reeled and spun silk, but in the 1850s it was more profitable to export raw silk directly to Lombardy.[52]

Both lands had reason to complain of the slow pace in railway building. Austria began well, constructing the second of all Italian lines, Milan-Monza, in 1840. In 1846 there was the link between Padua and Venice. In the postrevolutionary period Bruck and Andreas von Baumgartner nationalized most of the private lines and developed new projects at state expense. The treasury's crisis of 1854 forced retrenchment, and a company organized by the Rothschilds bought the Lombardy-Venetian railways for 100 million francs in May 1856. At that time the final connection between Milan and Venice was a year from completion. By 1859 Lombardy boasted of but 202 kilometers of railroad; Venetia, 469 kilometers. In Vienna there was great interest in linking that city with Trieste and Verona with Innsbruck, but corporate enterprise seemed no more speedy than imperial. Only the excellent road system and the impressive Lloyd service that carried freight and passengers from Trieste and

Venice along the Po to Pavia and beyond to the Lake Maggiore-Ticino area muffled the protests of the mercantile interests of the kingdom.[53]

In retrospect economists see Lombardy forging ahead industrially in the early 1850s, despite undercapitalization and the side effects of the crises in silk and wine production. Austrian tariffs favored the growth of cotton mills and inhibited metallurgy. Conscious governmental policy was less of a factor in sericulture than were the vagaries of world supply and demand. A depressed peasantry, whether in hovels or small factories, kept labor costs low. Law did not permit workers' coalitions, and it would have been surprising if the least skilled had dreamed of challenging their employers. In the urban areas the artisans lived much as before, and the landed proprietors by the middle of the decade were superficially as interested in "scientific agriculture" as in Italianism. The businessmen and journalists of Milan implied their dissatisfaction with the competition posed by the transalpine crown lands and with railway policy, and in Venetia both farming and manufacturing were languishing. But no one expected another upheaval based on material factors alone. The nobility and bourgeoisie had demonstrated in Milan in 1853 that they distrusted the common folk. For the short run they were willing to live with Austrian willfulness and neglect.

Trieste

After the reconquest of Venice by Habsburg arms in August 1849, the ministers in Vienna devoted several sessions to the rewards which should be bestowed on Trieste, the only demonstrably loyal segment of the imperial domain in Italy. Gyulai argued for a return to normal conditions. Of those principally compromised, many were liable for duty in the militia and should be drafted. He had presided over the defense of the port when a Piedmontese-Venetian-Neapolitan squadron had instituted a blockade, and he had vowed to the citizens he would remember their merits and their interests. To demonstrate Francis Joseph's particular regard for his Triestine subjects, the cabinet ordered suspension of military law on September 7. Thanks to Bruck, it was decided to attach Istria and Gorizia to

Trieste to form one crown land. The city's determined stance, he declared, had paralyzed Italian influence in Istria. Francis Joseph decreed that the governor was to reside in what was soon defined as a "city immediately under the crown."[54]

Trieste's great irredentist historian, Attilio Tamaro, was anguished that "the government continued to keep the city in the firm clutches of alien and nationally indifferent mercantile elements."[55] His more realistic colleagues are generally agreed that there was good reason for the populace's disinclination to break the ties with Vienna. The artisans and shopkeepers feared they would lose what little the city's commerce guaranteed them. There were few Italian nationalists among the businessmen, and those in the professions were only beginning to develop a consciousness of something more than a cultural affinity with the rest of the peninsula. The bureaucracy enforced the use of German as the official language, in contrast to the situation in Lombardy-Venetia, and a decisive number of the citizenry would have echoed Bruck's apostrophe of 1847, "Long live the cosmopolitans!"[56]

On April 12, 1850, the government published a new *Statuto* for the city, providing for a podestà with ample powers and a council of fifty-four to be chosen by voters who met educational and pecuniary prerequisites. The working class and the employees of private businesses were excluded from the franchise.[57] In May, Francis Joseph appeared to lay the first stone for the Tergestina railway station, though few would have anticipated from his parting words that the completion of the line to Vienna was seven years distant. "The sojourn among my dear Triestines and the many proofs given me of their truly sincere attachment will never disappear from my memory." Lack of capital, the challenges of geography, and Austria's hesitation over the port's ultimate importance weighed more than the monarch's gratitude.

Electioneering for the municipal council was discreet. The liberals promised probity and political moderation. The conservatives reminded the voters that sage conduct had earned the city its unique status. Those elected should be known for their unfailing affection for the august imperial house, for their common sense, their integrity, and their civic pride. In the first meeting of September 22, 1850, twenty-six of the propertied and business classes sat with six lawyers, four physicians, four bureaucrats, three underwriters, two manufacturers, two professors, two clerics, two licensed brokers, and an architect. Of these, only twenty-nine would last until the final session of March 18, 1861. The religious affiliations of the first fifty-two elected confirmed Bruck's emphasis upon the port's cosmopolitanism: forty-three were Roman Catholic, four Jewish, three Orthodox, and two Lutheran.[58]

Their most important debate of 1851 concerned the language of instruction in the *Gymnasium*. Everyone emphasized the need to know German in the world of business, and only seventeen of fifty-two dared to vote for a total conversion of classes to Italian. The winning combination, 32 to 10, prescribed Italian for the first four years, German for the last four. The authorities in Vienna decided otherwise. The *Gymnasium* remained German, save for a few classes at the lower level.[59] The autocratic tendencies of the ministries in Vienna increased on all fronts in 1851. Before Francis Joseph's brief autumnal stop, his advisers dissolved Trieste's "national guard."[60] Bruck, the port's greatest advocate, declared in ministerial council that there should be no special treatment for its inhabitants in tax matters, and in October the cabinet extended the income tax to the area.[61]

Worse, Bach was soon explaining to his colleagues why Trieste, Fiume, and Buccari should not be exempt from conscription. Trieste's status as a free port was sufficient privilege. The men taken would be sent to the navy, where they would be more useful. An imperial ordinance of February 9, 1852, called for 160 men from the Triestine area, and families of long residence protested by appeals to Charles VI's grant of immunity. The emperor relented and on March 10 suspended the draft for the coming six years.[62] The Austrian Lloyd received the right to send ships by way of the Po as far as Lake Maggiore, and the great insurance firms extended their branches and investments to other parts of Italy. It did not seem to matter that a subdued municipal council dallied with plans for urban expansion and regulations to ensure general cleanliness. Early in 1852 Bach had ended the publication of summaries of its sessions, and in July 1853 he announced there would be no more elections until the empire decided upon new communal regulations. When vacancies occurred, he nominated the replacements.[63]

A general trend toward stagnation in maritime activity developed
in 1854. Total traffic amounted to 200,700,000 florins in 1853,
205,800,000 in 1857. Extraneous factors were involved: increasing
reliance upon steam, the changing of traditional routes, and the
delay in completing the railway to Vienna. Economic liberalism and
the lower costs of manufacturing in more advanced states discouraged industrial enterprise in the city, and the port, until the opening
of the Suez Canal, was increasingly a servicing agent for the products of the Austrian hinterland and the origin of much that was
destined for the Italian states.[64] The Austrian Lloyd, never lacking
an annual subvention from the government, doubled the number of
its ships and almost tripled their gross tonnage between 1850 and
1860. With marked increases in passengers and goods carried, it
provided a stability that alleviated economic dislocations and
diminished the possibility of political movement.[65]

In 1854 the city's most important citizens gave no sign of
dissatisfaction with Habsburg rule. The voluntary loan was quite
successful, amounting to more than 22 million florins in Trieste and
the Littoral (about 4 percent of all subscribed in the empire). The
Comitato centrale triestino, packed with the city's leading tycoons,
announced a subscription on February 28 to build a frigate for the
imperial fleet. It was to carry thirty-one cannon, dispose of 300
horsepower, and bear Radetzky's name. On October 12 the gift arrived from an English shipyard and was presented to Archduke
Maximilian for the navy early in 1855.

Maximilian's duties as governor-general of Lombardy-Venetia
after 1857 did not preclude welcome furloughs to Miramare, and his
popularity in Trieste was marked. The newly rich liked to bask in
the glitter of his court, while the modest and the poor admired him
for his goodness, generosity, and courtesy. Tamaro concluded that
he was dangerous, for his fascinating manner worked against the
patriots.[66] Trieste suffered from the panic of 1857, largely because
of overextension of credit to the dealers in colonial goods. The first
locomotive pulled in to the station on June 20, 1857, but the trunk
line to Ljubljana was not very efficient and the freight costs were
high.[67]

The moratorium on conscription was to end in 1858, and the
municipal council petitioned Francis Joseph for a continuation of

the exemption. He compromised, announcing that in the 1860s the state would draft half of the prescribed quota. Trieste, in return, would maintain the existing battalion of militia. It was not easy to find men to fill the vacancies on the council. The podestà, Muzio Tommasini, wrote in 1858 of the insults and denigrations in the press that faced appointees. Persons of merit were not enthusiastic for such duty, chiefly because they were not elected by their fellow citizens.[68] At the end of the decade the great craze was for a canal through the isthmus of Suez.[69] Visions of unparalleled prosperity did much to dull the appeal of Italian nationalism.

Austria, Parma, and Modena, 1849–1856

In 1848, the Austrians had considered partitioning Parma with Piedmont, but Queen Victoria's strong interest in the young Bourbon couple destined by treaty to rule the tiny state of some 500,000 souls saved one of Europe's less consequential pawns for another decade. Charles III, who had married Louise Marie, sister to the chief French pretender, the count of Chambord, had thoroughly outraged the Austrians in 1848, but his very proper behavior with wife and tiny children as an exile in England helped to preclude proscription by Vienna.

D'Aspre had entered Parma on April 15, 1849, in the name of Charles II, but before the month was over, that dispirited gentleman had abdicated in favor of his son, who would be Charles III. Lithe, sleepy-eyed, ill-tempered, yet undoubtedly bright, the new duke had tried to serve with Charles Albert in 1848 against the Austrians. It was no wonder that Schwarzenberg had written to him on April 19 that Austria deemed itself free of the defensive alliance made with Parma, since he had run to fight in the ranks of the emperor's enemies. Schwarzenberg nonetheless promised to defend Parmese rights and to support the demand for an indemnity from Piedmont. Austria was always ready to be of assistance, in conformity with justice, social order, and the satisfaction of the legitimate wishes of the people of Italy.[1] Charles and Louise Marie tarried some months yet in England. Before embarking, he asked the Austrian minister-president to forget the past, when he was so young and inexperienced. Now he would depend on the prince's guidance.[2]

The duchy of Modena was under a Habsburg, Francis V, who had ruled for two years when the revolution drove him to appoint a council of regency and depart for Vienna. He abstained from fighting in the Austrian army, however, for he had long been conscious of his position as an Italian prince. Quite a realist, he also knew that Austrian forces alone guaranteed his return, which took place on

August 10, 1848. He and the duke of Parma would have resented Schwarzenberg's instructions to Count Giovanni Allegri, the minister appointed to both courts in late 1849, for they both struggled to prove they were not mere puppets.

The minister-president noted the ties which bound the duchies to Austria: dynastic relationships, the rights of reversion, the treaties of alliance, the geographic factors, and the general political situation. Allegri was particularly to combat opposition in the duchies to a customs union and to persuade the duke of Parma to abide by the treaty of 28 November, 1844, which admittedly gave Parma the least attractive of the lands divided up at that time. The duke should remember that Austria could have made peace much earlier with Sardinia at Parma's cost. Too, there could be no connection between his demand for the return of Guastalla (which, with Parma and Piacenza, had been Marie Louise's "bequest" from the Congress of Vienna) and the negotiation of a customs union.

Waxing philosophic, Schwarzenberg declaimed that Germany and Italy were somewhat alike as far as small states were concerned. They lacked the strength to withstand the ever more formidable intrusions of radical revolution. Forced to turn to more powerful political organisms, they had to sacrifice some of their sovereign rights to save the rest. Allegri would have to develop this truth in the minds of these princes, so jealous of their rights, without arousing their susceptibilities.[3] Charles III had ordered Baron Thomas Ward, his family's English counselor, to make Radetzky understand that he was "not to interfere too much with me, my government and my troops, as I am a free sovereign and not an Austrian Governor."[4] The remark no doubt had reached Schwarzenberg.

When the Austrian minister arrived, the bitterness between the two rulers over Guastalla seemed insurmountable. Francis V demanded to know if his "dear cousin" seriously was challenging a treaty guaranteed by an Austrian emperor. The duke of Parma instructed Ward in Vienna to tell Schwarzenberg that he could answer such an ungentlemanly and unprincely question only with sword and cannon.[5] Charles was already a puzzle to his wife and courtiers, for he was much given to sudden crusades which he soon deserted for other forays. In March, Charles visited the duke of Modena, but they did not "talk business." A week later, the latter returned the courtesy, to Francis Joseph's great relief.[6] The respite would be short-lived, for the duke of Parma thought he had discovered a richer lode.

It was announced in March 1850 that the members of the regency, which had been transformed into a provisional government in April 1848, would pay heavy fines for damages done the state during their tenure. Charles was never fond of the great landlords, and he probably wished to destroy the wealth of the very prominent San Vitale family, whose head was in exile in Piedmont. The accused appealed to Allegri, who asked Schwarzenberg if Austria, without encroaching on ducal prerogative, might accord them the protection they requested. It would add to Austria's influence, for the fines had made a painful impression even upon "the good party" in Parma.[7] Schwarzenberg was disgusted by an act that seemed to attaint the very sovereign power which had appointed these men as regents. Had Charles III no filial piety? He should draw a veil over the events of 1848 or else run the risk of having his and his father's conduct examined.[8]

By September, however, the young ruler had sequestered the revenues of the ex-regents and had confiscated the decorations his father had bestowed upon them.[9] They would have no relief as long as he reigned, and his decree that a landlord could not evict a peasant tenant without a hearing before a judge intensified the landed proprietors' indignation. By early 1851 Allegri reported that everyone was afraid of the duke. His ministers hesitated to manifest the slightest opposition to his desires. His troops cost too much, for there was an excess of officers. His extended trips caused general discontent, as did the court's stay at Castellammare for several months. As the days passed, Allegri grew even more disturbed. Could Radetzky tell Charles there was a need to cut his troops? The plan to form "Royal Volunteer Reservists" from the peasantry had failed despite considerable inducements, the Austrian envoy was happy to report, but too many of the regulars were concentrated in the capital. During 1851 Charles stayed nine months out of his domain. Only the customs duties and the alienation of the crown lands maintained the court's credit.[10]

Charles was steadfast in his claims to part of the Sardinian indemnity. The Austrian cabinet debated the extent of a settlement in

September 1850 and, thanks to Bruck, decided that Parma would receive 2,200,000 lire for war damages and upkeep of troops. Bruck predicted that the decision would speed the tariff union.[11] Months later the ministers were still debating their answer to the duke's demands for 372,262 lire in excess of what they had decided upon for the maintenance of Austrian troops. Schwarzenberg was willing to pay more than what equity demanded for "purely political reasons of great importance." Bach, Thun, and Anton Csorich, minister of war, agreed, but the other four members of the cabinet demurred.[12] Ward dragged his way from office to office, "humbugg'd day after day and week after week first by one and the other. . . . this is the fourth day I am an antichambre customer of Schwarzenberg from 12 until 4 which ends every day in 'The Prince wishes himself to be excused for today.' "[13]

When no lire reached the Parmese treasury in 1852, Ward protested vigorously to the minister-president. Infuriated, the latter reminded the Parmese envoy that he had better resort to more diplomatic language. When Charles came to Ward's defense, Schwarzenberg threatened to treat Parma retroactively as a belligerent against Austria. Then it would be the duke's fate to pay an indemnity.[14] A month after the prince's death, Ward negotiated a settlement that substantially bettered the sum which Austria originally offered and brought Parma three times the money granted Modena.[15]

Austria's financial woes, as noted before, inevitably worsened its relations with its satellites. Parma had already agreed to a customs union, though Allegri noticed that public opinion in the duchy was totally opposed to the idea in early stages of the talks.[16] Too, the duke dropped his attempt to recover Guastalla when Schwarzenberg informed him that the treaty of 1844 was beyond challenge and his protests were null and void.[17] Once Parma acquiesced in a customs union, Austria invited Francis of Modena to join. Schwarzenberg tried to cajole him into accepting a million francs a year from the joint revenue, but the duke appealed directly to Francis Joseph for a larger share. Surely the Austrian ruler did not wish the league to become an object of aversion to the Modenese and their government.[18] A year later Francis was sufficiently frustrated to write to his august relative that he and his consort were ready to leave Modena

unless his "sovereign rights" were restored. In August 1852, however, he commented to Count Giuseppe Forni, his chief minister,
"that we are tiny and that we are dealing with a big one."[19] On the
ninth of that month Modena joined with Parma and Austria in a
customs union that would run from 1853 to 1857.

Economic unification through railroad construction was another
goal. Austria, Tuscany, the Holy See, Modena, and Parma concluded an agreement in 1851 to creat a Central Italian Railway,
which would link Piacenza, Parma, Reggio, Mantua, Modena, and
Bologna. Later, a line would connect Bologna with Florence via
Pistoia or Prato. The general administration and a supreme commission sat in Modena, but little was accomplished in the first
years.[20] Parma, without consulting Austria, made an agreement
with English railway builders that put Buol in a near panic. He appealed to Francis of Modena to parry this English feint, since there
could be no connection of any importance between Tuscany and
Piedmont save through Modenese territory. The duke replied that
the proper remedy was the acceleration of the building of the Central Italian Railway.[21] He could not have foreseen that completed
track would stretch only from Bologna to his frontier by the summer
of 1859

Both dukes during 1853 proposed that Austrian troops retire from
their domains or, at least, that Austria assume the costs of their
maintenance. Buol's tardy response emphasized the worsening international situation and the redoubled efforts of the revolutionary
party in Italy. Vienna wanted both duchies to negotiate military
conventions which would stipulate the precise number of soldiers
each would place with the Austrian army should disorders occur.[22]

Carl von Lederer, who had succeeded Allegri as minister resident,
was contemptuous of Modena's troops. The officers were largely
anti-Austrian, the regulars too weak to defend the capital. He could
not deliver Buol's note to the duke of Parma, who was again on a
trip. Charles's chief adviser, Vincenzo Cornacchia, welcomed
Austria's constant pressure to have his sovereign reduce his troops,
but he warned Lederer that his master would not hear of this.[23] Indeed, the capricious Bourbon was embarking on schemes which
would provoke an astonishing question from Francis Joseph. In a
secret dispatch meant for the eyes of the king of Naples, the emperor

asked if there was a way to make the duke of Parma abdicate volun-
tarily. If not, did the laws of the Bourbon family provide a remedy?
The duke's mode of governing and his private life were destroying
the last trace of prestige which authority should enjoy with the people. His abuses threatened the public repose of the peninsula.[24]

Ferdinand agreed that Charles had neither character nor moral-
ity and should be put where he could no longer influence the education of his children. It would be dangerous for the other Italian
sovereigns if he were forced to abdicate, however, for the party of
subversion would exploit such a sensation. The king promised to
write the duke a letter and suggested that soon thereafter Francis
Joseph summon the young man to Vienna to put him "on the right
road."[25] Ferdinand's trepidation over a deposition impressed the
emperor, who suggested that the proposed letter omit all mention of
abdication.[26]

Certainly it was not the latest news from Parma which induced
Francis Joseph to greater caution, for Charles decreed a compulsory
loan on March 1. The greatest landlords would suffer the most, and
property of religious orders was not excluded. Since half of the
state's income went for court and military expenses, there were
threats scribbled on the city's walls. The aggrieved repeated the
stories of the high cost of uniforms, extended trips abroad, a swollen
"army," bands, ballerinas, and the invitation to the emperor's wedding in Vienna. On March 14 the duke ordered the issuance of
treasury bonds, ostensibly to pay his bills. To the bourgeoisie, who
also owned land, it seemed an invitation to bankruptcy.

Buol fumed to Ward that the duke could not pretend to keep up
such a force of soldiery when his finances were "worn out." He had
no one to fight, and, candidly, Austria was loath to count on their
loyal assistance. For some time Charles III had been enamoured of
Marchioness Emma Guadagni, whom he had married off to a Neapolitan diplomat named Schmucker, and Buol was very much outraged. In Ward's plain English, the Austrian government was of the
opinion that "a Sovereign cannot expose Himself constantly running
about and leaveing His duchies to themselves whilst He is running
after Madame Schmucker." Francis Joseph "regarded the whole affair as unheard-of madness and absolutely incompatible with the
dignity of a Sovereign." The lady in question tried to establish her-

self in Milan, but the shocked ruler ordered her departure. Ward tried to distinguish between the duke's loyalty to the emperor and his right to his own private affairs. Buol simply noted that rulers had few affairs that might be considered private.[27]

Charles would not be around to absorb such counsel. On a Sunday in late March he took a walk, as was his custom, with a trusted lieutenant of artillery. While Charles gaped at a dancer who appeared at her window, a man of small stature approached and drove a knife into his abdomen. Next day the duke died, and Louise Marie assumed the regency for her small son. The assassin was apprehended but released, thanks to a convincing alibi. There is little doubt today that he, a saddler, belonged to the party of subversion that Buol and the king of Naples despised and feared. The widowed duchess had always interested herself in the politics of her diminutive state, much to her husband's resentment, and she moved rapidly to consolidate her position.

She named a commission to plan the reduction of the army, revoked the decrees on the forced loan and the treasury bonds, restored the fines levied upon the ex-regents, and ordered the sale of forty horses and twenty carriages. Lederer was bothered by her appointment of Giuseppe Cattani to the vital Interior post, because he felt that this man stood for liberalism, which would play into Piedmont's hands. The duchess thanked Lederer courteously for his honesty but assured him she would tolerate no minister who did not understand that she was "in charge." The rather obtuse envoy then warned her against courting popularity, and again this stalwart legitimist and clerical had to assert her detestation of revolution and her determination to allow no liberal decrees and no popular demonstrations.[28] Buol warned Lederer to refrain from exerting too strong an influence upon the regent's governmental decisions,[29] and in June, Baron Odoard Lebzeltern replaced Lederer at the two courts.

On July 22 some thirty conspirators, vaguely Mazzinian, attempted a revolution which the 3,000 troops that were available crushed easily. The duchess instituted a rigorous state of siege, gladly accepted Radetzky's reinforcements, and did nothing to stop the execution of three of the chief plotters. Feldmarschall Leutnant Felix Prince Jablonowski, the titular commander of the regular Austrian forces in Parma, protested to Marquis Giuseppe Pallavicino that the rebels had been questioned and executed in too great haste. The duchess's adviser dryly replied there was need to restore tranquillity as soon as possible, and the cabinet backed his response. He and the regent were not uninformed of the rumors which asserted that they wanted to wipe out everyone who knew anything of Charles's death. When Jablonowski went on holiday, Cattani, whom Lederer had not been able to displace, requested in the duchess's name that the protesting commander be recalled. He had been brusque and had mixed a little too much in her government. In the end, Verona acquiesced.[30]

The duke's death had occasioned a hiatus in the negotiation of a new military convention binding Austria and the duchies, but a formula was ready for Francis Joseph's perusal in October 1854. The Austrian documents indicate that Modena particularly wanted an end to the Austrian control of the citadel in the capital, and the final proposal surrendered the Austrian "right" to garrison Modena, Parma, and Brescello. In return the duchies would state precisely the number of soldiers they could furnish in a time of disturbance and would promise to subordinate such troops eventually to the Austrian high command.[31]

Francis of Modena's reiterated requests for the retirement of Austrian forces had their basis in Vienna's failure to pay on time for the upkeep of the troops. It is also true that he scouted the chances of a revolution in Italy and believed his own troops could maintain order. In March, Buol asked if Modena was willing to have the troops leave simultaneously with the withdrawal from Tuscany, and the duke immediately and thankfully assented.[32] On May 1, after two days of farewell banquets and balls, the ducal pair and their officials accompanied the Twentieth Jäger Battalion a short distance from the city. In Parma a wave of murders prevented similar scenes. Pallavicino blamed the crimes upon the rift between military and civilian authorities and admitted that the students in the university were increasingly given to nationalistic comments.[33] Buol blamed the scandal and danger upon the government. Why did not the regent and her ministers enforce the state of siege rigorously, as the Austrian military had recommended?[34]

To prepare for the day when she would face her people without the support of Austrian bayonets, the duchess ordered an end to the state of siege, the dissolution of the council of war, and the restoration of regular courts (save for a mixed commission for political offenses) in June 1855. A major part of the prosecutions for infractions during the state of siege were dropped. On August 13 Generalmajor Franz Count Folliot de Crenneville arrived as Jablonowski's replacement. When the stabbing of a ducal military official on March 17, 1856, forced the reinstitution of the state of siege, he assumed command of all troops, and the regent requested Auditor Kraus's services in interrogations of suspects.[35]

By summer, relations between Louise Marie and the Austrians were tense. She refused to honor financial claims made by Ward, whom she had cashiered on assuming power. In Vienna he was most persistent in pleading for Austrian intervention, and Buol told Lebzeltern to press for a speedy settlement. Did not the Parmese government wish to keep private some of the particular circumstances which had been kept secret out of regard for the deceased's memory?[36] The duchess was discovering that Crenneville and Kraus were intent upon a full investigation of her husband's death. Indirectly she let her reactivated council of war know that it should not exceed its mandate by requestioning men already consigned to the Austrian prison in Mantua. A question of competence between Crenneville and the council automatically arose, and Pallavicino replied by private letter. The Austrian commander immediately returned it, adding that he would expect nothing less than an order from the duchess in regard to any "inhibiting" of proceedings against the regicides. Thoroughly outraged, the regent asked Radetzky to remove Crenneville. When the governor-general replied in a fatherly but inconclusive manner, Louise Marie declared she would write Francis Joseph.

The letter was extremely firm, for the regent accented the inviolability of Parmese law and Crenneville's demands contrary to such law. The emperor yielded to her request for the recall of his general and Kraus, but he asked some blunt questions. Had not the state of siege been proclaimed because the civil tribunals had failed to extirpate the "leprosy" of political assassination? What was a council of war supposed to do, if not hunt down the hired murderers? Sooner or later the full weight of the consequences would fall upon the ducal government and add to the difficulties against which "we all have to fight, especially in Italy." Since leaks to the press had revealed practically all of the controversy to the public, Radetzky had *La Specola d'Italia* publish in Verona on July 14 a long explanation. Toward the end, the article declared that the events proved that a state occupied by the Austrians did not cease to be independent. Its government could have an opinion different from Austria's.[37]

Two weeks before Buol had commented to Lebzeltern on rumors that the duchess would proclaim an amnesty and lift the state of siege. The emperor felt it was his duty as a friend to suggest that these measures would have disastrous effects. Under such pressure the duchess yielded and suspended a measure which the public would have "saluted."[38] Her cooperative humor did not last long, for she ended the state of siege throughout the duchy on September 10.

Several weeks later Count Teodoro Bayard De Volo presented his credentials as Modena's envoy to Francis Joseph. Distinctly exercised by the duchess of Parma's show of independence, the emperor warned that a state abandoned by Austria would have to turn to those who panted for that state's very destruction. He had heard that demonstrations in Piacenza against the customs union were poorly repressed, if not tolerated, by the authorities. The customs union had to be considered in terms of its political importance. Austria had suffered financially, too, from its operation, but he would come to the aid of the duchies to mitigate their losses. He hoped the duke of Modena would give the regent of Parma opportune and reasonable advice, for she was allowing herself to be led into decisions contrary to her own interests.[39]

Both states had heard promises of help before, and both rulers had an excellent idea of the strain put upon the Austrian treasury by the Near Eastern crisis. On October 27 the Parmese announced that they would leave the customs union as of October 31, 1857. To add to Austrian discontent, the duchess continued to contest Ward's claims. When the imperial couple made their way to Venice, Francis Joseph conferred with Louise Marie and asked if he might retire his troops without inconvenience. The duchess replied she would like to confer with her ministers, who concluded that the evacuation would be rather useful from the point of view of general policy.

Radetzky gave the orders, and the emperor asked if, in return for promise of aid in future contingencies, Parma would pledge not to make other military conventions without his permission. This assurance Pallavicino renewed at the end of the year.[40]

To Francis Joseph and his ministers, Modena was more important than Parma, though its population was only 100,000 ahead of the smaller duchy's. Francis V was an archduke who was not likely ever to have dealings with Napoleon III. If he dreamed of an Italian confederation of conservative rulers, in which he might play the leading role, it was easy to let his rivals cut him down. His city was a natural point of concentration for troops which might have to discipline Bologna and the Papal Legations, and the occupation forces which departed at his request in 1855 would need no more than a day to get back. He fretted over his dependence upon Vienna, but he was quite incapable of developing a following among his subjects which might release him from his status as a very weak satellite.

The antics of Charles III and the show of independence staged by his widow took up more time in Vienna than Parma was worth. Bourbons in northern Italy were at a discount when a Bonaparte was enthroned in Paris, and Louse Marie's attempts to save something for her son by wooing moderate opinion irritated Francis Joseph. Her secession from the customs union and obvious relief to have the Austrian soldiers evacuated did not auger well for the future of Austro-Parmese relations. Had not the Piedmontese continued to be abrasive, the emperor might well have reconsidered partition. Austria employed but one diplomat to deal with both courts. For the moment the diminutive states were allowed to survive.

Austria and Tuscany, 1849–1855

LEOPOLD II of Tuscany succeeded his father in 1824, and his first tussle was with a haughty Austrian minister who demanded an audience with "Archduke Leopold." In time Metternich accepted the young man's assumption of the title of grand duke, but Emperor Francis did not hesitate to declare that the empire would annex Tuscany should the junior line of Habsburg-Lorraine die out. By a second marriage to Maria Antonietta of Naples, sister to Ferdinand II, Leopold begot the necessary sons, but, retiring as well as a bit lazy, he never moved too far from the Austrian shadow.

In 1848 Leopold joined Charles Albert in the war against Austria because he feared for "order" and for his own tenure had he failed to rebel against his own house. He granted a *Statuto*, inaugurated the sessions of a senate and chamber of deputies, and struggled to accommodate himself to strange counselors and their liberal doctrine. In early 1849 he deserted his capital and denounced the provisional government which proclaimed that he had abandoned his people. From Porto San Stefano on the Tuscan coast he indited letters to Francis Joseph and Charles Albert. The latter had offered to send forces to reestablish grand-ducal sovereignty, but Leopold declined. The powers which were planning the restoration of the pope's temporal power would never allow such an isolated Piedmontese action, in his opinion, and Austria would immediately respond with armed action should Sardinian forces move toward Tuscan territory. To the Austrian emperor he stated that his horror of anarchy and civil war had forced him to make every kind of sacrifice, including the temporary interruption of those political and familial relations that had always obtained between Austria and Tuscany.[1]

The grand duke then departed for Gaeta in Neapolitan territory, and in a second letter of February 26 he appealed to Francis Joseph's benevolent sentiments. There was a foxiness in his colorless phrasing, but how else might he slip back into Austria's graces without a direct public entreaty that would ruin his chances forever with the Tuscans? Early March brought news of Charles Albert's renewal of hostilities and rather blunt talk in Gaeta that Austria would occupy Tuscany when it was opportune and then weigh the matter of restoring or dispossessing the Habsburg-Lorraine branch.[2]

Very much worried, Leopold wrote in plain German on March 19 that he and a majority of his people would welcome a friendly Austrian intervention (*Einschreiten*) to end the terrorists' regime.[3] Before his letter reached Olmütz, Francis Joseph, no doubt under Schwarzenberg's eyes, dictated a caustic reply on March 27. It was grievous that an Austrian archduke could desert "our glorious house" and seek aid from its enemy. Relenting a bit, the young monarch implied he was not insensitive to his relatives' fate. He already had ordered his government to take all necessary steps to protect Habsburg rights in Tuscany.[4] Leopold II dispatched a confidential agent to Vienna to seek a fuller explanation of the rather ominous reference to Habsburg rights in what had been his domain. There an irritable Schwarzenberg repeated several times, "Tuscany, that's Austria." The Austrians would never abandon the territory, and measures to this effect had already been taken. The prince clearly wished Ottaviano Lenzoni to return as Tuscan envoy, and he expressed hope that the grand duke would not hinder the course Austria planned to follow in Tuscan affairs by other negotiations.[5]

Schwarzenberg warned Radetzky on April 5 to shift part of his troops in preparation for an occupation of Tuscany. He had taken the precaution of advising the powers of Austria's special relationship with that state.[6] A counterrevolution in Florence on April 11-12 proclaimed the reestablishment of constitutional monarchy, and the new regime lodged Francesco Domenico Guerrazzi, the leading member of the provisional government, in the Belvedere to save him from a mob. The new Tuscan "governmental commission" was in something of a frenzy to prevent an Austrian entry. A delegation went to Gaeta to persuade Leopold to come back, and he notified them that he would send an extraordinary commission to restore the constitutional regime through measures that would stave off future disorders.[7]

The grand duke secretly sent a trusted French legitimist who frequented his court, Marie-Joseph-Prévôt de Saint-Marc, to confer

with Radetzky on the size of the Austrian forces destined for
Tuscany. Learning that 20,000 would breach the frontier on May 6,
Saint-Marc demurred, but with no success. D'Aspre was to command a corps of 15,000, Count Franz Wimpffen, 10,000. D'Aspre
was a man obsessed with disgust for Italian revolutionaries. Born in
Brussels in 1787, he served in the last campaigns against the first
Napoleon, and he had distinguished himself in the defeats inflicted
upon Charles Albert. In his manifesto of May 5 he promised a
restoration of the grand duke's rights, and he recognized the legal
authority of General Luigi Serristori, appointed on May 1 by Leopold II to be his "extraordinary commissioner." The document
mentioned Leopold's constitutional institutions, which alone could
"establish strong roots and produce good and bountiful fruit." Any
sign of resistance, however, would force him to resort to arms.[8] First,
he would purge Leghorn of its "scum."

Leghorn, like Genoa, was a turbulent port where old municipal
egoisms blended with mercantile bravado to create an atmosphere
of recklessness in the face of every outside threat. Men defeated in
the reverses of 1848–49 joined with democratic refugees recently
forced out of Florence to swell the ranks of stevedores, porters, and
merchants who disdained the warnings of their own short-lived
"governmental commission." By May 9 the Austrians were under the
walls of the city, which had confided its fate to a junta of momentarily popular tribunes and some 2,000 determined zealots.

Austrian artillery, employed because of the vigorous resistance,
triumphed by the afternoon of May 11, and there were the usual executions. Crenneville was left to enforce rigid controls and to supervise the collection of an indemnity which would be assigned to the
grand duke. In Gaeta the ruler in exile sensed that an Austrian occupation of Florence would outrage most of his subjects, and he
dispatched a special envoy to ask D'Aspre to halt at Leghorn.
Perplexed by such a direct request, the Austrian commander suspended operations and asked for further orders.

Radetzky's response was a curt order to resume the advance and
to issue a proclamation explaining the reasons for Austrian actions.
D'Aspre thereupon disseminated a statement that the grand duke
had called for Austria's aid in ending anarchy. More, ties of blood
that united him to the house of Austria and treaties which imposed

upon the Austrian emperor the defense of Tuscany's integrity justified the repression in Leghorn and the march into Florence.[9] The
capital accepted the inevitable on May 25 in a rather chilly fashion,
or so it seemed to D'Aspre after the warm welcome his troops had
received in the smaller towns. The day after the Austrians arrived, a
new ministry nominated by Leopold II assumed the responsibility of
regulating Tuscany's relations with the army of occupation. Giovanni Baldasseroni was president of the council, and he pleased the
Austrians with an immediate prohibition of the tricolor that symbolized Italian national aspirations.[10] His colleagues represented
both extremely conservative and moderately liberal opinion, but the
important Interior post went to Leonida Landucci, fervently pro-
Austrian, while Andrea Corsini, the duke of Casigliano, deemed to
be loyal to the idea of collaboration with Vienna, took over Foreign
Affairs.[11]

From the evening of June 7 to the morning of June 10, Radetzky
visited Florence. He boasted to Schwarzenberg of the rapturous applause he experienced as he passed through the Tuscan countryside.
Most of the time the cries were "Long live Austria! Long live our
liberators!" He had to admit that his reception in Florence was less
noisy, though a crowd outside his hotel cheered his appearances on a
balcony and broke up only at midnight. Next afternoon thousands
pushed into the Cascine park to see the renowned commander
review his soldiers. Leghorn also provided a triumph, and upon
Radetzky's return to Florence, the regimental bands beat a great
tattoo as the regulars snaked along the Arno in a torchlight parade.
The show attracted a great concourse, and the French envoy, Count
Alexandre Walewski, reported that the early atmosphere of sadness
dissipated as a numerous and splendid headquarters staff put their
money in circulation. The hundred or so urchins who swarmed
around Radetzky with their vivas were the same who had shouted,
"Death to the Austrians, long live Guerrazzi!"[12]

Toward the end of June, Austrian military authorities discovered
copies of a proclamation from Kossuth which enjoined all Hungarian soldiers in the Austrian forces to desert and come home to continue the struggle for Hungarian independence. On June 29 a court-
martial executed a youth of Pistoia for his appeals to troopers he
thought were Hungarian. As justification, D'Aspre delivered to

Baldasseroni a copy of stern orders from Radetzky, dated June 28. The Tuscan regime was guilty of inertia. It was to impose collective responsibility upon cities and towns for disorder, crack down on secret societies and the press, exile dangerous aliens, compel communes to deliver materials ordered by Austrian commanders, and apply military law. If the ministers resisted, D'Aspre was authorized to institute a state of siege.

Baldasseroni replied that the "requests" were excessive from a legal point of view and in fact impractical. The ministry would resign rather than participate in measures that would create long-lasting hatred. To the grand duke he wrote that the Austrian attitude was truly hostile, irrational, and prejudicial to Leopold's sovereign rights and interests. The military's fury would admirably further the anarchists' cause and propagate distrust and aversion, with the most tragic of consequences. Baldasseroni decided to warn all citizens of the penalties that would be exacted under the state of siege and urged the grand duke to return.[13] When Schwarzenberg heard of the confrontation, he applauded D'Aspre's tough policy. The Tuscan ministry should be left in no doubt of Austria's determination to maintain the safety of its forces.[14]

Casigliano's instructions to Lenzoni indicated that the ministers were quite aware that Tuscany required an Austrian presence. The envoy was to see to it that the occupation lasted until the government, with its own forces, could provide for the security of society. He was to fight any contrary disposition. With the greatest of delicacy, however, he should strive for that quota of troops actually needed, in view of the danger to the treasury. It was hoped that Vienna would reduce the costs of supplying the soldiers and recognize their status as "auxiliaries" offered a friendly and independent state.[15]

On July 25 the grand duke and his family disembarked at Viareggio rather than at "disloyal" Leghorn. He had ordered an Austrian uniform from Florence but refused to appear in it, despite his wife's warnings that the emperor would not forgive him a third time. Casigliano and Landucci proposed a compromise. Their ruler would enter Florence in Tuscan regalia, to prove his independence. On other occasions he would wear the Austrian uniform, and he would avow his obligation to Austria in an article for the press. Baldasseroni tried to sweeten matters by scattering decorations among the chief Austrian officers, and he, Landucci, and Marquis Cesare Boccella, the minister of public instruction, promised they would resign if the grand duke did not "march in the Austrian direction."

For his reunion with his subjects, many of them from the countryside, Leopold wore the white uniform of the Tuscan Order of St. Stephan. Bells, cannon, military bands, and fireworks added to the festive atmosphere, and he dressed unequivocally as an Austrian general of cavalry when he received the chief Austrian officers and visited Archduke Albrecht.[16] Leopold promised D'Aspre he would not summon the chambers without consulting with him, and he spoke approvingly of sending his heir to Vienna for several years to profit from imperial guidance.

Schwarzenberg decided he needed fresh talent in Florence to accomplish a modus vivendi that would ensure Austrian preponderance at a minimum of cost. In the middle of August, Baron Karl von Hügel was appointed a mere chargé, with instructions to work out some kind of arrangement for the occupation.[17] His background put him on the side of conservative legitimacy, but he had seen enough of the world not to be unbending. Born in 1796, he attended the University of Heidelberg and then served in the Austrian army against Napoleon and in the operations in Naples in 1820–21. From 1830 to 1836 he traveled to Syria, the lands along the Red Sea, to the Himalayas, Tibet, and Australia, collecting ethnographic materials and plant specimens. In 1848 he accompanied Metternich to England.

Hügel submitted the bases for a pact on September 16, 1849. Austria agreed to accept "auxiliary force" as the term for its occupying troops, though the matters of command and discipline would be under Austrian control. Both governments would have to concur in the timing and mode of eventual evacuation. For the present a minimum of 10,000 would serve in towns whose fortresses had to be made defensible. Austria would pay the soldiers, while the Tuscans would meet all other expenses of maintaining their auxiliaries on a war footing.

Casigliano soon proposed modifications. If imperial forces in Lombardy and Venetia were placed on a peace footing, could the same measure apply in Tuscany? Second, would the commanding

Austrian general proclaim a state of siege only with the consent of the grand duke? Hügel rejected the first but recommended acceptance of the second, since it would strengthen the monarchical principle and comport with the concept of "auxiliary force." He added his firm conviction that Tuscan courts should have jurisdiction over all criminal trials, with the right to summon Austrian soldiers when necessary. Otherwise, convictions would be few, a development which the Tuscan ministers very much deplored.

Schwarzenberg and Gyulai, concerned by problems of discipline within the Austrian forces, insisted on leaving the power to proclaim a state of siege with their own command. The grand duke would merely ratify such a decision by issuing the necessary edict. Tuscan requests to give their ruler the right to reduce or withdraw the auxiliary troops met with absolute refusal. By the end of the year, negotiations were stalemated. Tuscany insisted on the right to try all criminal acts in Tuscan courts, even attempts to persuade Austrian soldiers to desert. The ministry also wished a statement of the circumstances under which the Austrian commander could declare a state of siege. The grand duke was to have the initiative in demanding the increase, reduction, or entire withdrawal of the Austrian troops. No ministry could sign a convention which surrendered such important elements of sovereignty. When Hügel replied that Austria could not risk the safety of its men by such concessions, Casigliano suggested the signing and publication of an economic arrangement. The "political" clauses would be left unstated, and the ministry would allow Austria full latitude in deciding what was best for both states. Hügel refused such a solution, and he reported to Schwarzenberg that the ministry secretly wanted to agree to all of the Austrian conditions. The fear of critical comments in Piedmontese and French newspapers, however, stiffened their resolve not to give way on political issues.[18]

The restoration of polite, not cordial, ties between Francis Joseph and Leopold II was much easier to accomplish than the convention regulating the auxiliary force. The Tuscan court celebrated the emperor's birthday with fitting pomp on August 18, and in a rather stilted birthday letter the grand duke thanked his nephew for the "intervention and presence of Austrian troops" and promised to strengthen familial and political bonds. The imperial response was an invitation to Schönbrunn, where Leopold endured reproofs and brusque treatment during a five-day stay in September. One positive result was Schwarzenberg's grudging approval of an amnesty for all save some forty Tuscans compromised by revolutionary activity.[19]

Negotiations for the military convention resumed in January 1850, and the most serious quarrel was over Schwarzenberg's ultimatum that both governments would have to agree on the size of the occupying contingent and on the date of evacuation. Hügel warned that Casigliano and Baldasseroni would starve before they would sign a dishonorable document, but in the end they surrendered. It seems clear they were afraid of revolution, uninformed of the weak points in Austrian policy, and despairing of French good offices.

Finally signed in Florence on April 22, the convention fixed the auxiliary force at 10,000, to be diminished, increased, or eliminated only by mutual consent. Austria would equip and train the men. Tuscany would provision and house them. The emperor had sole command, which was exercised at his will by an Austrian general. A special note confirmed the Austrian commander's unlimited privilege to institute a state of siege when the troops were endangered or public order compromised and after he had notified the grand duke. As for accusations of incitement to desertion or mutiny, Austria renounced jurisdiction over Tuscans unless they were arrested during a state of siege. Tuscan military law would try such persons, and Tuscany promised to adopt in a new military code the basic prescriptions of Austrian military justice.[20]

On the day of the signing, Boccella came to Hügel to disclose that the "Austrian" part of the cabinet, Baldasseroni, Landucci, Casigliano, and himself, wished to play high politics in Vienna during the grand duke's second visit to Francis Joseph's court. They wished to concert with Vienna a postponement of the Tuscan chambers for at least a year. Casigliano accompanied Leopold II in May and reported to Baldasseroni that their ruler listened with approval to Austrian suggestions that he rid himself of the *Statuto*. On June 4 Hügel received a rather astonishing proposal from the chief Tuscan minister. The grand duke was bound by a formal promise to convoke the chambers, and the demagogues constantly cried for action. The Tuscan ministry by itself was not strong enough to withstand such pressure. Could Austria, the first Italian power, initiate a conference attended by representatives of Rome, Naples, Florence, Modena, and Parma to postpone indefinitely all the parliamentary bodies which had been promised?[21] In a letter to Casigliano, Baldasseroni mentioned the possibility of "reviving the idea, rancid a little time ago, of the Holy Alliance."[22]

Schwarzenberg was wary of any kind of joint Italian action and was hardly a devotee of the Holy Alliance. He had expressed satisfaction in September 1849 that Tuscany wanted an entente among all the Italian states on the proper means to obviate the dangers of a free press, but he had not moved beyond pious sentiment.[23] Nevertheless, to hear that Baldasseroni, still somewhat suspect, wanted to stymie Tuscan liberalism was excellent news. Early in June, Leopold II relayed from Vienna the emperor's desire to see "the soul of the ministry, the man of wisdom and experience in affairs." Schwarzenberg and others would most willingly have discourse with him.

Baldasseroni complied, only to discover that no one had talked seriously with the grand duke or with Casigliano. No intimacy had developed between the two families, and the grand duchess had lost none of her loathing for Germans. After all, in exile in Naples in 1849, she had recommended Germans as better than Neapolitans or Swiss for "clean-up operations." The consequent odium would fall on them, rather than upon her husband.[24]

In an informal scene with Schwarzenberg, Baldasseroni held up well in responding to the prince's, "What are we, what should we be, friends or enemies?" The shrewd Florentine reply was that family relationships made the grand duke the natural friend but not the dependent of Austria. "Friends, then?" Surely, was the answer, but it was in the interest of each not to parade this friendship overmuch. The prince assented, gave the commoner his hand, and concluded with a melodramatic "faithful to our word unto death." Francis Joseph impressed the Tuscan visitor with his military frankness, his great kindliness, and his very good Italian. When the younger man insisted that governments be strong, Baldasseroni countered that he would neither apologize for nor censure all the Tuscan government's acts in the past two years. When a tempest felled great oaks, little trees scarcely could stay in place. "Your Majesty saw the revolution triumph in Vienna, and so it is no great thing that the grand duke saw the same in Florence." The minister's candor was effective. The emperor lowered his eyes and suggested a change in topic. Later, the grand duke teased Baldasseroni but insisted he had made a good impression.[25]

In a second meeting Schwarzenberg convinced Baldasseroni of the inappropriateness of a congress to discuss the Tuscan government's desire to scuttle the representative system. Rather, on July 9, after the Tuscan's departure, he circularized the conservative Italian courts for their reactions to the question. While he definitely wanted no restoration of the *Statuto*, he warned that there could be no return to the abuses of arbitrariness that had occurred in the past. Energy, prudence, and moderation should be the weapons in a society that still was agitated.[26] The replies were generally favorable to the Tuscan ministry's objective. Giustino Fortunato, prime minister in Naples, declared that a restoration of the parliamentary system would ruin any country. The papacy proclaimed that every parliamentary regime was a menace to the free exercise of the spiritual power. Modena was sensitive to the dangers which would ensue if the party of movement in Tuscany could enjoy the freedoms which the *Statuto* promised. Parma predicted an outburst of violent and subversive passions if Tuscany restored the *Statuto*.

Schwarzenberg's response to the comments from the conservative states was a recommendation that they initiate municipal franchises and provincial liberties consonant with the rights of landed property. He deprecated the idea of formal conferences, which might give a foreign power a pretext to intrigue with Italian factions. For the same reason Austria would not participate in the preliminary negotiations.[27] In the shadow of these inconclusive exchanges, the grand duke suspended the constitution indefinitely and decreed a stricter control of the press on September 21, 1850.

In early November 1850 the idea of a general front of conservative Italian states reemerged in a note from Fortunato to Antonelli. Ferdinand II, it seemed, was willing to press for a certain degree of conformity in the organic laws of the various states and to consult on measures to facilitate internal stability. Francis of Modena had for some years cherished the thought of an Italian confederation linked by Austria with the German Confederation, and he offered his own project in December. Open to the five conservative states and to Lombardy-Venetia, if Vienna so desired, the union would strive to repress revolution and to forward economic cooperation. There would be coordination of police and military to war on subversion, as well as identical laws restricting the press, establishing censorship, denying the right of assembly, and forbidding the maintenance of a national guard. Uniformity of tariffs, a telegraph net, and system of railways connecting the entire peninsula with the Austrian provinces would ensure greater prosperity for all. Baldasseroni was enthusiastic once again, for he assumed the duke had Vienna's approval. In reality, Hügel and Schwarzenberg were quite reserved. To what extent could the empire encourage a positive retreat from the pre-1848 norms in Italy without stimulating anew the drift to Italian national union?

The Austrian cabinet was evolving plans for a highly centralized empire which would force Milan and Venice to look northward. Schwarzenberg liked the idea of a league which would make police forces and procedures uniform, but he could not encourage the conservative states to collaborate militarily and diplomatically. Baldasseroni saw the union as a means of avoiding the most abject dependence upon Austria, but he well knew that the liberals of Tuscany would hardly settle for pure reaction. Ferdinand II of Naples was constantly in a state of alarm over Austrian machinations and in time would tell Baldasseroni that he wanted a great "Chinese wall" to seal off his kingdom from international complications and liberal plots. In Rome the badly shaken papal administration would need proof that the union would be a surety against another round of agitation for fundamental reforms.[28]

Baldasseroni took the road south to discuss the Modenese suggestions with Ferdinand of the Two Sicilies. A first day at Caserta went quite well. Next day it was evident that the Bourbon state wanted nothing which had been wrought since 1847. The king indicated he would not offer a single soldier unless the cause directly involved his state. He was suspicious of Schwarzenberg's counsels and would brook no treaty or note which might afford Austria a pretext to interfere with his style of governing. Jealous of his independence, he believed a league might diminish his prestige. Austrian domination of a league would bring England and France together, a coalition he very much feared. In Vienna, Schwarzenberg seemed pleased that the pourparlers did not stress an immediate need for a military pact requiring all to assist a threatened signatory. More importantly, he warned that the reconstruction of the empire prevented any engagement that might link Lombardy and Venetia with the league, though the emperor would always lend his moral support. Between Ferdinand's intransigence and Schwarzenberg's diffidence over open Austrian collaboration, the idea of a league foundered.[29]

Three months after the signing of the military convention, Baldasseroni and Casigliano confessed they could not come up with the 100,000 florins due. Could the Austrian forces be reduced to 7,500? The land enjoyed profound calm, so there was little need to maintain the men on a wartime footing. More, the mountainous terrain and the system of railroads decreased the importance of cavalry, the more expensive branch. Schwarzenberg conferred with the military and declined the entreaties. There was quiet precisely because the Austrians were present in such strength and on such a footing. At most, Radetzky would receive orders to replace a division of hussars with a battalion of light infantry.

When Leopold II in the autumn of 1851 wrote Francis Joseph for some relief, Schwarzenberg's reply was brutal. The empire had suffered too much from recent revolutionary events to permit a modification of the moderate sums required. Tuscany should without further delay remit the monthly charge. Baldasseroni wrote Lenzoni in Vienna that one might well ask if Tuscany were at war with Austria. The government was not asking for remission, but postponement.[30]

New taxes, a public borrowing of 12 million lire in 1851, and the cashiering of some state employees meant the definite improvement of grand-ducal finance during that year. The deficit was small, a bit more than 200,000 lire. In 1852 there would be a slight surplus, about 600,000. It was the ministry's own competence and diligence that weakened its case in Vienna.[31]

On December 31, 1851, Francis Joseph canceled the March Constitution and assumed full responsibility for the affairs of the empire. Leopold II was in transports over his nephew's dismantling of constitutionalism and equally inspired by the prince-president's energetic measures in France. Baldasseroni complained to Hügel of his ruler's increasing drift toward reaction. He deliberately avoided asking his ministers about their specific areas of jurisdiction. He wanted to exclude all non-Catholics from educational facilities. Hügel reported to Vienna that the grand duke was intent on securing total independence from the head of the dynasty. He was dissatisfied with his ministry because he deemed it to be pro-Austrian.

In July 1852 Leopold II outraged Hügel by vetoing his ministers' and Austria's route for the railway from Florence to the Roman frontier. They wanted to go via Siena while he opted for the Arezzo route, and no reproof from the Austrian envoy, detailing added expenditures and broken promises, had the slightest effect on him. He increasingly discounted the need for any counsel and boasted to Hügel of his ability to steer the ship of state through tempests and shoals. Such grandiloquence, added to a querulous disregard for anyone's opinion, persuaded Baldasseroni to resign one day, then respond to his ruler's sudden change of mind by reassuming office next day.[32]

A sign of Austria's appreciation of Baldasseroni's insecure tenure was a reduction in troop strength. Lenzoni on January 28, 1852, asked that the forces be cut to 6,000. The Austrian reply was an offer to keep the same complements in Florence and Leghorn while departing from Siena, Lucca, Pisa, and Pistoia. A year later, in response to renewed Tuscan pleas, Francis Joseph consented to a maximum of 6,000. In the autumn of 1853 there were additional signs of a relaxation of tensions. The grand duke decided to pardon some of those convicted at the Leghorn trials, but he first cleared the matter with Vienna. Buol quickly acceded, noting that he understood there would be no general Tuscan amnesty and reaffirming the Austrian military's right to try persons who were accused of high treason or of attacks upon the security of Austrian troops in areas in a state of siege. Baldasseroni fully admitted the propriety of such reservations.[33]

The outbreak of hostilities between Turkey and Russia late in 1853 and the gradual involvement of the rest of the European powers in settling the Near Eastern crisis improved Tuscan chances to secure a complete clearing of their territory. When Radetzky ordered the "Grand Duke of Tuscany's Own Dragoons" to quit Tuscany for Styria in November 1854, Casigliano requested the

departure of all of the auxiliary forces in the near future and the
ending of the state of siege in Leghorn. Hügel confirmed his assertions that the Tuscan deficit was growing and that the port was free
of radical ferment. After conferring with the military, Francis
Joseph decided to withdraw his troops in the spring of 1855.[34]

On May 5 Leopold II and his sons in a driving rain accompanied
the last columns to leave Florence. In a rather touching confidential
note to Buol, Hügel admitted that he would have been at the end of
his rope if the troops had not departed. The daily torment and
tribulations were over. In a report for the record, he declared that
incidents between Tuscans and Austrians ceased after the first few
months of the occupation. Florence returned to normal — insouci-
ant, indolent, gossipy. There was one notable change. The Floren-
tines paid Leopold little respect, and he failed to order that hats be
doffed when he and his family entered a theater. In Pisa the professors lauded the liberties of Greece, Genoa, and Venice and ignored the faults of the British constitutional system. The theater was
another poison, inculcating materialism and self-indulgence.
Despite quarrels between peasants and landlords, the rural population was pious and peace-loving and posed no problems for the
government. The new soldiers looked good, if their true qualities remained questionable. Baldasseroni remained for Hügel the only
man of political capacity in the land. His expertise in a variety of
fields, his industriousness, and his skill in expressing his thoughts
reduced his colleagues to under secretaries. Hated by the constitutionalists and persecuted by the clericals, he had well served Austria
"not through ignorance or weakness but by conviction and because
of devotion to his sovereign."[35]

Austria's distrust of Leopold II did not abate after his restoration.
No Habsburg had gone as far as he in trying to appease nationalism
and revolution, and his quirks and lack of dignity increasingly compromised the family's future in Tuscany. Public indifference did not
connote active dislike, however, and many of the propertied preferred a dull ruler to a repetition of the scenes at Leghorn prior to
the Austrian capture of that port. Baldasseroni rather quickly won
Vienna's esteem, and his pivotal role in Tuscan affairs made the
grand duke's flightiness a matter of lessening concern. Like any
good administrator, he complained of the costs of the occupation,

but he came up with the necessary funds when his entreaties were refused. Save for the shocks of the earliest days, the relations between the Tuscans and the whitecoats were decent, probably because there were few activists in the land.

Baldasseroni's attempt to secure confederative action against parliamentarianism and "press abuses" was a response to Leopold's promises to summon the chambers. It had but one issue. Schwarzenberg took advantage of the parleys, which he hoped would fail, to stress every conservative state's need to allow municipal and provincial franchises. In 1848 he had learned that Austria was hard put to deal with a general conflagration. To satisfy the respectable in society, he wanted interplay between ruler and subject at the local level. The prince did not live long enough to continue his missionary work, but the superior performance of the Baldasseroni ministry defused much of the potential resistance in Tuscany. That land was one of Europe's calmest spots when Francis Joseph recalled his troops in 1855. Nowhere else in Italy had his men incurred less resentment. If and when Leopold II might fall, the blame would be primarily his own.

Austria and the
Papacy,
1849–1856

SCHWARZENBERG'S Italian policy explicitly called for the restoration of the pope's temporal power. He so declared in his first interview with Viale in December 1848, and throughout 1849 he demonstrated great skill in collaborating with the suspicious French in clearing the way for Pius IX's return to Rome as sovereign. After the turbulence of 1849 and the flight to Gaeta, the pope had appealed for help, without strings, from all the Christian states of Europe.[1] From that dull Neapolitan port Cardinal Antonelli wrote Viale to insist that Austria act only to restore the pope to his see and to give him free possession of his dominions. Only the Holy Father should grant his subjects those institutions he deemed best.[2]

After a complicated journey Count Moriz Esterházy reached the exiled curia on February 4, where, in his words, he was awaited like the Messiah. The pontiff showered him with attention and asked for immediate armed intervention by Austria. In a few days he would repeat his pleas to all the powers, but he wanted Schwarzenberg to know that he counted only on Habsburg might.[3] Antonelli exhorted his envoy in Vienna to use all of his persuasive gifts to energize the Austrians, and early in March an Austrian descent on Ferrara momentarily lifted his spirits. Though somewhat shocked by the fine levied and the hostages taken in retaliation for attacks on the Austrian consulate, he was much troubled when the troops withdrew.[4] Almost in a state of panic, he sent the nuncio in Paris an encoded admonition to eliminate French opposition to an Austrian intervention. A single day's delay could be the source of infinite and irreparable evils.[5]

Schwarzenberg had no intention of proceeding into papal territory without an entente with Louis Napoleon's France. The nuncio in Paris, Raffaele Fornari, predicted that the cabinet would never make a public agreement with Austria, for they and the president feared reproofs from the assembly. But it seemed that separate invasions of the rebellious areas would be quite all right. While diplomats from France, Austria, Spain, and Naples bickered in Gaeta over the proper procedures for a complete restoration of the temporal power, the French foreign minister, Edouard Drouyn de Lhuys, told Fornari of negotiations with Schwarzenberg that would assign Bologna and the Papal Legations to the Austrian sphere. The French government wanted the chance to insist to the assembly that Austrian intervention forced a French descent on Rome.[6] On April 17 a surprisingly large majority of the deputies voted to send 8,000 men to recapture the capital for Pius IX. Bonaparte wanted immediate glory, the conservatives and clericals writhed over the Holy See's humiliations, while liberal and democratic circles were sensitive to a Habsburg preponderance in Italy.

The French landed at Civitavecchia on April 25 as Austrian forces moved toward Bologna. Schwarzenberg was critical of the orders which Antonelli had given the pontifical commissioners who would accompany the troops. They were too reactionary.[7] At Gaeta and Paris, the French repeated their demands for a papal proclamation that would reflect the pope's beneficent and generous ideas of prerevolutionary days.[8] More agitated by French pressure than by news of Garibaldi's presence in Rome, Antonelli urged the Austrians in early May to take the city. Wimpffen forced Bologna to capitulate on May 16 and wheeled toward Ancona. When Radetzky had the keys to Bologna delivered to Pius IX, the cardinal renewed his intimations that the whitecoats should occupy the capital.[9]

Schwarzenberg had enough to do without challenging the French at Rome. He told the nuncio he would offer his counsels on the introduction of a wise and moderate administration and would not yield to French suggestions to impose conditions on the Holy See.[10] Time was on the side of the pope, and Esterházy was to avoid wounding French susceptibilities at Gaeta. At the same time Pius IX was to manifest invincible passive resistance to every attempt upon his imprescriptible rights.[11] Ironically, Austrian commanders were the first to threaten these rights.

The Austrians had fined Ferrara for damage done their consulate, and they would not hesitate, when affronted, to renew collective reprisals. Thoroughly shaken by the extent of rebelliousness in 1848-49, they relied on the state of siege and military tribunals to restore order. It should be said that they had been assigned one of the most crime-ridden sections of Italy. Brigandage sometimes masqueraded as popular retribution upon the rich and the corrupt. Its very presence was a provocation to the correct Austrian military, whatever its pretensions might be. To halt violence, the Austrian orders were predictable: no more civic guards, political clubs, or circles, suspension of the liberty of the press, stringent regulations of restaurants and cafés, surrender of all arms, prohibition of the tricolor in any form, and a curfew.[12] A *Notificazione* signed by General Gorzkowski on June 5, 1849, for the legations of Bologna, Ferrara, Ravenna, and Forlì carefully detailed capital offenses and less serious infractions. Persons guilty of high treason, traffic in or possession of arms, rebellion, sedition, suborning troops, resistance to sentinels, patrols, or carabinieri, robbery, or plundering would receive the death penalty. Councils of war would try cases involving the diffusion of revolutionary propaganda, insults to military personnel, wearing insignia of any entity that was not Austrian or papal, singing revolutionary songs, public demonstrations, disregard of orders or suggestions from the military, violations of the curfew, failure to heed the rules of preventive censorship, offering refuge to aliens without notifying the authorities, and malicious damage to pontifical heraldic symbols. Those found guilty would serve from one month to two years, with a corresponding fine. These were the regulations which lasted until May 19, 1857.[13]

With the surrender of Ancona on June 19, the Austrian forces could settle down to the task of pacifying an area that long had been famed for its refractory behavior. They were short of supplies and of cloth for the repair or replacement of uniforms, and Gorzkowski informed Gaetano Bedini, the extraordinary pontifical commissioner, that he had to have such items as quickly as possible. Antonelli sent a shocked protest to Vienna. It was difficult enough to supply food to the troops. The latest exaction had the effect of a forced contribution from provinces already suffering from anarchy. The nuncio should know (and, no doubt, tell Schwarzenberg) that the other intervening powers had demanded nothing for their services.[14] Radetzky protested that Austria had not planned any kind of contribution. Gorzkowski was desperate, for he could find little in Lombardy and Venetia, and it was always the army's purpose to repay in full. If the treasury could not pay for everything immediately, there would be an agreement between the governments for eventual compensation.[15] The first unpleasantness over supplies for the troops was over.

Less pleasant for Antonelli were the reports which indicated that Schwarzenberg was absolutely against a return to the system which Pius IX had inherited. The prince insisted upon a considerable secularization of the administration, though he readily admitted that the effervescence of the moment prohibited a representative system. The pope might allow his *Consulta* to vote on accidental or extraordinary expenses and still reserve to himself the control of the normal and indispensable disbursements. Austria favored an amnesty which, like Francis Joseph's, excused the seduced. He approved of the French recommendation of a law code and hoped it would be based on the Neapolitan model. There was no need to abolish the Inquisition, but the curia should change its name and modify its attributes. Bishops should have legal jurisdiction over purely ecclesiastical matters and nothing else. Austria had need of good relations with France, and so the papacy had to do something to satisfy France.[16]

On September 12 Pius IX issued a motu proprio in Portici which outlined the administration he would permit. It granted no deliberative vote to the council of state or to the council of state for finance. It allowed the propertied to vote for communal councillors, but the pope would choose all other public officials (on occasion, from lists compiled by other administrators). The same day Schwarzenberg was insisting that the curia had no time to lose in remedying the domain's abnormal condition. A code of law should provide for oral defense, which would be made public. The *Consulta* should vote on extraordinary expenses. Aulic courts should treat aulic affairs, such as matrimony, and not extend themselves to purely civil cases.[17]

When the question of a formal recognition of papal neutrality came up at the Gaeta conference of August 13, Schwarzenberg reacted with an interesting statement of Austria's position. The pope's chief enemies were the revolutionary factions in his lands. Neighboring states had no intention of dismembering these territories, nor would the great powers sanction such changes. If the pope should be menaced by rebellion, states which more or less catered to sedition would oppose any kind of intervention to restore legal order. Should adjoining states and Austria be precluded from coming to the rescue? Should there be any excuse to prevent Austrian rights to garrison Ferrara and Comacchio? If the king of Naples should call on Vienna for assistance against an uprising, would not a guarantee of papal neutrality forestall the movement of imperial troops through the States of the Church? Rather, the four Catholic powers represented at Gaeta should declare their interest in assuring the maintenance of the temporal power and the integrity of the papal frontiers.[18]

Esterházy's estimate of the man whom the Austrians might again have to rescue was not very complimentary, though he did believe that the pontiff had sincerely repented of his fling at liberalism. He lacked depth and obeyed the instincts of the moment or listened to the persons who insinuated themselves into his presence. Also, he seemed to be pro-French. Antonelli was the envoy's hero, for he was upright and honorable in colloquy. Born in 1806 to a very modest family, this Giacomo Antonelli always showed a propensity for the worldlier concerns of the church. He studied law rather than theology and affected elegance rather than piety. He had gone no further than the diaconate when Gregory XVI put him in charge of papal finances in 1845. His family had speculated aggressively and fortunately, and his brother Filippo, a "country businessman," helped Giacomo accomplish the "repurchase" of a much desired appanage. For the rest of Giacomo's life, he would never escape gossip that linked his family's fortune with his own meteoric rise under Pius IX. At thirty-nine he received the red hat.

In 1848 he favored an anti-Austrian league until he realized that the papacy could not afford national preferences. As secretary of state he helped prepare the flight to Gaeta and became the most influential man of the curia there. The motu proprio of September 12, 1849, was his, in words and in sentiment. The most reactionary of the cardinals censured him for the tincture of representationalism he allowed in the document. Many probably despised him as a parvenu. He was calculating, but at least he was one of the few who ran all of the risks the pope had run in 1848. For both Schwarzenberg and Esterházy, Antonelli was Austria's best friend in the curia.[19]

Pius IX's return to Rome on April 12, 1850, coincided with Austria's first moves toward a concordat. Two rescripts of April 18 and 23 permitted the bishops and their congregations to communicate freely with Rome and ended the restrictions upon the publication of papal bulls and encyclicals. Bishops could henceforth discipline their clergy and count on the state's enforcement of canonical penalties. The emperor still appointed the bishops, but after proper advice from the interested members of the hierarchy in the empire. The church in Austria dealt with other clerical appointments and controlled the seminaries and the curriculum and teaching staff of theological faculties.[20] The curia was grateful, but Austria's political plans for Lombardy-Venetia continued to create great uneasiness. If the kingdom received a representative assembly, could the papacy fend off demands for the same?

Schwarzenberg was as importunate as ever in his insistence that the pope's return should be the beginning of a new era. The papal cabinet should move swiftly to realize the reforms promised in the motu proprio. He wanted no more exceptions to the amnesty, for the malevolent were blaming Austria for such rigor. The pope had intended to forgive the lesser officials who had been compromised, and they should not be denied his grace. Antonelli complied with a confidential disclosure of the proposed laws, and the prince applauded the procedures for provincial and communal councils and the definite limitation upon the *Consulta*. If put into effect, they would end that incertitude of spirits upon which anarchy fed.[21]

When Schwarzenberg responded favorably to Baldasseroni's campaign against restoration of parliamentary systems, he warned Viale that the curia could avoid constitutionalism only if it adopted a system of administration that was good for its citizenry. The people had a right to be well governed. A bad administration was the revolution's best auxiliary. Administrators required surveillance.[22]

In two well-expressed rejoinders Antonelli agreed that the Italians had not yet sufficiently recovered from their delirium over new forms of government. The papacy would never accede to demands for a representative system, and it hoped its neighbors would postpone such a concession for an indefinite time. The moderates forwarded parliamentary ideas, but not because they believed they could better the condition of the people. They believed rather that such a regime would strengthen the concepts of nationality and independence. The proposed municipal and provincial councils were not yet instituted for two reasons. First, the treasury was in a most difficult situation. Second, the papal advisers knew that the constitutional party, inspired by Piedmont's revolutionaries, would try to obstruct anything that was not a part of the papal *Statuto* of 1848.[23] Esterházy perceived that the curia feared what might be granted Lombardy-Venetia more than it feared the republicanism of France.[24]

Schwarzenberg knew of the ultraconservative faction of cardinals, and he realized, from the reports of the Gaeta conferences, that Esterházy was not an avid proponent of papal reform. He admonished his envoy never to make common cause with those papal councillors who desired passivity in the face of the people's pressing needs and the dangers to the social order. He saluted Esterházy's veto of a celebration of Francis Joseph's birthday in Rome, and he took care to note that he had warned Radetzky against provocateurs who were trying to influence the inhabitants of the Legations in favor of annexation to Austria.[25]

The institution of the municipal and provincial councils at the end of 1850 placated Vienna, but the question of papal financial responsibility for part of the upkeep of the occupying Austrian forces seriously strained relations in 1851–52. Both states were suffering from severe fiscal problems, and Antonelli was fearful that his treasury would have to assume all expenses minus the rather inconsequential sum promised the papacy for cloth supplied during the first phase of the occupation. Radetzky was the soul of honor, promising to repay personally in hard cash the debt of 1849, but Vienna's continued silence reduced the secretary of state to despair. Surely the emperor would not exact more onerous conditions than those agreed to for the interventions of 1832 and 1837. Viale added to Antonelli's discomfort by expressing doubt that the Austrians wanted to settle the matter. In Schwarzenberg's last days, he complained that he was sent from one minister to another, "from Herod to Pilate." Such subterfuges were unworthy of a government, and he suggested that interim payments cease.[26]

Viale's and Antonelli's scandalized protests reached the emperor's ear, and Francis Joseph dictated a compromise. Because of his special regard for the pope, he would renounce whatever surplus his treasury was due in the accounting of papal obligations for 1849-52. Each state would recognize it had no claim on the other for past expenditures and payments. There was one exception. The papal treasury had to return 150,000 florins to the Lombard-Venetian "war chest" for what the treasury had received for supplying clothing to the troops in 1849. Austria would maintain 12,000 soldiers in its area of occupation. Increases or decreases of the forces would be a matter of common accord, as would the question of eventual evacuation. The papacy agreed to Radetzky's plea for first-class maintenance and fortification of the citadels used by the troops. In the future Austria would receive 36,000 florins monthly for general upkeep of the troops, but papal authorities also were to furnish lodging, light, and fire for officers, men and military employees plus stalls for 1,400 horses. Civilian or military hospitals would care for sick soldiers at the papacy's expense. Most transportation and official mail and package costs also were the responsibility of the papacy.[27] Viale estimated that the treasury would pay half of what Tuscany paid, and Buol consequently wanted to keep the agreement under wraps. The result was a confidential protocol rather than a public convention.[28]

Antonelli and Pius IX were delighted with the pact. The former asked for clarification of the phrase, "in case of war," for the Papal States could appeal to the Austrians only in case of legitimate defense or internal upheaval. He also insisted on a careful definition of "state of siege," which always was a burden on the treasury. Buol quickly assented to Antonelli's qualifications of both terms.[29] What had been a rather unpleasant issue between the two courts ended in quite a show of imperial generosity. It was not surprising that two months later Francis Joseph was thanking the pope for allowing the negotiations for a concordat to take place in Vienna.[30]

Much had happened since the first imperial letter had reached the pontiff in Gaeta in late 1848 or early 1849. Then, with some asperity, Francis Joseph declared he would forget that his ambassador had been forced from Rome and think no more of the reasons and conditions which led to that event. Pius IX took this as a reproof, he remembered twenty years later, but he blamed the ill-chosen words on youthful inexperience. By September 1849 the more secure emperor promised moral and, when necessary, material help for the tremendously urgent reorganization of the administration in the Papal States. In May 1850 he affirmed the basic concept behind the April rescripts: the full freedom of the Roman Catholic Church in his provinces. After his escape from assassination, he seconded the pope's maxim that only "our most holy religion" could remedy the tainted ideas and corrupt principles of the century.[31]

The young dynast was deferential to the pope and certainly sincere in his hopes for a satisfactory concordat. Yet one wonders how he reacted to an extremely frank briefing which Esterházy dispatched to Buol in the summer of 1852. The discontented in the pope's domain were all those who were not in power. A kind of political immorality was so profound and contagious that it affected even the best consciences. There was special contempt for the pope because of his remoteness and hatred for his director of finances. Antonelli's weak side was his family's growing wealth. He had no friends, and the ultraconservatives in the Sacred College accused him of docility in issuing the motu proprio of Portici. The cardinals who said they were for Austria actually were suspicious of Austria. Austria's real or pretended friends were often imprudent and embarrassing, and Antonelli tried to isolate Pius IX from them. Daily reports of their criticisms reached the pope's desk, but it would have been chancy for any foreign power to try to conciliate the factions. For Esterházy, anything that would hurt Antonelli's position would be bad, especially for Austria.[32]

During the first four years of Austrian occupation there were incidents that pretty well proved that talk of a popular desire for annexation to Austria was, in Schwarzenberg's phrase, an "absurd lie." The Bolognese did not invite Austrian officers to their casino, so the police shut it down. In March 1850 a few slammed shut their windows to avoid seeing and hearing a review celebrating the victory at Novara. The "offenders" were fined, and that night the Teatro Communale was bare of Italians.[33] In Perugia the Austrian command forbade red caps, *Ernani* style, as well as ribbons and shoes decorated with the three revolutionary colors. In 1851 another campaign to coerce smokers into abstaining from tobacco got under way, particularly in Faenza and Ancona. In place of cigars, men put straws or flowers in their mouths and sometimes earned a beating

for their pains. When the authorities of Forlì executed four persons
in June 1852 for political offenses committed in 1848, the town's
shopkeepers closed their places of business in protest. They ignored
the pontifical delegate's order to reopen, whereupon the Austrians
fined seventy-two.[34] Mazzini had sympathizers in these towns, but a
simple carpenter of the period admitted "there was a great distance
from words to deeds." The rigor of the reaction frightened the
people, who had lost the energy of '48.[35]

A few individuals in Rimini on a chill January night of 1853
roused the Austrians to a surprising level of indignation by disfigur-
ing the imperial coat of arms which adorned the Austrian vice-
consulate. The military dispatched from Bologna a regiment of
1,000 to exact reparation. The city had to pay a fine of 2,000 scudi,
while, under duress, certain citizens furnished lodging and a monetary allowance.[36] Antonelli, told by Esterházy that Austria would accept no official *démarche,* wrote a confidential letter begging for
mitigation of the penalty and promising to remove the governor and
the police commissioner of Rimini.[37] Radetzky withstood all of the
cardinal's remonstrances until Christmas time, when he decreed
that the money might go to charity, but not a copper coin for
Rimini or its inhabitants. Buol intervened, and the city's poor
received 500 scudi directly while 1,500 scudi were allocated for
public works on which the most indigent would be employed.[38]

Antonelli was winning another campaign early in 1854. When
Esterházy went on leave in the summer of 1853, he carried with him
a request to reduce the Austrian presence to garrisons in Bologna,
Ancona, and Ferrara. The papal militia was almost up to strength
and a foreign regiment almost complete. Antonelli needed quarters
for them. By autumn the French intimated they would confine
themselves to Rome and Civitavecchia if Austria would limit its
troops to Bologna and Ancona. The cardinal projected a maximum
of 8,000 French, 10,000 Austrians. Most of all, the papal regime
wished a reduction in the number of places occupied. A note from
Buol in November acquiesced in the concentration of troops within
Bologna and Ancona. Finally, in January 1854 he assured the nuncio that Austria would cut the contingent by 2,000, which
automatically meant financial relief as well as more barracks for the
papal authorities.[39] Because of a continuing shortage of accommo-

dations in the two cities, the Austrians did not evacuate the rest of the bases until October 29, 1856.

The tendency of the Austrian command meanwhile to impose its will upon pontifical authorities seemed to grow day by day, complained Antonelli. Especially grievous was the action of the military in conceding commutations and pardons to papal subjects. Such acts of grace were the pontiff's prerogative. The permission to bear arms should have been on papal authority, subject to ultimate ratification by the Austrians. The generals should have notified local officials when units were transferred, since such changes involved specific communities. More, why should the papacy have paid for troop movements which benefited Tuscany?[40] When the Austrians concentrated in Bologna and Ancona, they issued an ordinance proclaiming their right to establish a state of siege in towns garrisoned only by papal elements. From Ancona, General Hoyos had ordered a rigorous disarmament of Perugia's delegation. How then could these men protect the people from robbers? Why should Hoyos regulate carnival festivities where he had no forces? Austria should end such interference with papal sovereignty.[41] The clash of authority continued into 1855, when Antonelli complained about intrusions upon the papal administration of justice in Bologna. He was just as bitter over the high cost of lodging officers. Their constant change in assignments and unending demands for what they considered proper housing was a serious burden. Could there be some regulations to reduce the exorbitant allocations?[42]

The lifting of the state of siege in Lombardy and Venetia encouraged Antonelli in February 1856 to request the same for the Austrian-occupied towns. The military answer was simple. The Legations and the Marches did not offer the security which had been attained in the kingdom. The local authorities could not protect property or fend off the revolutionary party. The ministers agreed that the party of subversion, dismayed by the conclusion of peace when they had counted on a general conflagration, was bound to show signs of life. Francis Joseph accordingly approved a suggestion to have Bach tell the curia that it was in their own interests to keep the state of siege. It was also decided, however, to offer something of a compromise. Military commanders might surrender to papal jurisdiction the direction of preventive censorship and control of aliens, curfews, and cases of damage to papal insignia.[43] With such crumbs Antonelli would have to be satisfied.

The conclusion of the concordat in the late summer of 1855 had been a great boost to morale in Rome, however. As early as January 1849 Archbishop Friedrich zu Schwarzenberg of Salzburg, Felix's brother, had joined with Joseph Othmar von Rauscher, the emperor's onetime tutor in philosophy, in pressing for a greater episcopal role in church-state affairs. The ministers had bitter remembrances of the role the clergy had played in the disturbances in Italy and Hungary and had no taste for a surrender to either episcopacy or Rome. At one time or another, however, Bach, Thun, Bruck, and Schwarzenberg argued that a concordat would forward Austrian policy, particularly in Germany and Italy.[44]

Antonelli respected Francis Joseph's insistence upon an empire-wide conformity in negotiating the agreement, but he warned that Italian practices were quite unlike those in the rest of the Habsburg domains. Tense over increasing signs that the ruler would not relent, the secretary of state composed a rather petulant dispatch evaluating the young man's pious intentions. They had almost become a dead letter. The church's interests in Lombardy-Venetia were in decline, and Viale was to use all of his energy and zeal to redress the situation. Again, the Holy See would never consent to a law that would confuse Roman Catholicism with "false sects" or put the Roman communion on a par with such sects. This was particularly true of Italy, where there were no other faiths.[45]

The curia feared pernicious books as much as pernicious sects in Austrian Italy. Pius IX wanted Francis Joseph to give the hierarchy the right to end the importation of "evil literature" and to exercise preventive censorship. Concurrently, they should have the power to publish and circulate pastoral letters without seeking authorization from the government.[46] Viale saw no chance for such ecclesiastical controls, for the emperor was adamant in regard to any distinction between the kingdom and the rest of his realm. The curia should accept the inevitable, which was an Austrian guarantee to suppress anti-Roman Catholic literature.[47]

In the last meeting between the nuncio and Rauscher, the latter warned that the state never could surrender its right to move against a bishop who violated imperial law, above all against one accused of high treason. Viale agreed to accept this principle in a secret article.[48] Even so, the negotiations almost foundered over Article XXIV. This proviso counted upon the Holy See to exhort bishops not to appoint to benefices priests who were displeasing to the state. No matter what Gregory XVI had taught, Francis Joseph would brook no repetition of what some clerics had committed in Italy, Hungary, and Galicia. When Rauscher insisted that he had been promised such a statement in Rome, the nuncio yielded.[49]

Article IX of the concordat promised that the state would impede the circulation of books forbidden by the church. In January 1856 the archbishops of Lombardy and Venetia placed severe restraints on booksellers and insisted on police enforcement of such regulations. Thun supported their pleas, but Bach appealed to the wording of the concordat to demolish their case. The state had promised to respect a bishop's request to have the authorities examine a book he deemed damnable. Its judgment was totally independent, however, and any infringement of this principle would lead to endless demands. A majority of the ministers forced Thun to withdraw his motion.

Viale was appalled by the archbishops' lack of prudence. They would delight the church's enemies in Germany and Italy and tempt the lower imperial bureaucrats to sabotage what had been negotiated. Antonelli admitted that the clerics had made a bad impression, but the Holy See would not manifest the slightest disapprobation of what they had done. They were following the canons of the Fifth Lateran Council and the Council of Trent.[50]

Thun revived the controversy in an April session of the cabinet, but Krauss led the counterattack by declaring that nowhere did the concordat allow a bishop the right to ban a book. Why should the Italians receive something the others had not requested? A majority again prevailed against Thun.[51] Viale conferred with the Italian delegation that came to Vienna that month to discuss the implementation of the agreement with the other bishops of the realm, and he found that only the bishop of Bergamo still demanded what amounted to preventive censorship. The rest realized the emperor would never agree and shrank from petitioning him for it.[52] Like the rest of the leaders of the church in the monarchy, they must have appreciated the advantages which the concordat of 1855 afforded Roman Catholicism.

The concessions made to the clergy in Lombardy and Venetia un-

doubtedly intensified liberal distaste for the Austrians there, but the
important effect was to be seen in the rest of the peninsula. The contrast between Piedmont's campaign to curb the religious and Francis Joseph's conscious effort to rally the faithful to his empire had
great impact even upon those Italians who regretted the actions
taken in Turin. It was easy to equate Habsburg authoritarianism
with Roman immobility. After 1856 a Cavour might fret over the
prospect of a more beneficent Austrian regime in the kingdom. He
did not need to give more than lip service to ideas of a confederacy
over which a pope might preside.

Esterházy had played practically no part in the elaboration of the
concordat, for he had fallen into an inertia that probably was a form
of mental depression. As early as July 1852 Buol had reprimanded
him for a silence of three months. In January 1856 Francis Joseph
replaced him with Count Franz Colloredo, then in London. The
new envoy consequently knew of the poor reputation which the pope
and his government had among the English. Pius IX had suspended
elections to the communal councils in 1853, and the Rothschilds,
despite their resentment of the depressed status of Jews in the Papal
States, had advanced a loan of some 4 million scudi in September
1854. The financial disarray continued, and the peacemakers at the
Congress of Paris were bound to ask themselves what could be done
to remedy the situation.[53]

In his first conversation with Buol in February 1856, Napoleon III
insisted there had to be an end to the occupation of Rome, which
was so costly. The Austrians also wished to get out, replied their
foreign minister, but there were obstacles: disordered finances,
faulty administration, and a poor police system. Empress Eugénie
suggested a subsidization of the pope by all of the powers, and Buol
indicated that Francis Joseph would be happy to participate in such
a subscription. But, he added, he had no permission to deal with
"the Roman question."[54]

Thanks to Cavour's frantic insistences, the earl of Clarendon and
Napoleon III agreed to raise "Italian questions" at the Congress's
twenty-second session of April 8. Walewski spoke of France's hope
for a speedy removal of its troops from Rome and politely invited the
Austrians to associate themselves in general evacuation. Clarendon
asserted the need to end "abnormal" occupations and to seek a

remedy for justified discontent. For eight years Bologna had been under a state of siege while brigands tormented the countryside. The Papal States should have a secularized government.

Buol insisted that he had instructions to deal only with the affairs of the Levant, but he did associate himself completely with Walewski's comment on foreign forces in papal lands. He would not discuss Clarendon's recommendations or the length of the Austrian stay in the States of the Church. Alexander von Hübner, the Austrian ambassador to Paris, argued that the reduction of strength in the Legations was ample indication of the imperial cabinet's intention to recall the soldiers when that measure was opportune. Cavour retorted that the Austrian presence day by day assumed the character of permanency. After seven years there were no signs of improvement in their areas. Was not the continuation of a rigorous state of siege in Bologna sufficient proof? Austrian troops in the Legations and in Parma destroyed the political equilibrium in Italy and constituted a real danger for Sardinia. Europe should pay attention to the abnormal state of affairs resulting from Austria's indefinite occupation of a great part of Italy. Hübner testily noted Cavour's failure to mention the French in Rome and the Sardinian occupation of Menton and Roquebrune, which belonged to Monaco. The latter, declared Cavour, would end when the prince could return without running grave risks. The Piedmontese government also wanted the French to quit papal territory, but it was the Austrian army which was far more dangerous for the independent states of Italy.[55]

A month after this bruising encounter, Buol completed instructions for Colloredo which indicated that France and Austria were determined to insist upon fundamental remedies. The Papal States were weak, and the officials, not up to their responsibilities, had mishandled what reforms were instituted in 1850. The French had charged their ambassador to collaborate with Colloredo in studying the internal situation and in recommending policies to ameliorate the critical state of affairs. A most urgent need was a gendarmerie, for France and Austria were moving toward removal of their forces. The papacy seemed not yet ready for this, despite the comments made at the Congress of Paris. Given the financial confusion, there would have to be an increase in taxes, though this would aggravate discontent. Finally, Colloredo was to remember that the emperor expected an absolutely scrupulous enforcement of the concordat.[56]

The criticism of papal government and the questioning of foreign troops in the papal lands at the Congress of Paris vexed Buol more than his public utterances would indicate. In June 1856 he invited Viale to have dinner and a little talk with Baron Adolphe de Bourqueney, the French envoy. In a rather vague manner Buol and the French ambassador wondered if the Holy See might be prepared for an end to the occupation. They only wanted Viale's ideas. Again, rather lightly, they touched upon the administration of the Papal States. Viale properly refused to consider the dinner a "conference" and remarked that his twenty-eight years of diplomatic service had kept him from any involvement in internal affairs. He suggested that their ambassadors to the curia knew or could find out the answers, and Buol responded that this was exactly what the two cabinets planned to do.[57]

Antonelli replied that the sentiments of the two cabinets were well known to him. There was constant study of means to improve public administration, which suffered only from those defects which the Piedmontese chambers chose to find. Where was there a government without flaws? It was hardly a good time to accept advice. Would there be a repetition of the events after 1831, when contesting powers vied in an attempt to destroy the temporal power?[58]

The secretary of state knew well that Francis Joseph and Napoleon III would not be parties to a destruction of the pope's temporal sovereignty. In 1849 the remembrances of Napoleon I's trickery in interpreting the French concordat and brutality toward Pius VII impelled Antonelli to seek an Austrian occupation of Rome. The French who preempted the Austrians in the Holy City, no doubt with Schwarzenberg's sincere approval, were surprisingly well-liked by the Romans, and their presence did not begin to cost what the Austrians demanded. Though Vienna and Paris consistently recommended greater laicization of the administration and reforms which might restore some public faith in the officials, the fact that both had rival establishments in the Patrimony of Saint Peter aided Antonelli when he avoided commitments. Relegated to the northern areas, the Austrians had to contend with resentments that were essentially anticuria, anti-Rome as well as poverty that encouraged crime. It was no secret that the taxpayers were contributing to the upkeep of the Habsburg troops, and the enforcement of strict regulations against political activity added to the unpopularity of the Austrians.

Francis Joseph was as irritated as his ministers over what seemed to be an administration that constantly hinted at its desire to be free of foreign legions and just as constantly failed to take steps which would guarantee its continued existence. His impatience, however, did not prevent the conclusion of a concordat which affronted liberals and anticlericals everywhere in Europe. The modifications of Josephinism were considerable, for the emperor willed the restoration of much episcopal power. There were limits, as the Lombard and Venetian prelates discovered. Uniformity of procedure was all-important to Francis Joseph. What was good for a Galician bishop was equally good for an Italian. The Austrian concordat sharpened the debate over the degree of influence which the church might exert in a predominantly Roman Catholic state. When Cavour challenged the papal conduct of its own affairs at the Congress of Paris, his auditors were aware of the strife between government and church in Piedmont. The alliance of rationalism and nationalism was plain to see, the "Syllabus of Errors" less than a decade away.

Austria and
the Two Sicilies,
1849–1856

FERDINAND II was the true isolationist among Italian rulers. Born under British protection in Palermo, he never rid himself of the dread that the English navy would someday establish a sphere of influence in Sicily, if not add it to the empire. Matrimonially bound by his second wife to Austria, he was chary of propositions that seemed to advance the Habsburg predominance in the peninsula. French republicanism was anathema to him, and though the first to recognize Louis Napoleon as emperor of the French, he did not forget the relationship between the Bonapartes and the Murats. His best friend was Nicholas I, thanks to their common views on government and the distance which separated them. As king of the Two Sicilies, he referred to the salt water and the holy water which surrounded him and his realm without placing absolute faith in either.

Schwarzenberg was the imperial envoy to Naples when he was summoned to assume the post of chief adviser to Francis Joseph in late 1848. The prince had watched with loathing Ferdinand's grant of a constitution in that chaotic year, but he also had an excellent idea of the corruption and oppressiveness which had outraged the liberals and had driven the Sicilians to separatism. Schwarzenberg's shrewdest move was sending Anton von Martini, a senior naval and army officer, as ambassador in February 1849. His exquisite courtesy charmed a monarch who preferred to converse in Neapolitan dialect but who was quite aware of the demands of Spanish etiquette.[1] Martini quickly realized that Ferdinand was very much alarmed by the Austrian regime's failure to invalidate its promised constitutionalism in Lombardy-Venetia. Prince Giovanni di Petrulla, the new ambassador to Vienna, was to bring royal expostulations. If Vienna did not listen, he would go to St. Petersburg to see the tsar.[2]

Schwarzenberg countered adroitly with the statement that he had received reports that the Two Sicilies would return to "pure monarchy," getting rid of all constitutional forms. Should Martini be queried as to what should be done, he was to make a noncommittal answer. Naples had all of Austria's sympathies in restoring confidence and order, but the king alone had the choice and responsibility for the means to attain this end.[3] Ferdinand dispatched a special envoy, Commander Marsilio, to Vienna in the summer of 1850 to ask for friendly counsel on the system of government Naples should follow. Schwarzenberg believed that Ferdinand had already made up his mind on the *Statuto* of 1848, and he warned Martini to be most reserved.

The Austrian cabinet devoted two sessions to the formulation of a reply. Schwarzenberg seemed to feel that the king would like to copy what Austria planned for Lombardy and Venetia, and there was unanimous agreement that the differences between the two areas were great. Local conditions should determine the course of political development. Bach and Krauss were concerned that the *Statuto* might be voided. If Austria were associated with such a repudiation, the empire's position in Italy would be weakened. The latter doubted that a majority in the Two Sicilies wanted its abolition, even if the past two years showed that the populace was not ripe for representative government. Schwarzenberg and Bruck, referring to their own personal knowledge of Italian affairs, predicted ruin for states which insisted on constitutions. It was not to their interest, or Austria's, to hang on to such an impossible *Staatsform*. Schmerling and Thun would have recommended to the king a revision of the *Statuto*, but Ritter Ferdinand von Thinnfeld, the minister of agriculture and mines, was suspicious that Ferdinand was not really seeking counsel. In case of necessity he wanted to be able to cite "Austrian advice." The Ministerrat concurred, and it was decided to give Martini comments which he could deliver orally. There would be no written document which could be filed away.[4]

Schwarzenberg's *mémoire* was masterful. The Austrian cabinet wished to stress the essential difference between the abrogation of a written charter and the return pure and simple to the indolence and *laisser-aller* of the "good old days." A retrogressive turn of this nature could only lead to new catastrophes. The kingdom had enjoyed municipal franchises, provincial councils, and a supreme *Consulta*. Now was the time to modify them more or less according to circumstances and to put them to work. They would be an effica-

cious control upon the administrators and would guarantee the
people the first of their rights, which was to be governed by a just,
strong, and enlightened regime. Add to these institutions a body of
fundamental laws, and the king would have bestowed upon his subjects the best of constitutions.[5]

Martini read the message to Ferdinand at Caserta. The ruler was
most attentive but made no comment whatsoever. *Il Risorgimento*
published a report from Naples dated July 3 which virtually quoted
Schwarzenberg's phrases. Without trying to guess the source of the
disclosure, Martini noted that this unanticipated language from
Austria had upset the reactionary plans of the ministers and of the
obscurantist party.[6] He already had given Schwarzenberg his opinion of Naples and its king. The people were inconstant and crafty.
The king's moods were variable, and any kind of incident could
bring about the abandonment of the wisest calculations and convert
the firmest of decisions to a fountainhead of confusion.[7] Martini was
cynical when Fortunato passionately offered aid to Austria in case of
hostilities with Piedmont. "I give no importance to this *élan*, knowing well enough through experience how quick they are to hold their
fire and to rectify their promises when it is a matter of fulfilling
them."[8]

King Ferdinand gave color to Martini's assumptions early in 1851
when there was talk of a Neapolitan replacement of the French in
Rome. Though the armed forces undoubtedly were oversize for the
question of defense, their commander-in-chief indicated he would
never accept a police assignment. His government would stay on the
defensive, isolate itself, and avoid entangling innovations.[9]

Then came William Ewart Gladstone's *Two Letters to Lord Aberdeen on the State Prosecutions of the Neapolitan Government*, one
of the most famous philippics of the nineteenth century. After several months' residence in Naples, the Conservative M.P. had attended the first trial of persons accused of plots to end Bourbon rule
and had visited several of the condemned. Thoroughly horrified by
the treatment of some of Naples' finest minds, he first addressed a
letter dated April 7, 1851, to the earl of Aberdeen. The latter forwarded it to a "fellow conservative," Schwarzenberg, on May 2, with
a concluding statement, "Your Highness will best judge whether
anything ought, or can with propriety, be attempted."

Obviously embarrassed, Schwarzenberg did not write Naples of Aberdeen's ambiguous communication until July 8. He declared that he had reminded his English friend in a reply dated June 30 of English repressions in Ireland and of Austrian repressions in Hungary. These two Englishmen were Conservatives, however, and he wanted Martini to emphasize that someday they probably would return to power. His ambassador could show the letter to Fortunato and to the king, as long as they maintained confidentiality. Possibly Gladstone's allegations would put the government on the trail of real abuses. Perhaps it would be wise to indicate what was erroneous and exaggerated in the English parliamentarian's report. Incidentally, neither Aberdeen's letter nor Schwarzenberg's dispatch suggested that better treatment of the prisoners would prevent publication of Gladstone's letter.[10]

Ferdinand expressed gratification with Schwarzenberg's reply to Aberdeen, and he obviously was quite unprepared for the sensation which Gladstone created by publishing the first and a second letter (with additional evidence of tyrannical procedures) in the summer of 1851. The sentence "This is the negation of God erected into a system of Government" became famous wherever censorship did not forbid its reproduction. Schwarzenberg could only ask Martini to relay to Fortunato the "most unfortunate impression" which Gladstone's move had made upon the Austrian government. The prince was disgusted, however, when a Neapolitan commission was extremely generous in awarding damages to English citizens for losses suffered during the Sicilian revolution. Palmerston would be more exigent than ever, and the audacity of his protégés would increase.[11]

When Buol succeeded Schwarzenberg, Martini furnished the usual sketch of the ruler of the Two Sicilies. The king resented states which tried to dominate and coerce him, and he was aware, in a period when navies executed intimidating maneuvers, that Austria lacked a fleet. He also had lost none of his conviction that he had to maintain his liberty of action vis-à-vis the other Italian states.[12] The quarrel over the Holy Places in Palestine stripped him of his chance to remain in isolation. Pro-Romanov, he undoubtedly would have liked to accord to Nicholas I the advantages of benevolent neutrality. The presence of the English and French squadrons should have demonstrated that he could not afford ambiguous gestures.

Ferdinand, however, disliked infectious diseases of all kinds, cholera as much as liberalism, and his officials in October 1853 refused to allow two French officers to leave quarantine at Capri before the appointed time. One of them, Pierre-Emmanuel-Albert Du Casse, had edited the ten volumes of Joseph Bonaparte's *Mémoires et correspondance politique et militaire*, and the Bourbon ruler probably suspected he would propagandize for a restoration of the Murats. The French broke off diplomatic relations, but only for a month. In early December, Drouyn informed Emidio Antonini, the Neapolitan envoy, that the Anglo-French alliance wanted 40,000 men and three ships from his monarch. "Everyone is with us, and you will do as the others do."[13]

Petrulla reported to Buol his king's decision to remain strictly neutral and asked if the Two Sicilies could count on Austrian support in case of an attack by a Western power. Not charmed by such a direct question, Buol tried to squirm his way out of a commitment. If war became general, it was only too probable that the revolutionary party would try to advance its projects. Then all governments would have to join those belligerents who promised to maintain existing frontiers and legality. Austria would never default in this regard. "If the king of Naples, rallying to the Emperor Francis Joseph's flag . . ." Buol drifted off into an extremely vague evocation of concerted action.[14] Sardinia, rather than Naples, would provide the troops for the Crimea, but Ferdinand continued to irritate the French by prohibiting the export of sulfur from Sicily and of 1,000 head of cattle from Apulia, which the French forces needed. Buol secretly worried that France might exact vengeance by stirring up rebellion, but he tried to reassure Ferdinand by emphasizing the French pledge of collaboration against such tactics in Italy. The king should avoid giving umbrage without, of course, sacrificing his rights or his principles.[15]

Military deadlock in the Crimea meant increasing Allied impatience with Ferdinand, but it also hastened what Buol was seeking, security in Italy. On December 22, 1854, Vienna and Paris secretly contracted to maintain the status quo in the peninsula. In case of military cooperation in the Near East, the two powers also would cooperate in Italy.[16] Austria continued to make representations against the "indiscreet zeal" of the police in the Two Sicilies and urged the king to offer to the maritime powers all the facilities that were compatible with duty and neutrality.[17]

Ferdinand and his officials seemed to pay no heed. The chief of police, Orazio Mazza, caught the first attaché of the British legation, George Fagan, violating a silly ordinance, and William Temple, the queen's minister and Palmerston's brother, decided that majesty and honor were at stake. After some weeks of increasing tension the British let Buol know that they were dispatching a squadron to force Mazza's removal. By telegram from Ischl, Francis Joseph ordered Martini to contrive the official's removal. Buol urged the king to get rid of Mazza at once. This would give his action the character of spontaneity, save his dignity, and prevent the coercive measures England irrevocably had decided upon.[18] Two days later the Austrian envoy notified Vienna that Mazza had been relieved of duty and that the ruler was most grateful for the emperor's intervention.

A second incident originated on August 15, when the commandant of the citadel at Messina refused to raise his flag in returning a salute from a French ship that day, which was Napoleon III's birthday. The French demanded an apology and, after two months of indecision in Naples, warned Vienna that they would recall their minister, short of proper satisfaction. Far less offended than the British, they edited a note which would save Ferdinand's dignity. Martini persuaded him to sign it, and again he relayed his thanks for Austria's *démarche*.[19] The Austrian emperor had been careful not to suggest a relaxation of the Neapolitan ban on certain exports. He and Buol were insistent, however, that the king make amends for palpable insults.

Sick of Austrian evenhandedness, Ferdinand warned Austria that the pressures from England and France made it impossible to control the revolutionary hydra. Vienna had every reason to show interest in order and tranquillity, principally in Italy, and the Austrian cabinet did not allow the press to run wild in its territories. For a long time, however, Vienna had not restrained its journals when they commented on his kingdom. It was as if Austria wished to make common cause with those who were not pleased with the actual state of affairs in Italy.[20]

At the famous conference of April 8, 1856, of the Congress of

Paris, the peacemakers turned to Italian questions despite Buol's strenuous protests. Walewski rather lightly announced that, having attained the principal purposes of the Congress, the conferees might turn to problems which might disturb the peace. Without undue accentuation he expressed the hope that certain Italian governments would modify those policies that stimulated demagogy. It would be a service to the regime in Naples to point out its wrong path (*fausse voie*). Clarendon denounced the "deplorable and abnormal" state of affairs in that kingdom. Though interference in the internal business of another state was regrettable, civilized powers should urge justice and humanity upon the king in such a peremptory manner that he would feel constrained to accede. After Buol's categorical refusal to accept the Congress's right to discuss a sovereign's interests, particularly in the absence of that sovereign's representative, Cavour argued that Ferdinand's conduct discredited the concept of monarchy and augmented the threat of the revolutionary party. The diplomats also considered the Papal States and the foreign troops stationed there, it will be remembered, as well as issues relating to Greece, Belgium, and international law.[21] For the rest of 1856, however, it was Naples which seemed most vulnerable to projects of reformation. Thoroughly affronted, Ferdinand decided he would not yield, and thanks to the inherent rivalries of the great powers in the Mediterranean, he survived.

In May the English and the French presented admonitory notes, stressing amnesty and reform. Ferdinand ordered Luigi Carafa di Truetto, his "provisional" director of foreign affairs, to reply verbally that no power had the right to mix in the internal business of his government.[22] On June 30 he dictated even more provocative statements for London and Paris. Walewski's response was rather menacing when he wrote to Bourqueney in Vienna on July 12. Buol had indicated that Austria would be very much vexed if France worked with England on an Italian question without Austria. If such were the case, Buol could give the king of Naples some salutary advice by the end of the month. Walewski truly did not know what France would do, but a rupture of relations and probably a threat to rectify in twenty-four hours the pending claims of some French nationals would seem to him the minimal actions one could expect.

Buol reacted to the French hints by dispatching a strong note to

Naples. "Our emperor" wished the king to consider the grave consequences of the displeasure his reply had aroused in Paris and London. Austria believed that Naples had firmly maintained its rights to autonomy by protesting all foreign interference. Having satisfied honor and dignity, might not the king yield to an impulse to be clement? There should not be too sweeping an amnesty. Only those who had sincerely repented and who personally begged for pardon should receive it. Austria's only motive was to uphold the common interest which Vienna and Naples had in assuring public tranquillity in Italy and to avert the dangers which were imminent if the king persisted in his peremptory refusal. In a reserved annex Buol warned Felix Wimpffen to avoid every appearance of mediation. The emperor had remained a stranger to the notes delivered by the Western allies and planned to remain so. His representative should explain the gravity of the situation, no more. It was up to the king to take the part which prudence and his people's interests demanded.[23]

Ferdinand did pardon some persons of minor consequence on July 28, thanks to Austrian advice.[24] Neither London nor Paris responded favorably to the very limited amnesty or to the king's formal excuses for his note of June 30. Walewski's innate conservatism and Napoleon III's intuition that France needed some months of repose, however, dictated a check upon Clarendon's zeal. On October 21 there was still no sign of a general liberation of political prisoners in the Bourbon kingdom, and the ministers of the maritime powers gave notice they were leaving. Nevertheless, the French emperor had proposed to the English the postponement of any action by the fleets.[25] Ferdinand had avoided armed intervention, and he had proved to himself that he was his own best ally.

The salt water which he had relied upon was not much of a defense against France and England. Rather, the Austro-French pact to maintain the status quo in Italy during the preliminaries to the Crimean War was his best hope to stave off the effects of outraged opinion in the West. Francis Joseph and his advisers worried over his intransigence and applauded his eventual yielding to the Mediterranean partners. Vienna had no brief for restoration of the *Statuto*, which would have inspired constitutionalists in Tuscany, the Papal States, Parma, and Modena. The Piedmontese example was enough of a challenge. Schwarzenberg had stressed the value of utilizing local representative bodies and the *Consulta* and the benefits of law codes which were enforced and respected. Buol did not depart from such counsels, for it was inconceivable that Austria could dispatch another expedition to quell troubles in Naples or Sicily at a time of international tension in the Near East. Habsburg policy required tranquillity in southern Italy. That entailed a subtle blend of persuasion and, on occasion, the emperor's direct interference. Given the character of Ferdinand II and the impatience which he aroused in London and Paris, there could have been no other approach.

Buol and
Cavour, 1852–1857

IN 1853 the relatively decent rapport between Vienna and Turin suffered from Austrian complaints over the Piedmontese press and from Austrian suspicions that the Lombard exiles were behind the February rising in Milan. Radetzky lost little time in sequestering the properties of the Lombard émigrés, even those who had secured the right to emigrate and subsequently had been naturalized as Sardinians. At the end of the year neither state had a representative of ministerial rank in the other's capital, and the focus of international complications was in the Near East.

The executions in December 1852 of anti-Austrian conspirators at Mantua had evoked a tremendous outcry in the Piedmontese press, and Buol demanded that Turin, in accord with Azeglio's promise, answer such outbursts with a statement in the official journal. He was especially outraged by articles which implied that Francis Joseph was an assassin.[1] Dabormida asked Buol to convey his colleagues' sincere regrets to the emperor, but the wording of the printed reproof was quite guarded. Buol took the text to Francis Joseph and explained the difficulty Sardinia would have in adding even a few lines to the statement. The ruler agreed, but he insisted on a positive and formal engagement that Turin would unilaterally denounce any future calumnies.[2] Dabormida answered that a self-respecting government could not accept a procedure imposed by another state. The French were also applying pressure, however, and James Hudson, who had been the British minister since February 1852, wrote Lord John Russell that "unless your Lordship and her Majesty's government come quickly to our assistance, Piedmont will be wiped from the list of constitutional states."[3] With considerable aplomb, Dabormida told the French that he was surprised to see them play the part of Austria's auxiliary. The cabinet would resign if France forced restrictions on the Piedmontese press.[4]

The unexpected Mazzinian rising in Milan on February 6 surprised both governments and convinced the Sardinians that their reputation with the rest of Europe was compromised. The presence of resentful émigrés in Piedmont cast suspicion upon them, despite the effective Austrian interdiction at the frontier of the more effusive Turinese and Genoese newpapers. On the morning of the rebellion, Dabormida apprised Apponyi of the departure of twenty to thirty émigrés from Turin for Milan. His government telegraphed all frontier posts to intercept potential troublemakers, and Apponyi immediately warned the military in Milan. The rebellion was so short-lived that the Austrian envoy, at Dabormida's invitation, was reporting on February 8 that he had inspected the Sardinian orders to the frontier officials, which he judged to be very precise. He also received a promise that all compromised émigrés would be expelled.[5] The apprehensive cabinet asked for an Austrian note on press excesses, promising to reply that it highly disapproved of past and future attacks on the person of the emperor and incitements to rebellion. The ministry guaranteed it would employ every legal power to repress future excesses and to maintain good relations with Austria.[6]

Apponyi praised the Piedmontese government's denunciation of the rising and the strict surveillance of suspicious émigrés and sensitive frontier areas. The *Questura* in Turin had annulled all residence permits held by émigrés. None would be renewed unless the petitioners could demonstrate good behavior and sufficiency of means. The people of Turin were showing no sympathy for radicals who were arrested and transported through the street by carabinieri.[7] Dabormida informed Revel that he would ask the American chargé for passports for those émigrés who had abused Sardinian hospitality.[8]

Buol expressed his appreciation of Sardinia's energy and promptness in acting to maintain general tranquillity and good neighborliness. He and Dabormida nevertheless continued to haggle over a formula which would satisfy each state's sensitivity to press affairs. In the end Buol indicated that Austria would accept the general promises which Dabormida had made.[9] The administration in Lombardy and Venetia believed it had a far more potent weapon against the émigrés who nourished the provocations of the press. On February 13 Radetzky sequestered their properties. The decree directly linked the emigration with the recent events in Milan. Affected were all who were excluded from amnesty, whether or not they had permission to emigrate. Also included were those stripped of Austrian citizenship and declared legal emigrants by the decree of December 29, 1850[10]. Francis Joseph's bitterness over the Milanese affair, Radetzky's undying distaste for the treacherous émigrés, and Buol's exasperation with Piedmontese journalism dictated reprisals that would hurt. It is not surprising that the emperor, bleeding from an assassin's sharp knife on February 18, exclaimed to Archduke Rainer, "Now they have even tried the Milanese story on me."[11]

Though the commercial treaty of 1851 declared that Sardinian property in Lombardy and Venetia could be expropriated only through regular condemnation procedures, Buol informed Revel that the decree applied to all émigrés without distinction. Even the officers who remained in royal service might find their incomes cut off.[12] In a second and tempestuous encounter Buol did not attempt to deny that the decree was illegal in an international sense and an act of hostility against Piedmont. The leading personalities of the emigration did not take part in the rising, but the 500 who came to the frontier were not on a pleasure trip. Turin might believe Austria would leave Lombardy some day. Rather, Austria would sacrifice its last drop of blood and its last florin.[13]

The frank disclosure of Austria's motives coincided with Dabormida's attempt to enforce the laws on the press to Vienna's satisfaction. The repression in Milan provoked the radical press to the greatest violence Apponyi had yet experienced. *La Maga* of Genoa referred to Francis Joseph's assailant with the assertion that "not being able to print János Libényi's name in golden letters, one must be content with capitals." A scandalized council of ministers ordered immediate prosecution of this "apology for assassination," but Dabormida begged Apponyi to lodge a formal request for legal redress to avert a trial by jury. Buol indicated to Revel that he did not oppose an Austrian appeal to Sardinian law, but the emperor continued to show an invincible repugnance for such a procedure.[14]

Dabormida continued to argue that the decree of sequestration violated the spirit of the peace treaty of 1849 and the letter of the treaty of commerce of 1851. Where was the proof that Piedmont was the center of conspiracies against Austria? Buol retorted that sequestration was not a punishment, but a provisional precautionary measure. When Austria granted legal emigration, the document did not sanction Sardinian naturalization or the exploitation of revenues to underwrite the spirit of revolution.[15] On April 12 Revel received orders to go on leave. Simultaneously the cabinet in Turin circulated a memorandum, aimed primarily at Britain and France, which repeated the legal and moral flaws in sequestration. The tone was measured, the reasoning impressive.[16] Dabormida had requested that Apponyi remain in Turin, and Buol agreed to his provisional stay on April 17.

Apponyi reported in late June that the polemics had subsided. The Sardinian protests had aroused little French or British support, and this fact embarrassed the cabinet. The days left to Apponyi in Turin were few, for Revel had not returned to Vienna and Buol had to think of appearances. The minister would go on leave "to take care of personal affairs," and Ludwig Paar would remain as chargé ad interim.[17] The war of nerves over Lombardy had entered a quiescent stage, though a decree of November 12 tightened the screws on those absentee landholders whom the Austrians wished to squeeze. In principle, only debts existing prior to 1847 were legal. Other rules hampered a widow's recovery of her dowry, impeded the pensions of servants and dependents of persons whose lands were sequestered, and encouraged heirs living in Austrian territories to separate themselves from their absentee parents.[18]

Discreet inquiries in Vienna revealed that there was no likelihood of a successor to Apponyi anytime soon. Paar went through the usual New Year's audience with Victor Emmanuel, who summarized matters neatly. "It would appear that *our* position is quite delicate." Paar let the expression pass without comment.[19] The vendetta between the two states was increasingly obscured by the worsening situation in the Near East.

Revel died of cholera at the end of July 1854, thereby ending the comedy of his "leave." Cavour's chief worry was the increasing evidence of greater intimacy between Austria and the Crimean allies. Buol took care to notify all the Italian courts that Austrian troop movements in Italy meant no diminution of effectives and no relaxation of the watch on the revolutionaries.[20] After lengthy negotiations Austria did join the Western powers in an alliance on December 2. In Turin, Hudson showed Cavour the telegraphic notification, and Victor Emmanuel ordered Dabormida to do his best to ascertain the secret conditions which secured Austria's adhesion. He did not want any articles that promised the maintenance of the territorial integrity of the Italian states.[21] The king was assuming that he would be asked to join the alliance, and he was hoping for some territorial compensation.

In Vienna the English and French envoys informed Giovanni Cantono de Ceva, the Sardinian chargé, that a secret convention would be signed by France and Austria, with English approval, to guarantee the tranquillity and the existing frontiers of the Italian states. Bourqueney stressed the antirevolutionary nature of the pact and assured Cantono there was no direct or indirect allusion to Piedmont.[22] The convention manifestly had destroyed Piedmont's bargaining power when the Western allies virtually coerced the small state into promising troops for the Crimea. Dabormida had dreamed that the Italian question would be reexamined, even of territorial accessions. Cavour and the king, however, were ready to pledge 15,000 men for a mere face-saving protocol, not to be made public, in which France and England would explain why they could not agree to Dabormida's conditions. After a great battle within the cabinet, Dabormida departed from the Ministry of Foreign Affairs.[23] Clarendon had made quite clear that the allies would not "use all their efforts to induce Austria to remove the sequestration upon the properties of Sardinian subjects." While recognizing that the states of Italy imperatively demanded improvement, "Her Majesty's government must reserve to themselves the unfettered right of acting at the time and in the manner that they think most expedient and most likely to be attended with success."[24]

Cavour braved his reluctant colleagues and what would be an inflamed democratic press because he was sure that, by adhering to the alliance, he would cancel England's and France's suspicions of Piedmont's past ties with revolution.[25] He wanted to give his country's policy a European dimension. His allies expected him to normalize relations with Austria. Word from Cantono was reassuring. Buol was not bitter about Sardinia's action as long as there was no question of bringing Turin into the agreement of December 2. It also seemed to the Sardinian chargé that the reduction by 20,000 of the Austrian troops in Italy was a direct result of Cavour's joining the Western allies.[26]

The English and the French had declined to put pressure upon

Vienna for an end to the sequestrations when they secured Piedmont as an active ally, but they had made discreet representations to Austria throughout the early part of 1855. Their growing estrangement from Austria over the terms to be submitted to Russia inevitably strengthened Cavour's hand. It is true that he worried in April 1855 over dispatching his troops to the Crimea during a time of tension, but Palmerston and Clarendon denied there would be treachery. The latter was his usual blunt self when he wrote to Turin that "we cannot for a moment suppose that Piedmont runs any more risk from Austria, on account of having sent away 15,000 men, than if she retained them at home."[27] The troops departed, and the absence of a regularly accredited Sardinian representative at the conferences in Vienna did not keep Cavour from knowing that Austria would not play the Anglo-French game in neutralizing the Black Sea. Austria wanted some security against Russian revenge by land, and Cavour was quick to gain advantage of the resulting acrimony.[28]

Now that the Austrians had taken to their tents while the Piedmontese troops readied themselves for the assault, should not the Western powers treat Turin a little better, he asked his representatives in Paris and London. In June his allies agreed there would be a Sardinian plenipotentiary at the peace conference. He would participate in all discussions that involved his country's interests. His French and English colleagues would keep him fully informed of all general discussions. By late summer Buol was informing Cantono that he saw no point in trying to reconcile the differing principles which Austria and Piedmont had adopted in trying to settle the question of the sequester. About seventy-three persons were involved, and there should be a separate treatment of each case. Those who asked to return would be granted permission to do so, with restoration of their property. Those who were denied readmission could petition for their property, which would be restituted. Cantono understood that those who wished to remain in Piedmont and who could advance reasons for such a decision also would have their properties returned. In a coded message the chargé worried that those in the last category would have to sell their property, though Buol had not mentioned this. He felt, however, that the Austrians were making a real concession by lifting the sequester upon the properties of those they would not allow to come back.[29]

In November and December, Victor Emmanuel made his long-delayed state visits to Paris and London. Cavour, who accompanied him, realized that Napoleon III wanted an end to the war, though the French did not apprise him of their negotiations with Austria for an Austrian ultimatum to Russia. The valiant Sardinian action at Chernaya in mid-August had improved his bargaining position, and there was no little rivalry between his allies in recognizing his new status. Napoleon III easily outtrumped the English when the king and Cavour returned to Paris. Reasonably sure that Russia would accept the Austrian ultimatum, he could renew, at the height of his prestige, earlier dreams. A rapprochement with Russia annulled his fancies for a restored Poland. In the crusade to liberate the nationalities, Italy offered the appropriate terrain. There it was not likely that Prussia and Russia would rush to save Austria's position. Yet who would deny that Cavour was thunderstruck by the famous imperative uttered the evening of December 7, "Write confidentially to Walewski what you believe I can do for Piedmont and for Italy"? There was a brief and feverish exchange of ideas. Possibly Wallachia and Moldavia for Austria, in return for Lombardy and Venetia? Relieve the pope of any further tribulations with the Romagna? It was not surprising that Cavour wrote to Emanuele d'Azeglio on New Year's Day, 1856: "The time to act has come. Up to now we have left our allies alone; now we have to harass them, give them no more repose."

Cavour did not know that Francis Joseph and his ministers had decided to "cleanse" themselves of the question of the émigrés in November 1855. There was no precise agreement on the terms to be offered, but Cavour was sooner rather than later going to lose the strongest issue he possessed in his campaign to goad his allies. With the prospect of peace he decided to stir up his friends with some frank conjectures on the future map of Europe. Was not Austria replacing Russia as the preponderant power in the Near East? Was it not to Austria's profit that the treaty would assign half of Bessarabia and the mouths of the Danube to the Danubian Principalities? Austria would extend from the Ticino to the Black Sea, with exclusive control of the Po and the Danube. Should Europe be left to the mercy of two such antagonistic powers (he said to Hudson) as France and Austria? Was it right for Austria, "who had not fired a single shot and who had tricked all Parties more or less," to reap all the advantages? Rather, it was time to regularize Austria's position in Italy, if there was any desire for that European equilibrium for which the war had been fought.[30]

The tsar's acceptance in January 1856 of an Austrian ultimatum to enter into peace negotiations shifted the scales against Turin once again. The news reached the capital on January 18, and Cavour admitted he was crushed. Paar gleefully wrote of the "consternation" in Turin, which the newspapers could hardly hide. It was Austrian diplomacy, not the arms of France or the fleets of England, which had achieved an armistice.[31] Cavour discarded a lengthy memorial which Massimo d'Azeglio had composed in reply to Napoleon III's "what can we do for Italy?" The sudden emergence of the Habsburg state as the pivot of European affairs required a bill of particulars that would read well in London and Paris newspapers. Austria should govern Lombardy-Venetia with greater mildness, there should be a reformation of the absurd regime in Naples, Austrian troops should evacuate Romagna and the Legations (these lands could be placed under Tuscany or Modena or be allowed absolute administrative independence), and Austria should end the sequestrations and relax "her measures of commercial rigour" against Piedmont.[32] In early January, Cantono had told Buol that Sardinia was very much disposed to accept what Austria would offer in ending the sequester. He had explained to Count Luigi Cibrario, the minister of foreign affairs, that each case would be treated on its own merits. It was his belief that Turin would have no great objection to Austria's prohibiting the return of an émigré, even one with Sardinian citizenship, as long as Austria lifted the sequester.[33]

The Russian collapse forced a reversal. When Francis Joseph's rescript of February 8 prescribed forced sales for those who made no move whatsoever to take advantage of the conditions for ending sequestration, Cibrario retreated to the earlier legal position. His government could not admit that those who asked for recognition as expatriates might be forced to sell their property in a certain period of time. It did not agree that Austria could refuse to honor the naturalization of former subjects by Sardinia unless they asked for and received the right to remain abroad. Rather nastily, Cibrario added that he well believed that Austria would return the income, minus expenses, it had realized under sequestration. After all, the Vienna cabinet had always hotly disavowed accusations of confiscation. A few days later he was indignant when Paar asked the Sardinian government to suggest to the émigrés that they petition for authorization to return to Lombardy-Venetia. The cabinet would do nothing of the kind. The rescript was anything but well publicized, and Sardinians did not regard their citizenship as a transitory makeshift.[34] By this time Cavour was in Paris for the great congress which was to establish peace. He was quite busy, among other things, in composing a stern critique of the rescript of February 8.

His memorandum of March 8, transmitted to the maritime powers, admitted that Francis Joseph had never declined to grant to any émigré a recognition that he was an authorized émigré. He implied that he believed Buol's prediction that the emperor would approve most of the requests for the right to return or the right to remain abroad with free disposition of properties. His state, however, would continue to protest if Austria demanded declarations that were offensive to the status acquired by new Sardinian citizens. The cabinet would also deprecate a system of exceptions, which would entail the continuing sequestration of some properties and the forced sale of other properties. Buol chose to declare that the issue had been purged of both cause and substance (*Stoff und Boden*). If the Sardinian cabinet declined to apprise indirectly the émigrés of the content of the rescript, that was, of course, its business.[35]

After the famous session of April 8 at the Congress of Paris, Cavour was again in an excited state as he prepared to return home. He had deduced from a private talk with Clarendon on April 11 that, in time of embarrassment, Piedmont could count on England. To this day there is mystery over the interchange, for Clarendon denied in 1862 that he had given any hint of possible English assistance.[36] Through an exaggerated estimate of what had been accomplished on April 8 or simply as a result of misunderstanding Clarendon's French, Cavour felt he could again remind his allies of Austria's role as troublemaker in Italy. His note of April 16 asked if England and France realized what Austria had accomplished by blocking a discussion of remedies for Italy. The outraged inhabitants of the peninsula would revert to conspiracy and disorder that would explode at the slightest commotion on the continent. The revolutionary party was a threat to Europe as well as to monarchy in Piedmont. Austrian hegemony in Italy was the second great menace. To survive subversion and constant Habsburg enmity, his government might be forced at any time to extreme measures whose consequences would be incalculable. The maritime powers should consider well the state of affairs and concert with Sardinia the steps to be taken.

On May 6 he analyzed for the Chamber of Deputies what had happened in Paris. On balance, not a great deal had been achieved. Europe had witnessed a denunciation of Italy's anomalous and unhappy condition, however, and England and France had declared that some kind of remedy was necessary. Then, with monumental bravado, Cavour asserted that the negotiations had done nothing to improve relations with Austria. He and Buol had parted company courteously and with no personal animosity, but each knew that the principles of his state were irreconcilable with the other's. There would be difficulties and dangers, but Piedmontese policy would not change. The Italian cause had been brought before the court of public opinion. Piedmont would await the verdict with confidence.

Next morning he was surprised to read of an Anglo-French-Austrian treaty which upheld the integrity of the Ottoman Empire. Buol had exacted his price for Austria's decisive ultimatum to Russia. Vienna had no special regard for the Turkish state, but the thought of facing renewed Russian expansion in a decade was sobering. Cavour retreated a bit in a second speech to the deputies. He had not said that a breach with Austria was at hand. Rather, the Paris conferences had brought no rapprochement. Should there be complications, he could only promise that the government would follow a path that would lead most directly to the improvement of Italy.

The note of April 16 and the speeches of May 6 and 7 caused such a lively reaction in Vienna that some of Cantono's colleagues asked if he was expecting his passports. He assured Cavour that he did not anticipate such a precipitate move, but he was alarmed that the note seemed to justify a possible support of the revolutionary element by his own country.[37] In an audience with Hercule de Serre, the French chargé, Buol denounced the note as a tissue of calumnies, an impudent provocation, an undisguised appeal to the subversive passions of all Italy. He sincerely desired to keep the peace, however. He did not wish to pick up the glove thrown down by Cavour.[38] His circular of May 18 to the conservative courts of Italy accented restraint. Austria did not recognize Cavour's assumption of a mission to speak for Italy. Paar was to be calm, firm, and reserved in his language. If seven years of peace between the two monarchies had not afforded better relations, whose was the fault?[39]

En route to St. Petersburg to render his king's compliments to the tsar, General Dabormida paid a courtesy call on Buol. He argued that the note of April 16 in no way aimed at exciting revolutionary passions. The Austrian spoke courteously of Cavour and admitted that the Sardinian government's position and the exigencies it faced should be considered in any evaluation of its acts. Dabormida concluded that Buol still wanted to have good relations with Turin.[40] There were other signs of diminishing tension. In February the Sardinian cabinet had protested "constant violence" done their citizens by Austrian customs agents along the border. In early June, Buol promised severe punishment for these men, whose actions, on examination, clearly exceeded the agreement of 1851.[41] Several weeks later the two states finally signed a railway convention that ostensibly would link Lombardy with Piedmont. Within three years Austria would complete the thirty-five kilometers from Milan to the Ticino, while Piedmont would build a line from Novara to the frontier. Implied was the long-discussed junction at the bridge of Buffalora.[42]

In July 1856, however, Cavour announced that he wanted a million lire to strengthen the fortress of Alessandria as a counter to Austria's "permanent menace to Piedmont" at Piacenza.[43] Cantono reported that some in Vienna were worried over such plans, but he discounted the precautions the Austrian military had taken. In certain army circles there was fear that revolution might break out in Piedmont, but no resolution to attack that state.[44] Cavour did not bother to convey anything of importance to his legation in Vienna during the second half of 1856, probably because of predictions that Austria would lift the sequester. Bourqueney warned Tancredi de Fortis, Cantono's substitute, to be most reserved. France was sorely trying Austrian dignity by asking for acts of clemency at Naples and the end of sequestrations in Lombardy.[45] Clarendon was less patient with Austrian dignity. If Buol was complaining about Turin's hostility, he should realize it derived from the question of the sequester, which had been a galling humiliation. There was every indication that Austrian occupation of lands not its own in Italy would be permanent. This was "contrary to the letter and the spirit of the Treaty of Vienna and a constant menace and danger to Sardinia."[46]

The "galling humiliation" ended with Francis Joseph's decree of December 2, which revoked the sequestration of all properties owned by émigrés, pardoned seventy who had been cited for high treason, and empowered Radetzky to allow the repatriation of those who requested it. Buol was obviously happy when he acquainted Cantono with the provisions and joked with the French and English ministers. To the former, he said, "Only good things are done on December 2," a pleasant allusion to Napoleon III's coup d'état, if not to the battle of Austerlitz. In speaking of Naples to Sir George Hamilton Seymour, he noted, "You see that we preach by example."[47]

Three years of bickering, the last of which had been marked by numerous voluntary repatriations to Lombardy and Venetia, had institutionalized mutual suspicion and rancor in the two capitals. In January 1857 the *Wiener Zeitung* reprinted an article from *L'Unione* which celebrated the assassinations of the king of the Moabites and of Holofernes. The first victim was compared to Francis Joseph, the second to Radetzky.[48] The imperial couple were in the midst of their progress through the kingdom, and Cavour was nervous enough to ask Cantono by coded telegram to ascertain most discreetly the details of Austrian troop dispositions in Italy.[49] Victor Emmanuel II had refrained from sending an emissary to Milan to bear his respects and greetings to Francis Joseph and Elizabeth. Indeed, he ostentatiously courted visiting Russian royalty on a visit to Nice, and there is no doubt he enraged his cousin. The day the emperor reached Milan, the authorities expelled Senator Giacomo Plezza, a much esteemed figure in Piedmontese parliamentary life. That very day, Cavour claimed, Turin was deciding what person would carry the king's compliments to the emperor. Nonetheless, Sardinia appreciated the end of the sequester. If Buol should make overtures for full resumption of diplomatic relations, directly or through the British and French ministers, Cantono should accept them. He was not to take the initiative, for Sardinia was the offended party in the diplomatic niceties that brought Revel home but sent Apponyi to a new post.[50]

On February 12 Paar quickly disabused Cavour of any worry that the emperor might wish normal relations. During the imperial visit to the kingdom, the Piedmontese press had poured abuse on the monarch and all of the acts of the Austrian administration there, declared Buol in a stiff note. What, too, of the open soliciting of foreigners to contribute to the Piedmontese defense system? What of the acceptance of a monument, reportedly from the emperor's subjects, which would commemorate the Sardinian army's feats? Did the cabinet really expect Austria to complain daily of the revolutionary press in Sardinia? The emperor owed it to his dignity not to leave the Piedmontese government unaware of his resentment of all of these actions.[51]

Cavour's dispatch to Buol was sharp. He regretted and condemned attacks on the emperor, but law did provide a remedy. The Austrian press, especially in Lombardy, was not innocent of attacks on the king of Sardinia and members of his family. Buol accused the Sardinian cabinet of indifference to polemics in its press. The same could not be said for Austria. "The articles which the official journals contain, which the imperial government inspires, prove that the cabinet of Vienna sanctions and directs the attacks of which we are the object." As for accusations that Sardinia provoked demonstrations, its delegates admittedly had called to the attention of the Congress of Paris the question of the condition of Italy. Austria had no reason to complain. Its recent acts proved that Piedmontese assertions were not without foundation. In answer to the complaint about the monument to be erected in Turin, the Sardinian government had nothing whatsoever to do with the project. It could not prevent the municipal council of Turin from accepting the offer, but it did see to it that the inscriptions gave no hint that the donors were Austrian subjects. He might list Sardinian complaints, but he could see no sense in further poisoning a discussion that could advantage neither state.[52]

Cavour continued to order Cantono to show a conciliatory spirit without leading the Austrians to think there would be some concessions. The western envoys were reporting by March 10 to their capitals that rupture was inevitable. Buol simply assured Seymour that the breach would be handled with the greatest possible discretion.[53] On March 12 the imperial couple returned to Vienna and to a tearful Archduchess Sophie, who had been most uneasy about her son's safety among Italians. After a day or so of meditation, Francis Joseph decided to recall Paar, and Buol had his final conference with Cantono. It is unlikely that there was regret in either capital, for audiences, *démarches*, and explanations all had failed to compose the basic differences which existed.

Constant recriminations over abusive newspaper articles and Cavour's aggressive behavior at the Congress of Paris accounted for the final rupture. Piedmontese behavior during the rising in Milan in 1853 had been impeccable, and Francis Joseph and his ministers had finally decided that sequestration of émigré property neither ended Lombard intrigues in Turin nor facilitated efforts to reconcile the kingdom's inhabitants to Habsburg suzerainty. It was obvious that Cavour and Victor Emmanuel were disappointed over their profitless engagement against the tsar, yet not without hope that their allies might persuade Austria to disgorge some Italian land. The king's failure to send his compliments to the imperial couple while they were in Milan was particularly offensive to a dynast who never permitted lapses in etiquette and who bridled at the suggestion that his officials should not banish any person they pleased from one of his cities. When an exchange of notes did nothing to compose bad relations, there was no sense in keeping inconsequential attachés in either capital. On this point, at least, Austria and Piedmont were agreed.

The Policy of Conciliation in Lombardy-Venetia, 1856–1859

FRENCH dispatches from Milan in 1855 depicted a land sunken in apathy. The citizens judged the decree which ordered the convocation of the central congregations to be a ruse to fool foreign powers. They were equally unimpressed with the concordat, which gave the clergy prerogatives they had not even requested. To St.-Amand, the Second Empire's commercial agent, disorder and injustice reigned supreme in all branches of the administration, while the military were provocative and violent in their relations with the people.

The new year brought relaxations. The authorities cut the garrison in Milan by a third and abolished several of the guard posts. Friedrich Burger, the governor, seem to capture popular approval by standing up to the archbishop when that worthy insisted on shutting down all places of amusement after services in honor of Saint Ambrose. With the ratification of the peace, however, sadness and an extraordinary indifference to events returned.[1] Francis Joseph nevertheless advised Maximilian, en route to Berlin, not to be impressed with Prussian trumpetings of Austrian difficulties in Italy. "We are calm about Italy, and the Piedmontese government, even in Italy, has helped rather than hurt us with its foolish twaddle."[2]

It is not clear who persuaded the emperor to embark upon an elaborate progress through his Italian possessions in the autumn of 1856, though Buol, Bruck, and Bach must have believed that such a pageant would impress the rural masses and possibly diminish aristocratic hostility. On November 2 an imperial ordinance reminded the populace that the central congregations might respectfully present the needs, desires, and requests of the nation in all the realms of public administration. The monarch reserved for himself the right to choose the opportune moment to ask for advice.[3]

In Trieste on November 20 the imperial couple received the usual obeisance from the muncipal officials and then plunged into the inevitable reviews and inspections of schools, hospitals, railway station, and the Lloyd's facilities. The Venetians who gathered to watch the arrival of the imperial flotilla on November 25 manifested the indifference of previous years, but the empress was attended by ladies who bore such illustrious names as Grimani and Nani Mocenigo at a dinner for fifty-two of the aristocracy.

On December 2, Francis Joseph amnestied seventy political offenders and lifted the sequester of February 13, 1853. Buol was to instruct the imperial diplomatic missions to answer questions and rectify erroneous assumptions but not to offer official notifications to foreign governments. The end of the sequester was an act of grace, wrote the emperor, not a satisfaction of Piedmont.[4] There was a sincere ovation for the rulers at La Fenice on December 3, and Francis Joseph seemed almost to court popular approval by pardoning, the day after a regatta in the Grand Canal, a gondolier who had been accused of lese majesty and disturbance of the peace. Between fireworks and the theater he wrestled with the "Radetzky problem," for he had been uneasy over the governor-general's capacities since the rising in Milan in 1853. A vigorous twenty-six, aching to escape the ambiguities of the Venetians for a good duck hunt with compatible royalty, he faced up to the old warrior's senility and encompassed his resignation. Radetzky would have the privilege of residing in his accustomed manner in Monza or Vienna.

To end the "mess" in Verona, the ruler split the kingdom's civil administration from the army command. Maximilian, despite his fears that he could not function properly without military powers, finally agreed to serve as governor-general. The older brother hinted there would be need to meet complaints over burdensome taxes and the manner in which they were collected when harvests were bad. Most of the blame for the kingdom's unsatisfactory state he placed upon "a large part of the upper classes," who were unbelievably fearful of the revolutionary party and of the Piedmontese press.[5]

In the first weeks of the new year the sovereigns visited the chief cities of Venetia and Lombardy. In Bergamo the police erased from a wall, "The emperor arrives at 1500 — we will get him at 1600," but the French agent in Milan reported that the crowd of 100,000 who witnessed the formal entry into that capital was seemly (*convenable*) in attitude. After a Te Deum at the Duomo there was a reception at the palace and an evening at La Scala. St.-Amand found the monarch cold and composed, the empress gracious in her responses. An evening or so later Francis Joseph and Elizabeth promenaded along the brightly lighted Corso in an open calèche with no aide-de-camp or guard near the carriage. A crowd of peasants and townsmen, poor and well-off, was so dense that some were pressed against the footboards.

On January 25 the *Gazzetta Ufficiale di Milano* proclaimed an amnesty for all political offenders imprisoned in the kingdom, the suspension of all trials in progress, and the end of the special court in Mantua. The city celebrated with almost total (and voluntary) illumination, vivats and applause in front of the palace, and singing in the streets. While relations with Piedmont worsened, since Victor Emmanuel had sent no envoy with his compliments, Francis Joseph multiplied his benefactions: subventions to beautify the Giardino Pubblico, for the productions of the imperial theaters, and for the restoration of Sant'Ambrogio and the refectory where Leonardo had painted his *Last Supper*.[6]

In a letter of February 28, 1857, the emperor apprised Maximilian of his new duties. He was to strengthen dynastic loyalty among the people, to persuade the nobility to look to their (true) interests, and to develop in all classes an awareness of the advantages of a decent and impartial administration. He was to maintain the closest possible liaison with the commander of the Second Army. Should there be a serious conflict between the civil and military spheres, Francis Joseph would resolve the matter.[7] On March 10 the imperial couple returned to Vienna.

The archduke's entry into Venice promised little for the future. A flagpole in front of St. Mark's flew the Italian tricolor, despite gas illumination and sentries. Since the halyard had been removed, a sailor had to climb the pole to cut down the offending colors. Francis Joseph was irked by the event and by the coldness of the Venetian reception for his brother. He asked, however, if there had been gross irregularities in the process of conscription. There should be punishment of illegal demonstrations and childish tricks, but never with the slightest touch of arbitrariness.[8]

The emperor surmised that Venetian standoffishness had its origin in jealousy of Milan. If so, the Lombard capital gave no sign that it recognized any special standing under Austrian rule when Maximilian made his entry on April 19. Those close to his carriage uncovered sullenly, the rest kept their hats on. Not a cry from the crowd, not a handkerchief waved from a window, reported the rather scandalized French agent. The Milanese had been more cordial to Francis Joseph, perhaps out of fear. The new governor-general moved quickly to enlist some support. A few members of the nobility responded, particularly Count Giuseppe Archinto, Duke Lodovico Melzi, Marquis Luigi D'Adda, and Duke Antonio Litta. In receptions and attendance at religious rites, Maximilian moved elegantly and judiciously. When he learned that his appearance at the French theater caused a great rush to the exits, he decided to come no more.[9] In an early speech (he knew Italian as well as he knew German), he adverted to the Italian blood in his veins and spoke of taking up the cause of a nationality which his great-grandfather, Leopold II, had so much loved.[10]

Maximilian had little room to maneuver in espousing the cause of his charges. There is no reason to challenge Carlo Pagani's conclusion that he was the executive (*organum expositum*) of the ministries in Vienna. The Archducal Chancery was the organ of transmission of reports between the *Luogotenenze* and the central authorities. The governor-general could append his comments, but to break the chain of command he had to appeal directly or indirectly to his brother. Many institutions were in no way accountable to him: the prefecture of finance, the general direction of the post, the provincial delegations, the chambers of commerce and industry.[11] When Tobias Wildauer composed his retrospective account of the archduke's tenure in the kingdom, he noted Maximilian's desire to have Lombardy-Venetia seize from Piedmont the initiative and leadership in Italy. He wanted a great congress of princes at Monza. In the respites from hunting, theater, and balls, which would tempt Milanese society, there would be serious progress toward a customs union, telegraph system, and railway net. The emperor agreed, but Buol angrily and successfully intervened, ostensibly because it was impossible for so many princely persons to come to any agreement.[12] Again, the governor-general appealed to Archduke Wilhelm to postpone the draft in Lombardy in the autumn of 1857. He feared that the increased quota would hit hardest those who were decent in opinion and loyal to the dynasty. A second levy within twelve months would seem to be a special punishment in the very year of the emperor's lengthy visit. Almost 6,000 families would be upset. Wilhelm refused, declaring that the emperor found such a revision of the quota unsuitable.[13] In September 1857 Maximilian brought his bride, the Belgian Charlotte, to Milan. The population was cordial and seemed to like her gracious physiognomy and affable manner. The presence of a consort increased court expenditures, to the satisfaction of those in Milan who catered to such demands. The couple commissioned paintings for Miramare, their palace in Trieste, and ordered statues and restorative work for churches and public places. Demolitions created a new square before La Scala, and there were grandiose designs to enhance the Duomo's façade by enlarging the piazza before that great cathedral. Drainage of the Piano di Spagna, which the Spanish had turned into a marsh by building their fortress of Fuentes, was undertaken. To help the distressed silk industry, he urged Vienna to approve a discount bank for Lombardy, as proposed by businessmen and chambers of commerce, and an emergency fund to offer subventions to the stricken producers. While holding a regatta in October, he heard of the flooding of the Po and the Ticino and left in the night for the scene of disaster. To his sympathetic physical involvement he added donations from his own pocket. From May 4, 1857, to the end of 1858, he obtained pardons for several hundred of the politically compromised not covered by the amnesty. Of these, twenty-nine were destitute and he sometimes secured money grants from Francis Joseph to keep them alive.[14]

Dieudé Defly, the new French agent in the autumn of 1857, reported that an increased tax on newspapers and books caused resentment, though the business class, like the workers, feared that Maximilian would desert Milan for Venice. They did not wish to lose the court's patronage or the tourists attracted by the newsworthy couple. A majority of the aristocratic families boycotted official events whenever possible, and even the governor-general joked about the "pilgrimage to Nice" which many made to pay homage to the dowager tsarina. The workers doffed their hats when the archducal pair passed by, but strollers of other classes ignored the carriage. On Christmas Eve there was a party for 150 children of the poor: candles and shiny toys on great fir trees, a ducat and a prayer book for each guest, plus material for a dress or a suit, and a pretty basket of fruits and sweets. The workers were pleased by the gesture, but there was little hope of rallying most of the old families to the Habsburg eagles.[15]

From Venice, Charles-Edouard Herbet, the French consul general, reported favorably on Alessandro Marcello, the new podestà, who would be one of Maximilian's most loyal collaborators and who was struggling to bring some order to the city's tangled finances. He had uncovered corruption in the lower levels of the administration, but this was not the reason that "the rope was at the breaking point." The land was quiet, resigned. There was no need of an army big enough to cow an actively hostile area. Bad harvests and a draconic system of tax collection had reduced the landed families to despair. At Christmas time a cutback in naval construction meant the dismissal of several hundred workers from the Arsenal, and this coincided with a somewhat higher quota of recruits. The general picture was depressing.[16]

Cavour thought otherwise. Irritated by conservative successes in the recent general elections in Piedmont and frightened by French pressure to "discipline" his press after Felice Orsini's attempt on Napoleon III's life on January 14, 1858, he sent a message to the habitués of the Maffei salon. "It is urgent that you bring about the reimposition of the state of siege in Milan."[17] Orsini's letter to the French emperor circulated throughout Lombardy, as did Jules Favre's defense speech, right down to the haunts of the agricultural laborers. Maximilian admitted to his brother that there had been much public discussion of the letter, but he urged against premature steps that would indicate concern that the revolutionary movement could not be foiled.[18] The emperor was concerned, for he asked for a telegraphic report in cipher of the extent of the disaffection and of preparations to meet possible demonstrations.[19]

On March 16 several hundred students at the University of Padua went to Sant'Antonio for mass and circulated pamphlets calling for prayers for Orsini's soul. At the end of the regular service a few began a De profundis and were joined by the others. On March 22, the tenth anniversary of the Venetian revolution, members of Countess Giustiniani's salon decided to promenade in the square before St. Mark's. Quite a number of the elegant did assemble, and the archduke dispatched a military band to the scene. Second, he and Charlotte appeared to promenade in the square, and the demonstrators immediately departed. Common folk subsequently filled up the nearly empty area, and their friendliness encouraged the pair to stroll along the Riva degli Schiavoni as well. It should be noted that Maximilian had summoned a squadron of warships as early as March 11 "to inspect the harbor," and few Venetians failed to discern the muzzles of the cannon pointed at the city.

In Milan no one had heeded calls for an assemblage to memorialize Orsini, and there was no trouble from a fashionable audience that nearly filled La Scala to hear as sensitive a piece as *Guglielmo Tell* the night after Orsini's execution. Some of the university students in Pavia wore mourning, however, and 300 of them jammed the church of Il Gesù on March 20 for a commemorative mass. The leaders, as in Padua, were picked up by the police.[20] Francis Joseph, worried over Napoleon III's oscillation between conservatism and a search for popularity, warned Maximilian to crack down on even a partial rebellion in such nervous times. He found fault with the authorities, for how could 300 students get together without their knowledge?[21]

In late April, Maximilian and Charlotte went to Vienna for a lengthy stay. After a year's experience, he was convinced that he could never, without substantial reforms, attract a sufficient number of persons of rank to serve in his administration. To his brother he suggested a reformation of the kingdom's "representative system" that would persuade more nobles to participate in public life. Cavour had brought up "the Italian question," and Austria had to win over English and German opinion by establishing liberal institutions which would pave the way for similar reforms in the rest of the peninsula. If Austria failed to initiate such changes, only the sword could cut the knot.

Francis Joseph complimented his brother on what had been accomplished, and the two seemed to agree in their estimates of the situation in Italy.[22] The ministers were outraged, however, by a proposal which would give Lombardy and Venetia greater autonomy than that enjoyed by other elements of the empire, and their climactic encounter with Maximilian was a Ministerrat of July 12, presided over by the emperor. Arguing that stopgaps (*Kunststücke*) could no longer guarantee calm, the governor-general begged for a system of representation that would create an Austrian party. Otherwise, one might as well dismiss the central congregations, which enjoyed neither the confidence nor the esteem of the people or the officials. The kingdom awaited the fulfillment of promises made. Negotiations should get under way quickly. Bach retorted that it would be dangerous to open up the prospect of a parliamentary regime in lands whose provincial and central congregations already had extensive powers. Given the situation in the rest of the crown lands, could more be promised? Buol argued that such territories had greater right to consideration. Toggenburg worried that talk of reform would invite agitation in other parts of the empire, and Count Karl Grünne, Francis Joseph's chief military adviser, pointed to the petitions already received from the Magyar nobility. Maximilian observed that he could not hide the conditions in other crown lands that gave rise to concern. The defects of the existing system were undeniable. It was not dangerous to declare that it should be replaced by something better.[23] Two months later the archduke wrote his brother of four comments which had especially outraged him. Toggenburg had declared that a government party in Lombardy-Venetia was an impossibility. Buol had claimed that it was only Piedmont that kept Austria from managing well in the kingdom. Bach expressed the feeling that the lands had enough with their central congregations. Bruck had raised the possibility that past promises could not be kept.[24]

On July 16, however, Francis Joseph had acceded to some of Maximilian's suggestions. He appointed a commission to study the allegations that the property tax, in comparison with German-Slavic lands, was disproportionately high for Lombardy-Venetia. Second, all localities which enjoyed special fiscal privileges would no longer be able to claim them. Third, there would be reorganization of the academies of art in Milan and Venice. Fourth, Maximilian was to prepare an ordinance which would better the wages and status of district physicians. Fifth, the authorities were to cease their attempts to make up for the "draft deficits" in the kingdom. More, all married men and only sons were to be discharged from the forces. Maximilian would have the right to excuse from conscription all students at the two universities who distinguished themselves through talent, industry, knowledge, and deportment. A timely reform of the kingdom's representation was in principle conformable to the interests of both throne and land, but there never could be a government of the Italian provinces independent of the organs in Vienna or one in communication with them solely through a ministry of Italian affairs. The force of Austrian influence in Italy depended upon the solidity of the entire monarchy, not upon the intrinsic importance of the Italian lands and their development.[25]

Though discouraged, Maximilian returned to his assignment. In a circular of July 28, 1858, he told his officials that he hated and would punish illegality and arbitrariness, just as he would not tolerate weakness.[26] At Monza he conferred with advisers on the program for a commission on education. A note from Vienna ordered the discontinuance of such projects, and he decided to resign. He was furious that a minister of the crown (Thun) had implied that he wanted to turn Lombardy-Venetia into his own secundogeniture (that is, his own kingdom, which would revert to the elder branch of the family should he have no heirs). A trusted emissary was to assure his brother that he had avoided what would have increased his own popularity. Rather, he had tried to develop among the people affection for the supreme ruler.[27] The death of Archduchess Margarethe permitted the brothers a rendezvous in Bruck. The younger maintained that his position was hopelessly compromised. He did not wish to appear as a man who could not fulfill his promises. Francis Joseph refused to permit a resignation which might affect international affairs, but he allowed his unhappy viceroy to go on leave, with Charlotte and a small entourage, to Corfu and Sicily.[28]

On November 1, a day dreaded by Milanese businessmen, the currency reform that had been announced in April went into effect. A new silver florin was the basic coin, to replace the silver *svanzica* (the Italian version of *Zwanziger*) which had circulated for several decades. The svanziche were to be exchanged for the new florins at a 3 percent loss. Worse, the government refused to redeem svanziche of various German states, which had been supplements in the kingdom to the Austrian mintage. As a result, the railways, the banks, and commercial enterprises rejected such pieces. Had Vienna sent in a plentiful supply of florins, half-florins, and quarter-florins, a bit of the anger might have dissipated. In a matter of days, speculators were buying up the old svanziche and shipping them to

France for the purchase of gold napoleons. The virtual nonappearance of the new and the rapid disappearance of the old stripped the land of the wherewithal to make change. If the lower classes and the peasantry had ever acquiesced in Habsburg rule, that tepid allegiance now was threatened.[29]

These strata of society already were lamenting a modification of the conscription law, announced in early October. Instead of five classes, there would be seven, from which the authorities could draw men between the ages of twenty and twenty-seven. No male could marry before the age of twenty-three, since a husband ordinarily was excused. An only son could expect exemption only if his father was aged seventy. This was a distinct modification of previous practice. The well-to-do could secure substitutes for their sons, but this did not diminish the total assessed each commune. A third blow followed, an increase in the prices of tobacco and salt.

Maximilian had decided to leave Charlotte at Miramare, returning to Venice on November 9. He had written his brother that the latest ministerial decrees had destroyed his patient labors of the past two years, and from Mantua he used cipher to declare that he saw no way to restore confidence in the government.[30] On November 25, once again in Milan, he inscribed a despairing letter to his mother. There was but one voice in the land, the voice of indignation and disapproval. "We live now in a complete chaos and occasionally I myself begin to ask if conscience permits blind obedience to Vienna's orders; for loyalty's sake Radetzky was disobedient and we rightly and gratefully erect monuments to him, and therein lies a truth that goes very well with religion."[31]

In Milan, Maximilian walked along the Corso, ignored. He bombarded Francis Joseph with pleas for a more moderate policy. The patents on coinage and conscription were provoking meetings and pronouncements reminiscent of 1847–48. Already there was chaos within the bureaucracy and a very bad reaction among the peasantry. Maximilian begged for a larger role in any military action, should there be trouble. This would be one way to calm the more aggressive generals.[32] On December 16 some 200 students of the University of Pavia, wearing mourning, marched to Gravellone on the Piedmontese frontier, and some put clay pipes in their mouths to show their disdain for the state monopoly cigars.[33] The same day an assassin successfully attacked a professor, Emilio Briccio, who had ridiculed the students' nationalism. In Milan men who smoked in the streets were inviting a spray of acid, and on December 18 the government announced cuts in the number of men to be conscripted. In Lombardy the armed forces would take 6,844, which was 1,513 less than for 1858. In Venetia, the quota was 5,570, a decrease of 1,412. No one doubted that Maximilian deserved the credit for the modification, but the large and fashionable audience at the opening of La Scala showed its contempt by hissing the performance, which etiquette forbade in the presence of the court. Again the couple entertained poor children on Christmas Eve. The opposition commented that it was very easy to be generous with the people's money.[34]

The governor-general was not always on the side of leniency. A prince who failed to doff his hat to Charlotte was advised to "change air" within twenty-four hours and complied by moving to Genoa. Before Christmas a nest of "disloyal" railway employees was discovered at the central station in Verona. The emperor quickly seconded Maximilian's recommendation to get rid of them and moved to check on their superiors as well.[35] The day after Christmas he penned an unusually long note, denying the governor-general the supreme command of the troops in case of rebellion. The reasoning was simple. Sometime there probably would be a war. Its course would assuredly undermine his position as governor-general and as archduke should he be in charge of military operations. Far more reassuring would be his command of the fleet in case of hostilities. Maximilian should come to a full understanding with Gyulai to prepare for ugly eventualities. He should zealously carry out imperial decisions, whether he agreed with them or not. There should be no more ventilation in the foreign press of Maximilian's proposals when they were scarcely known in Vienna. That meant Francis Joseph earned all of the odium if he rejected them. Maximilian was to press for the suppression of the University of Pavia, to urge Beretta, the president of the court of appeal in Milan, to work for properly stern verdicts, and to carry out drainage and irrigation projects to show that increased tension could not bring such improvements to a standstill. "This is the most difficult time I have experienced and in this period I am counting, with the firmest confidence, on your loyal support."[36]

Maximilian also was enduring a most difficult time, for he wrote

Leopold I of the Belgians that it was terrible not to know how every day would end. His own wearisome work had been completely destroyed. He was never sure his actions would be approved by his own irresolute government. He had to live with the fear that his consort would be insulted, that both of them would be hissed at the theater, that neither might get home alive from a promenade.[37] Napoleon III's famous comment to Hübner on New Year's Day that he regretted relations were not as satisfactory as formerly and Victor Emmanuel's promise on January 10 that his country could not be insensible to "the cry of pain which rises toward us from so many parts of Italy" enhanced the anticipations of the nationalists in the kingdom. The famous "Guerra, guerra!" chorus in Bellini's *Norma* was tailor-made for excitable times, and in Milan on January 29 the spectators applauded the stanzas vociferously and shouted the word for "war" repeatedly in Gyulai's presence. Infuriated, the general unsheathed his saber and banged it on the flooring of his box. Austrian officers who were present followed his gesture and also shouted for war. In minutes the uniformed had quit the theater, but a similar outburst the following evening ended with a suspension of the performance.[38] The death of a young Count Emilio Dandolo, who had been one of the defenders of Rome in 1849, gave rise to a clash between the *italianissimi* and the police. Burger panicked when he heard that 12,000 would follow the bier but finally issued a permit when warned he would otherwise provoke serious trouble. Someone placed a tricolored crown upon the coffin as the procession left the church, but the police did not intervene. At the grave there were daring tributes, and the day after the funeral, police and cavalry had to come to the aid of persons who were manhandled when they came to La Scala for a masked ball. On March 2 the government countermanded another ball at the opera house. Defly noted that the city's tranquillity was at the mercy of incidents.[39] The governor-general had been in Venice during the obsequies, but he blamed the scandal on the ineptness of Milan's officials.[40]

Carnival was a sad affair in the two chief cities. In Venice only thirteen ladies deigned to appear at a court ball on February 22, and persons on their way to masked balls ran the risk of insults and worse. The police in Milan forbade masks and confetti on the streets. Young men along the Corso forced pedestrians to accept tricolors, which the accosted dared not throw away or keep. Other young men, anticipating the call-up of reserves or a special levy, were fleeing to Piedmont.[41] Early in April, Croat battalions moved into Venice and Milan. Francis Joseph informed his brother that Austria would force Sardinia to disarm if the great powers failed to persuade that state to do so. "Be ready to send your wife from Italy at short notice. All of this is for your eyes alone."[42] On April 16 Charlotte departed for Trieste, ostensibly for Holy Week. Her husband retired to Monza, to confer with the last of his trusted advisers on a program of administrative decentralization that would impress the powers, especially England.[43] On April 20 he was relieved of his responsibilities as governor-general. Two days later he departed Milan to inspect the fleet in Venice. The experiment in Lombardy-Venetia, which never had a chance with the emperor's highest advisers, was at an end.

There were two epitaphs of note. On June 12, James Howard Harris, third earl of Malmesbury, wrote his ambassador in Vienna that his government was pleased to affirm that Maximilian's administration had "been conducted with great talent and in the spirit of most honored liberalism."[44] Years later, when Victor Emmanuel II visited Vienna, Emilio Visconti-Venosta confided to an Austrian official, "One time only was our conspiracy in difficulties and gave us something to think about . . . that was when you sent Archduke Maximilian to us."[45]

Maximilian's chances to reconcile the Lombards and Venetians to Habsburg rule always were slight. In 1849 many within the dominant noble and bourgeois strata in Lombardy were disgusted with Piedmont's military awkwardness and by what seemed to be Charles Albert's preoccupation with his dynasty's advancement under cover of "fusion." The Venetians remembered no effective aid from the flotilla under Sardinian command, and the peasants of both lands had no reason to believe that a change in governors would solve their problems. Between 1849 and 1856, however, Austrian execution and incarceration of Italian patriots revived sentiment for Victor Emmanuel in the kingdom. Cavour's economic policies, when contrasted with recession in Venetia and Austrian dilatoriness in Lombardy, added to the dissatisfaction of the enterprising and the propertied. The amnesty of 1857, with the accompanying dismissal of political prosecutions, was an acknowledgment of poor insight, but these acts of grace did not obliterate remembrances of earlier rigors.

It is virtually useless to speculate on what might have happened if Maximilian had induced the emperor and his ministers to widen the competence of the central congregations, for the Austrian empire of the 1850's was committed to absolutism tempered by bureaucratic efficiency and legal propriety. How could the imperial advisers allow the Italians what was denied the Germans, the Croats, and the other nationalities? After the Ministerrat of July 12, 1858, the archduke's opportunities were foreclosed. It was not enough to promise a commission that would see if the Italian lands were discriminated against in taxation. It was impolitic to promise relief in the matter of conscription, then increase the quotas, and ultimately to decree a smaller levy. Worst of all, the currency reform threatened to tie the kingdom to the fluctuating paper of the rest of the empire. Few notables had rallied to Maximilian's call, and their enthusiasm, if it ever was that, diminished in the face of negatives from Vienna and veiled threats from the Turinese press. Cavour and the nationalists worried over the governor-general's intelligence and charm, but they had overestimated his influence with Francis Joseph. The dominant philosophy in Vienna precluded meaningful alteration of the status quo.

Austria and the Conservative Italian States, 1856–1859

THE policy of conciliation in Lombardy-Venetia after 1856 exacted circumspection from Austria's diplomatic representatives at the conservative courts. Acts of amnesty and rumors that the kingdom's congregations would enjoy a larger role in administration worried all of the rulers save, possibly, the duchess of Parma. Her show of independence and courting of public favor revealed her disquietude over Austria's future in the peninsula and imperiled Bruck's renewed pressure for a customs union that would counterbalance Piedmont's economic gains.

It was decided in Vienna that the duke of Modena could best reanimate the concept of economic unification. The note to Forni of March 12, 1857, stressed the advantages of linking two great networks, the Italian (obviously without Sardinia) and the Austro-German-Italian. Francis V was amenable and wrote for Leopold II's reaction. The Tuscan was elusive, avoiding a direct refusal and counseling further study. Since the duchess of Parma had shown no sign of moderating her distaste for a customs league, Francis V decided to proceed with direct negotiations in Vienna.[1]

Buol had visited the duchies in February 1857, and his instructions to Paar, the new Austrian minister-resident, might well have been written by a competent journalist of the period. If Parma was not to be led to the abyss, Paar would have to stress to Louise Marie and her government the necessity of sticking with Austria. A tariff union would be an excellent guarantee of conservative polity, but the Parmese ministers were changeable and offered but weak assurances. The terrain in Modena was infinitely more solid, though the duke's state of health raised the question of the succession. If there were difficulties at his court, it was not a matter of ill will but rather heaviness of spirit.[2]

The Austrians and the Modenese realized from the beginning of their negotiations that they could not settle for a simple commercial treaty. Such an instrument automatically would entitle Piedmont and the Zollverein to demand, thanks to previous most-favored-nation agreements, every concession the two signatories made to each other. A genuine customs union would render inoperative claims made by Turin or the Germans. After tense negotiations the conferees added secret articles to the treaty signed on October 15, 1857. Modena would work for a customs union with Tuscany, Parma, and the Papacy. Should Piedmont and the Zollverein try to exact from Modena those reductions which Austria had secured, Vienna would fight such moves. In due time the Zollverein and Cavour questioned the nature of the Austro-Modenese pact and demanded rates equal to those granted the duchy by Vienna. Buol had no stomach for a fight. France and Russia might be behind Piedmont. The other conservative courts had manifested no inclination for economic unity. After conferring with Vienna, Forni notified Turin on January 19, 1859, that, for motives independent of and anterior to Cavour's request, Austria and Modena would confer on a nullification of their pact.

Paar had asked Forni in December 1858 to authorize Bayard De Volo, the Modenese representative in Vienna, to undertake a secret mission to the conservative courts. He was to attempt to get general simplification of customs and police formalities as the Central Italian Railway moved toward completion. Forni refused to comply. No Italian government wished to give the French a pretext for action. Vienna should propose a league directly or advise the railway concessionaires to inaugurate discussions with the various states. Perturbed by Napoleon III's remarks to Hübner on New Year's, Buol found no reason to dispute Forni's comments. It was better not to stir up new alarms and rumors with talk of a union that would not succeed.[3]

Florence was the least important of Italian listening posts for Vienna in the period of the Crimean War and afterward. The grand duke's evasion of any commitment to a customs union was expected. When Hügel suggested that Tuscany concert with Rome and Naples a denunciation of Cavour's activism of 1856, Baldasseroni replied that his land was too weak to act alone but assuredly would follow what the papacy and the Two Sicilies did.[4] When word came of the birth of an heir to Francis Joseph and Elizabeth, Leopold was quite dilatory in commanding a Te Deum. Eventually Hügel could report a public celebration that entailed a brilliant cortege from the Pitti Palace to the Duomo and the thunder of gunfire. As Lenzoni, now minister of foreign affairs, put it, "One must above all be lavish with demonstrations when one does not wish to grant something else."[5]

The Tuscans had dispensed with an Austrian auxiliary force in relatively short order and managed their relationship with Vienna with finesse. In Rome, after Cavour's blasts at papal administration, Antonelli maneuvered to reduce the onerousness of the Austrian occupation without encouraging subversion or giving color to the rumor that he was pro-French. Colloredo quickly learned that the pope's subjects especially hated the Austrian soldiers for their clumsy and brutal acts. "It is not so much Austria that they hate as it is Austrians."[6]

In October 1856 Austria agreed to a relaxation of the regulations concerning the state of siege in the Legations. Papal police would control theaters, public spectacles, nonpolitical assemblages, cafés, and inns, enforce censorship, and issue passports. Austrian military justice would have competence over matters of high treason, secret associations, subversion, murders and woundings of a partisan nature, armed resistance, offenses against imperial or papal soldiers when on duty, attempts to tamper with soldiers' loyalty, armed robbery, possession of arms, public demonstrations, and refusals to obey officers or patrols. Powder for hunting and self-protection would be available in small quantities and under controls.[7] By the end of the month the Austrians garrisoned only Bologna and Ancona. Colloredo reported an "excellent reaction" to the changes, though he was dubious of the state of the papal army. His sources emphasized bad uniforms, poor pay, and rare reenlistments.[8]

In 1857 Antonelli worried over the high cost of the Austrian occupation while Colloredo dreaded the promises the pope might be inveigled into making as he traveled through his domains in the spring and summer. A mixed commission of Austrian officers and papal representatives bargained fruitlessly over lodgings, hospital costs, troop movements, and transportation allowances. In near despair the cardinal besought Antonino De Luca, who had been appointed nuncio on June 16, 1856, to take advantage of Francis Joseph's return from Italy in March 1857. Were three generals needed for such a restricted number of troops? Would not the emperor grant the terms of the convention of 1837 and thereby alleviate the papacy's financial distress?[9]

Pius IX's journey through part of the Legations was without benefit of French or Austrian troops, though both were offered. Antonelli stayed in Rome, to inspire the following pasquinade:

Poor flock, now that the shepherd is gone!

Relax, the dog's still here.

Colloredo surmised that the pope wanted the trip because he loved ovations. He wanted to combat the European press's opinion that he was unpopular and his government not respected.[10] When some Bolognese begged him to include their city on his itinerary, he had Antonelli ask the Austrians to lift the state of siege. Since there was ready compliance, the cardinal asked the same concession for Ancona. On June 9 De Luca notified Rome that the suspension was not provisional, but definitive.[11] Francis Joseph was as uneasy as Colloredo over what Pius IX might do if confronted with petitions, and he opted to end the restrictions. He warned the pontiff to consider most seriously the dangers of granting a general amnesty. It was better to supervise the administration more carefully, rather than venture upon radical reform.[12]

Pius IX's indirect comment was a letter from Bologna to Francis Joseph, asking for a decrease in the "fine and disciplined" troops and a return to the subsidy convention of 1837. The fewer the barracks, the greater the gratitude of the citizens. The fewer the soldiers, the greater the relief to the treasury. The emperor replied that he could not revert to the earlier agreement. He had ordered a reduction of troops and of the papal subvention.[13] In Rome, Antonelli assured Colloredo there would be no general amnesty. When conditions permitted, the church would like to see the French abandon Rome for Civitavecchia, while the Austrians would depart from Bologna to concentrate at Ancona. When stories drifted to Rome of a chilly reception given Pius IX in Bologna, Colloredo predicted there could be no political reforms. The pontifical government should try to remedy administrative vices, however, to show friendly powers that the curia was sincere in its intentions to heed Austrian and French advice.[14]

In July the French presented to the nuncio in Vienna a project of reform, which De Luca transmitted to Antonelli.[15] Buol wrote

Hübner that he was surprised and concerned, since the recommendations definitely infringed on political matters. Already there was "serious" liberal agitation in the Papal States. No accord should defer to revolutionary tendencies.[16] At this time Colloredo was presenting Antonelli with a *mémoire* on the customs union which Bruck so much wanted. The cardinal promised to appoint a commission to study the problem, but he noted that there would be problems for some industries sponsored by the government. In some disgust, Colloredo mused that the papal administration was repelled by anything new and disliked any kind of precise engagement. There would be the traditional caution and hesitation.[17]

Francis Joseph and Buol tried to reassure the curia without hiding their own convictions that change was imperative. The papal contribution to the upkeep of Austrian forces was cut by 30,000 florins monthly. Buol denied that his sovereign had asked him to make representations of a reformist nature to the papal government, since it was recognized that these would not be conducive to the prosperity and tranquillity of the pope's subjects. In an audience Francis Joseph declared that the pope was the best judge of reforms. He could count on Austrian support in every circumstance, though the Austrian ruler confessed that he had to be most circumspect with the French, whose designs in Italy were rather mysterious and not without danger.[18]

In time Vienna commented on the French proposals, and a comparison of the differing points of view is of interest. The Council of State, in the Austrian view, was to examine and discuss proposed laws and administrative regulations which had been submitted by the government. The French wanted the Council to elaborate and edit such propositions. Vienna wanted the councillors to be ecclesiastic as well as lay, while Paris recommended that at least fifteen of the twenty-five be laymen. There was no basic disagreement on the pope's right to name and dismiss his ministers or their right to sit on the Council of State. Both powers would have left to the pope a final decision on the dispositions arrived at by the councillors.

Both powers suggested *Consulte* to deal primarily with fiscal and commercial affairs. The French wanted them elected by the provincial councils, while the Austrians believed they should be appointed by the pope from candidates presented by the provincial councils.

The Austrian formula declared that the *Consulte* would examine and give advice on the budget. The French would have given these bodies the right to vote the budget. Both empires wished the restoration of the municipal councils in accordance with the edict of November 24, 1850, but only the French believed that these local bodies should elect directly the members of the provincial councils. Austria preferred that the pope pick the provincial councillors from men nominated by the municipal councils.

Napoleon III wanted a general amnesty with few exceptions, the abolition of extraordinary commissions, and the quashing of trials still pending. The Austrians would have avoided mention of a general amnesty. Francis Joseph's influence was obvious in a recommendation of clemency insofar as circumstances permitted for those who demonstrated repentance. Both states emphasized revision and codification of the laws and improvements in tax collection. Vienna added two counsels: reformation of the papal armed forces and papal appointment of the four cardinals destined to preside over the Legations.[19] Though stillborn, the project demonstrated the expected contrast between French impatience and Austrian reserve.

Austrian relations with the Kingdom of the Two Sicilies after the autumn of 1856 reflected as before the southern realm's poor reputation in West European minds. Ferdinand II was increasingly isolated from his subjects and hardly convinced that Francis Joseph was a reliable patron or friend. On the eve of the emperor's extended visit to Lombardy and Venetia, Buol flattered the king for showing his independence. He could consequently issue any pardons he wished, which would facilitate reconciliation and be in the interest of all the parties. Martini was to inform Carafa tactfully that Francis Joseph would amnesty many Lombards and Venetians. The king could then decide on his "opportune moment."[20]

While reviewing a regiment of light cavalry on December 8, 1856, Ferdinand escaped assassination by the timely intervention of his aide-de-camp. One Agesilao Milano had deliberately enlisted with the hope of eliminating the king. A few weeks before this incident, there had been an attempt to suborn hussars in Sicily by Francesco Bentivegna, who had been pardoned for previous political activism. Martini was frustrated, for the king had amnestied more than thirty in November, thanks, the Austrian felt, to Austrian persuasions.

True, he and Carafa refused to publicize these decisions, and after the attempted assassination Martini predicted that the king's angry mood would not soon change.[21]

Ferdinand applauded the Austro-Sardinian breach and talked of an all-Italian league to keep Turin's activities under surveillance. When Buol suggested that he demand prosecution of a provocative Piedmontese journal, however, Carafa declared that it would be useless to complain. Cavour always said that the aggrieved party should go to court.[22] Buol probably was not surprised. In June he admitted to Martini that the king was seemingly out of sorts with Austria and embarrassed by the emperor's acts of grace in Lombardy-Venetia. No Austrian blamed the other Italian princes if they could not be clement. The Austrian Foreign Office continued to preach moderation upon Paris and London and believed it had thereby helped the conservative states, especially Naples. It was difficult, however, to make Ferdinand realize that his manner of government was so unpopular that all foreign comments were alike. His own newspapers did nothing to establish the truth. Martini echoed Buol's verdict. The king was jealous and embittered, less disposed than ever to follow the examples of others, and unable to see the imperatives of the times. Carafa was a fine man, but passive, unproductive, and with no influence upon affairs.[23]

Carlo Pisacane's hijacking of the Sardinian ship *Cagliari* and his unsuccessful attempt to raise the flag of revolt on Neapolitan soil in June 1858 intensified Ferdinand's problems. His fleet seized the vessel and crew, which included two English engineers. All ended in Neapolitan jails, which had a most unsavory reputation in England, and Turin and London demanded release of ship and crew. After some bluster Ferdinand ordered the release of the Englishmen but declined to send the *Cagliari* home. English public opinion stood behind Cavour's protests, however, and the government decided to support a claim for release of the ship and the rest of the crew, plus an indemnity. Since Francis Joseph had counseled moderation and conciliation, the king had not the slightest hope of Austrian remonstrances. Too, the Russians were stressing the need for decent Anglo-Neapolitan relations. In the end the ship was returned and the engineers were awarded damages.[24] Martini's dispatches of 1858 contrasted the signs of economic revival with the evidence of political torpor. Ferdinand made only fleeting visits to Naples, and Felix Wimpffen wrote in August that the land was perfectly tranquil. In case of a serious shock from abroad, however, the king would find himself alone in the midst of his trusty 15,000 Swiss.[25]

Francis Joseph and his ministers had no illusions about the conservative Italian courts. "A serious shock from abroad" would dislodge Leopold as well as Ferdinand, and who could guarantee the integrity of the disaffected papal lands? In the grand melee that might arise, the future of Modena and Parma was even more dubious. Legitimacy was an outmoded concept. The Bourbon and Habsburg states of Italy symbolized international bargains of comparatively recent origin, and the *Realpolitik* of the Crimean era emphasized their transiency. What seemed more durable than their continuing rule was the threat posed by the party of movement on one hand and by Piedmontese ambition on the other.

The Coming of War

THE reaction of the great powers to the breach between Austria and Piedmont in March 1857 was mixed. Clarendon was distinctly upset, while Walewski, uneasy over Cavour's policies, was not eager to join the English in an attempt at mediation. The Russians were not displeased to see the Austrians as frustrated as the Russians had been over the Habsburg occupation of the Danubian Principalities during the Crimean War. Prince Alexander Gorchakov, minister of foreign affairs, sent a secret telegram to his minister in Turin, declaring that the clash in no way impaired his empire's good relations with Piedmont.[1] As the year progressed, Prussia made a serious effort to compose the differences, but both parties seemed disinclined to paper over their disagreements.

Clarendon was harsh in his comments to Henry Wellesley, Baron Cowley, his minister to Paris. Sardinia "could not establish a censorship of the press at the dictation of a foreign Government . . . without a complete loss of national dignity and independence, and the utmost danger to those constitutional principles . . . put in practice." As for the Austrians, they "have not a leg to stand on in this most stupid quarrel . . . it is entirely the Emperor's own doing, and he is as obstinate as a mule when his own personal feelings are concerned." Clarendon admitted that he was not satisfied with Cavour, "who is always making political capital out of his hatred to Austria, and who relies more than he is entitled to do upon the sympathy and the support of England and France."[2] In Paris, Hübner wrote in his diary that the breach was deplorable. Buol's language to Turin was inconceivable. It had wounded and irritated Napoleon III, who would back Piedmont. It was too bad that Vienna did not see the obvious: Cavour wanted the rupture.[3]

On March 20 Walewski expressed concern to Cowley over Cavour's "deep . . . and dangerous game" and Austria's "foolish conduct." Sensing a bid for Anglo-French mediation, Clarendon proposed that the two powers secure from Turin a pledge to respect existing treaties. After a month of frustrating exchanges, he realized that his maneuver was doomed. "We *can't* take up the press part of the question, and the French *won't* take up the treaty part."[4] Buol was polite at the end of April in receiving English admonitions to avoid "all measures which might be of a nature to give offense to the Sardinians" but insisted that the primary condition for the resumption of diplomatic ties was a Piedmontese response to the last Austrian note.[5] A Prussian move to reconcile Turin and Vienna in late July also met with resistance. Buol retailed the usual complaint that Cavour had deliberately courted the breach. More, the Sardinian leader's avowal that the unity of Italy was his goal was hardly consonant with the rights of the king of Lombardy and Venetia.[6]

Orsini's bombs of January 14, 1858, put Cavour in a predicament and gave Vienna hope that outraged Western opinion would put limits upon Piedmontese intransigence. Walewski was critical of the press in Turin and of Mazzini's seeming ability to move in and out of Genoa at will. His note of January 25 was an open invitation to muzzle the press and expel the political refugees. Cavour ordered a reorganization of the police and dispersed or exiled some of the more visible émigrés, but he declined to suppress directly *L'Italia del Popolo*, the journal which the French had singled out.[7] To placate the English, he complained that the papal government was issuing passports to dissidents and criminals who then became conspirators or lawbreakers in Piedmont. He also averred that "a vast number of Lombards have returned home without any evil result having ensued."[8]

Hübner reported from Paris that Cavour's dilatory responses had considerably diminished earlier French sympathies for a greater Piedmont and a constitutional regime in Italy.[9] Buol was delighted. Reality, he wrote Colloredo, was leading France to support the same international principles which Austria had so often invoked, particularly with Turin.[10] He hoped the tough French language would compel Cavour to reappraise his duties to his neighbors and to judge the other governments of Italy with greater forbearance.[11] Buol was in for a severe shock. Napoleon III had Orsini's second letter, aflame with Italian patriotism, transmitted to Cavour, obviously for publication. Its appearance in the official Piedmontese gazette on

March 31 was "a direct assault on Austria, not only on Piedmont's part, but also by the [French] emperor," boasted Cavour.[12]

The Sardinian cabinet had been preparing a more vigorous press law, to crack down on apologies for political assassinations, as well as laws which would increase the penalties for conspiracies against the rulers of foreign states and which would presumably guarantee that the jurors would be picked from responsible elements in society. To persuade a reluctant Chamber of Deputies to swallow the medicine, Cavour delivered one of his great speeches on April 16. He defended Victor Emmanuel's refusal to renounce Charles Albert's aspirations or to go along with England's austrophilism. He had harsh words for "Young Italy" and the man who had inveigled the radical sectaries into one terroristic blunder after another, but his peroration breathed defiance of any pressure beyond conscience itself.[13]

Buol lost his head and penned on April 19 what Hübner called an "incredible dispatch," which virtually demanded a French explanation of Cavour's remarks. To act otherwise, wrote Buol, might create illusions and doubts about the Austrian emperor's unshakable resolve to maintain tranquillity in Italy and to defend, if necessary, the rights, consecrated by treaties, which he had there. Napoleon III was soon telling Hübner that Austro-French relations were sour, for Austria "opposed me in matters great and small." Specifically, he listed the Balkan questions left over from the Crimean settlement and alleged that Count Anton Prokesch von Osten, the Austrian internuncio at Constantinople, constantly advised the Turks to ignore French counsels. When Hübner asked him to reassure the Italian governments in regard to the Orsini letters and Cavour's speech, he declined. He denied he was the revolutionaries' friend in Italy or that he had changed his policy there.[14]

At best the French emperor was telling half the truth. On May 9 he confirmed to Cavour's secret agent that he was willing to join in a war against Austria and convert Piedmont into a kingdom of Upper Italy in return for Prince Napoleon's marriage to Clotilde, daughter of Victor Emmanuel. At Plombières on July 20 he and Cavour agreed to an Italian confederation headed by the pope, to consist of a kingdom of Upper Italy, a kingdom of Central Italy, a Papal State limited to Lazio and Rome, and the Two Sicilies. Piedmont would annex Lombardy, Venetia, Parma, Modena, and the Legations. To provoke Austrian aggression, the two men canvassed possibilities that would absolve them from any accusations that they were trafficking with revolution. Cavour recommended that his king, replying to petitions drummed up in Massa and Carrara, write an unacceptable letter to the duke of Modena, who owned these territories. There would be an impertinent reply, supported by Austria, and war could begin. The French price at Plombières escalated, for the emperor in an offhand manner remarked that the question of Savoy could be arranged later.

In the months that followed, Clotilde acquiesced in what promised to be a distasteful union, and Napoleon III tried to secure a Russian pledge to go along with modifications of the 1815 settlement in Italy. Hints of a Franco-Russian entente, he assumed, would neutralize Prussia. The English government could be counted upon to offer compromises without end, but it was not likely to outrage the opinions of its citizens by taking active measures against Italian nationalism.[15] In December, Cavour reported that he had found a better pretext for war. He would secretly encourage Lombard and Venetian draftees to flee across the Ticino. The Austrians were bound to retaliate.

At about the same time the plan to exchange Lombardy for Wallachia and Moldavia surfaced again. Buol warned that any attempt to barter the emperor's rights in Italy for a Near Eastern settlement would meet with Austria's most decided opposition.[16] Hübner's entry in his diary for December 14 revealed that Napoleon III often hinted at such a solution. The French ruler refused to see that Austria would defend its Italian possessions to the death. He always was hoping to intimidate Francis Joseph, and he was making a complete miscalculation.[17] The famous intimidation was delivered to Hübner at the imperial reception on January 1. "I regret that our relations with your government are not as good as they have been. I beg you to say to the emperor that my personal sentiments have not been changed."

On January 10 Victor Emmanuel told his parliament that Piedmont had become powerful in the councils of Europe "because of the greatness of the ideas she represents, and the sympathies which she inspires . . . . We cannot disregard the cry of anguish which rises to us from so many parts of Italy." The Austrians immediately moved 30,000 fresh troops into Lombardy and revictualed their fleet. Francis Joseph wrote Maximilian that the increase in forces should have a calming effect, though he expected no outburst in the kingdom. Napoleon was playing with fire and might get himself into such a corner that war would be his only way out. Cavour would probably make his strike in Parma. Gyulai had orders, based on the existing military convention, to send troops into the duchy even if they were not requested. The Duke of Modena had promised to speak to the duchess of Parma about combined operations if she could not keep her state under control. He would call for Austrian aid only in case of a foreign invasion.[18]

The rumors of war were especially disturbing to Antonelli and Pius IX, since two of the putative antagonists had troops on papal soil. In January, Napoleon III told the nuncio that, whatever happened, the pope had nothing to fear.[19] Antonelli knew the delicacy of the situation, however, and queried De Luca in regard to an increase, later countermanded, of the garrisons in Ancona and Bologna. The response indicated that Austria would adhere scrupulously to the protocol of 1852 when changing the size of its forces.[20]

In February, Antonelli came to the conclusion that the total evacuation of French and Austrian troops was in the papacy's best interests. Francis Joseph responded that he would be overjoyed if the internal conditions of the Papal States could guarantee the temporal power. Pius IX consequently should initiate the request for Austrian withdrawal. Antonelli promised that the pope would ask both powers to get out, for the occupation had become an embarrassment.[21] Buol notified the English and the Prussians that Austria would honor the pope's petition without reference to what France did. He added that his emperor would never allow London or Berlin to interfere with Austria's particular treaties with Italian states.[22] By the end of February it was clear that the French would recall their reinforcements and that both powers would accede to a papal request for withdrawal. It was equally clear to Colloredo that Antonelli would stall the execution of the rest of the promises made in the motu proprio of Portici.[23] Tension steadily escalated in Turin, Paris, and Vienna during February. Cavour circularized his diplomats on February 4 with a justification of a new bond issue. Extraordinary Austrian military measures forced Turin to take protective measures. Whether disorders might erupt thanks to Austria or to revolution, Sardinia stood ready to combat them. At about the same time Buol appealed to all the German states to unite against either Sardinia or France. Prussia significantly responded by decrying talk of war, especially over the administration of the Papal States, and by pledging to work against a clash in both Paris and Vienna.[24] When Hübner indicated that Austria could not well ignore an insurrection of foreign inspiration in Parma or Modena, Walewski recommended that Vienna consider well the grave consequences which might follow a military intervention.

In a dispatch of February 25 to London, Buol defended Austria's right to aid Italian states with whom it had treaties and implied that Piedmont was evading a pledge to honor the existing frontiers in Italy. There were defects in the administrations of central and southern Italian governments, but improvement could come only after their independence was guaranteed.[25] "Off the record" Cavour was telling Henri-Godefroi de La Tour d'Auvergne, the French minister, that he was upset by the papal demand for total evacuation. If the Austrians departed, he would lose the best argument he had in winning over European opinion.[26]

It seemed wiser to denounce the Austrian administration of Lombardy and Venetia, which he did in a note of March 1 to the English and Prussian governments. The immense majority in the kingdom had an invincible repugnance for their governors, thanks to bureaucratic pedantry, unbearable taxes, the most rigorous system of conscription in Europe, and violence that did not even spare women. To avoid war or revolution, the Austrians should grant these lands a national and separate government and end their domination of the central Italian states. Modena and Parma should proclaim institutions comparable to Piedmont's, and the grand duke of Tuscany should restore the constitution of 1848. The Austrians should withdraw from the Romagna, and the pope should make administrative changes.[27]

Two days later the Austro-Sardinian commission which was to plan the linkup of railway lines near Buffalora broke up after fifteen sessions. The English sent Cowley to Vienna to attempt a settlement of the bitterness, but Marquis Gaston de Banneville, the French chargé, reported that Francis Joseph and his military entourage had become rigid in their opposition to any conciliatory moves. They had come to the conclusion that Napoleon III was determined to end the Austrian domination in Italy. The Austrian ruler's dignity did not permit any discussion of the treaties with the Italian states, and both public and government were eager for a solution, good or bad.[28]

Cavour was arguing that Austria's signing of the conventions of December 24, 1847, with Parma and Modena had deprived it of the right to pose as a defender of the settlement of 1815. If Austria could move in to thwart foreign aggression or internal disturbance, there was no sense in speaking of a balance agreed to at the Congress of Vienna. Buol refused to discuss the conventions with Cowley, and he warned the rulers of the duchies to yield nothing to Peter Scarlett, the chargé whom London had sent to Parma and Modena. His mission reflected an English supposition that Austria was not adamant about the treaties but wished to save face. If the tiny states unilaterally denounced the agreements, there would be a decrease in tension. By March 23 Buol could remit to Paar his feeling of satisfaction that the duchies had turned down Scarlett.[29]

The same day he reminded Tuscany of the treaty of June 12, 1815, which allied that state with Austria in case of a general Italian war. It would be well for the grand duke's government to prepare in silence the necessary measures, which included a contingent of at least 6,000 men.[30] A similar message went to Naples. What steps could be taken to honor the treaties of 1815 and 1819?[31] Antonelli had already formalized on March 11 a request for total evacuation in the course of the current year. Carlo Sacconi, the papal nuncio in Paris, suggested that both powers pledge they would not attack each other's forces on papal territory should war break out.[32]

Antonelli was more worried over a Russian proposal of March 18 for a congress that would settle Italian problems. The tsar had finally agreed to a treaty of March 3 with France that secretly and vaguely seemed to promise benevolent neutrality while the French were engaged in a war in Italy. Alexander II wished to avoid an embroilment with Prussia while hoping for Austria's humiliation. Too, a congress might ventilate the question of revising the Bessarabian and Black Sea clauses extracted from him in 1856. When Cavour learned that Piedmont would be excluded from such conferences, he warned Paris that overexcited persons might be driven to violence and acts of despair.[33] Buol was under no illusions as to the losses Austria and its clients would suffer at the hands of resentful Russia and Prussia and high-intentioned England and France. Before Austria would attend, Sardinia would have to disarm. Turin's countermove was a demand for a seat at the congress, withdrawal of Austrian and Sardinian forces from their common frontier, and general disarmament. There was talk of allowing the Italian states to send plenipotentiaries who would join discussions of direct relevance to their interests, but Buol counseled the conservative Italian courts to reject a concept "derogatory to the dignity of an independent and sovereign state."[34] The king of Naples concurred, and Antonelli announced that the pope would not allow himself to be summoned by other governments, especially non-Catholic, to answer for his system of government.[35] A more ominous message came from Florence. Lenzoni wished to secure Austria's permission to remain neutral. Thanks to Piedmontese propaganda, the small Tuscan army would go over to "the enemy" if ordered to fight alongside Austria. Hügel admitted to Buol that the Tuscan minister's fears were all too well justified. Young men were leaving to enroll in Victor Emmanuel's army, and clandestine appeals for a war of independence were multiplying. In regard to the Austrian suggestions to boycott the congress, the Tuscans noted that they had not received a proposal to send delegates.[36]

During these days Austrian policy toward the conservative Italian courts underwent quite a change. On April 3 Buol recommended to the rulers of Modena and Parma that they suppress Article III of the conventions, which obligated Austria, whether summoned or not, to move in to restore order in case of revolutionary activity. It would be preferable to reserve to Austria the right to come to the aid of the ducal rulers, who could continue to rely on the emperor's benevolent friendship. On the same day he asked Naples to agree to the abrogation of Article II of the secret treaty of June 12, 1815. This, if left intact, would have compelled the king to send a contingent to help Austria. If Naples declined to repudiate this clause and if the question should arise at a congress, the Austrians would announce unilaterally their refusal to avail themselves of the promise.[37] The volte-face alarmed the ducal rulers, while the dying ruler of the Two Sicilies took some time to respond. Forni declared in Modena that his ruler could not in conscience agree to the modification. Should a change be inevitable, he would not make claims that would intensify the existing complications.[38] Pallavicino concluded that suppression of the article would transform *security* to *trust* "for us," *obligation* to *favor* as far as Austria was concerned. It might be better to annul the entire convention and allow the Parmese to chance "the refuge of neutrality." Both rulers were advised that the emperor hoped they would see that the renunciation of Article III, not of the entire treaty, was the best way to avoid complications. Austria still would assure protection against internal trouble.[39]

The Tuscan inclination to neutrality seemed ill-advised to Buol. Austria did not need 6,000 men, but the grand duke could not compromise himself a second time. Hügel predicted privately to Buol that no one in Tuscany would lift his hand or his voice for Austria. At the moment war should break out, the grand duke would be on his way to exile. The army would fight neither the Sardinians nor the French. On April 16 Hügel cornered the ruler with the report that Tuscany would declare its neutrality. Leopold confessed that he would have to annul the treaty with Austria. He needed all of his troops to hold out against Piedmontese revolutionary activity. The envoy invoked the shade of Maria Theresa and the painful memories of 1848–49 in a conversation that lasted two and a half hours, and he had some hope the grand duke would remember his duty and his honor.[40]

In Vienna the emperor and his closest advisers were approaching a decision on war or peace. In a conference of April 6 Francis Joseph asserted that Napoleon III would use the time taken up by the congress to complete his preparations and to find an excuse for hostilities. He and Buol insisted there had to be disarmament of Piedmont and France before Austria would attend such a parley. When the ruler raised the question of a preventive attack that would destroy the Sardinian army before the French could intervene, Grünne and Feldzeugmeister Heinrich Baron von Hess warned that an ultimatum to Turin could put the empire in a serious dilemma. It would strip the emperor of allies. Was it possible financially to

establish a Rhine as well as an Italian front? Bach retorted that
public opinion would not accept continuing provocations and insinuations from Piedmont and France. With Austria's many military
resources, there was no reason to fear the French. Grünne stressed
the demands of a great war, but Bruck argued that the emperor
could yield no more. The present unendurable relations with
Piedmont had to end as quickly as possible. The unanimous decision
was to prepare for a major campaign and to send reinforcements to
Italy.

To ascertain Prussian intentions, Francis Joseph sent Archduke
Albrecht to Berlin on April 12, but Prince Regent William favored
the congress and discouraged the idea of directly challenging Turin.
Buol was pressing for an ultimatum, especially in view of his belief
that France was seeking a way out of the complication. At the
decisive ministerial conference of April 19 the emperor was in full
agreement, despite the lack of a pledge from the Hohenzollerns.
Was the ultimatum ready? Was it time to dispatch it to Turin? If the
reply should be negative, should Gyulai attack? Hess and Grünne
predicted a French response on both land and sea, and the former
wanted a blow along the Rhine to prevent France from aiding Sardinia and the revolution in Italy. They and Feldmarschall Leutnant
Karl Baron Schlitter urged immediate mobilization, but Buol
demurred. It was better to hold off until the French decision was
known. Francis Joseph ended the discussion by declaring he would
send a courier to Turin that very day.

Meanwhile Napoleon III, fearful of Prussia, ordered Cavour to
accept a British proposal which would guarantee Piedmont a seat at
the congress in return for disarmament. On April 19 Cavour gave
in. Two days later Europe heard of the Austrian ultimatum, which
two emissaries delivered to Cavour on April 23. He allowed the three
days' limit to expire and then rejected the demand to restore his
army to peace-footing and to disband the volunteers who were
gathering. On April 27 Francis Joseph and his counselors agreed on
an immediate offensive. Grünne, obviously upset, spoke of "finding
ourselves in a catastrophe," and he protested Buol's assumption that
Prussia, the rest of the German states, and England would declare
for Austria. The emperor ended the embarrassing exchange with
the statement that honor and duty left no doubt as to the decision to

take. Gyulai would receive the order to begin the attack against the Sardinians and the French allied with them.[41]

The same day a quiet revolution swept Leopold II from power. He tried to salvage his position by accepting the tricolor and allying Tuscany with Piedmont, but the leaders of the insurrection insisted upon his abdication, with the idea of compelling his son to ratify the change in foreign policy. Hügel, professing horror at such perfidy, insisted that the entire family depart, and he succeeded.[42] Toward evening four coaches took the Tuscan Habsburgs through impassive crowds to Bologna and eventual exile in Austria. On April 29 Austrian troops invaded Piedmont. On May 3 Napoleon III announced he would come to Victor Emmanuel's defense.

Throughout the month of May, Antonelli agonized over the chances that one of the occupying powers would find an excuse to attack the other. At the same time he fretted that the departure of sizable contingents from either corps would leave the curia at the mercy of pro-Piedmontese elements. On May 7 he protested that the Austrians in Ancona, without consultation, had imposed the state of siege and had shut down the lighthouse. They also were working on the fortifications despite the French promise to respect neutrality. Next day he telegraphed that the French would bombard the port if the Austrians did not end such activities. Buol quickly promised Austrian neutrality in the Papal States, and Francis Joseph decreed that nothing further would be done at Ancona. If the French kept their pledge, no change would be made in the garrisons of Bologna, Ancona, or Ferrara. When De Luca questioned Count Johann Bernhard von Rechberg und Rothenlöwen, who had succeeded the unlucky Buol on May 15, as to whether part of the garrison in Bologna would go to the relief of a threatened Modena, he received assurance this would not happen. Francis Joseph fully expected in return that the French and their allies would do nothing to breach the guarantees.[43]

Cavour had qualified his promise to respect the integrity of papal territory in his note of May 16. Piedmont wanted and expected to observe neutrality but could not agree to the areas of occupation still accorded Austria. More, Turin wanted a promise that the occupying Austrians would not move from their bases into Modena and Tuscany. Austria on the other hand wanted a more explicit pledge from Cavour, which did not come.[44] Austrian disappointments, if not surprises, were on the increase.

At the end of April the Two Sicilies announced neutrality. Buol was not pleased, but Petrulla gathered that Francis Joseph understood the state's need to keep its army at home on guard against Napoleon III or the subversives.[45] On May 22 Ferdinand II died. The Austrians had never counted on him and they were just as dubious of the duchess of Parma. On May 15 Paar relayed the news that her cabinet was frightened by Sardinian arguments that Modena was a belligerent because the duke allowed imperial troops to pass through his territory. Parma would protest if this should happen within Parmese frontiers. The duchess wanted Vienna to know that she would maintain neutrality. Rechberg replied that the emperor wished to avoid adding to Parma's embarrassments. Neutrality was most dangerous, however, for France and Sardinia would ignore such a declaration. Austria would have to uphold the convention against foreign aggression and internal disturbance.[46]

Francis V of Modena alone remained loyal. Sardinian troops had seized Massa and Carrara on April 28, and he had sent his consort away on April 30. As long as some Austrians remained in Bologna and Ancona, he had a degree of security. In early June a French frigate appeared in the harbor at Ancona, asking to be received in peace. Antonelli notified Vienna that neutrality compelled him to answer affirmatively. If he refused, there would be terrible consequences, including probably a French attack on Ferrara.[47] De Luca asked permission for a special convention between the commander of the Austrian garrison and the French ship's captain, but Francis Joseph declined. Neutrality called for total absence of contact between belligerents. Since there was no uniform recognition of papal neutrality, the emperor could only retire his troops from Bologna. On June 11 he carried out the threat.[48] As soon as the Austrians left the city, revolution broke out.

A disconsolate De Luca listed the grievances which had persuaded Francis Joseph to leave the Papal States to their fate. Cavour's reservations, the departure of armed volunteers and deserters to join the Piedmontese, the provisioning of French ships in papal ports outside the French *rayon*, and the threat of a French descent on Ferrara made an Austrian withdrawal imperative.[49] On June 9 Louise Marie released her troops from the oath of allegiance, suggested the nomination of a governing commission, and betook herself from Parma. Two days later Francis V instituted a regency and deserted Modena for Mantua.⁵⁰ A well-prepared Austrian army had not won at Magenta on June 4, thanks to, in Hübner's words, Gyulai's "pyramidal incompetence," and there was a second reverse at Solferino on June 24. They were still capable of a good fight, however, and Prussia mobilized the day of Solferino. Napoleon's quick victory was not forthcoming, and he proposed an armistice to Francis Joseph. At Villafranca the two agreed that Lombardy, minus Mantua and Peschiera, should be ceded to France as preliminary to its transfer to Victor Emmanuel. Venetia would remain under the Habsburgs, and the rulers of Parma, Modena, and Tuscany were to be restored, without the use of force and if they granted full indemnity to their subjects. There would be an Italian federation, under the pope and including Venetia. A European congress would confirm the new arrangements.

Thoroughly outraged, Cavour resigned. Representatives of the three former combatants met in Zurich to ratify on November 10 what had been decided upon at Villafranca. Meanwhile, in August and September, constituent assemblies in Modena, Florence, Bologna, and Parma voted the deposition of their former masters and declared their union with Piedmont. This Napoleon could not permit, but the liberal fusionists raised 30,000 men in central Italy to warn off Austria and the exiled royalty. A Piedmontese, Boncompagni, functioned as "governor of the united provinces of central Italy," but the assemblies actually were in control. In December a French pamphlet, *The Pope and the Congress*, infuriated the Austrians, who rightly detected in its arguments Napoleon's willingness to have the pope despoiled of everything save Rome. There was no more talk of a congress, and Cavour returned to office on January 20, 1860. A year earlier he had formally promised Nice as well as Savoy to the emperor in return for what Sardinia was promised at Plombières. If Venetia now was beyond grasp, what of central Italy? It was clear that force alone could bring back the Bourbons and the Habsburgs.

England suggested plebiscites in Tuscany and Emilia, and Austria, reluctant to challenge London and Paris, made a formal but perfunctory protest. The vote was overwhelmingly for union with Piedmont, whose king signed the appropriate decrees on March 18 and 22. Napoleon III forced the disclosure of the cession of Savoy and Nice on March 24, and in April the inhabitants proved by ballot they would be happy to be French. When Victor Emmanuel opened parliament on April 2, he spoke to deputies from Tuscany, Emilia, and the Romagna as well as to those from his inherited lands. Austria's last decade of predominance in Italy was at an end.

Conclusion

FRANCIS JOSEPH inherited from Maximilian and Charles V the compulsion to dominate Italy and from more remote ancestors a Germanic affection for the land where the lemon trees bloom. The years of the French Revolution and of Napoleon I's hegemony had induced a restlessness among Italians, already disenchanted with alien rule, and the settlements arrived at in 1815 thrust upon them the figure of the Austrian whitecoat as the archetypal barbarian Machiavelli had cursed. Whenever the restored rulers were threatened, their pleas for succor went to Vienna.

Of the peoples of the empire, only the Magyars surpassed the Italians in their frustrations over the debacle of 1849, and both had to endure for some years the treatment accorded rebels. Radetzky's relatively easy victory at Novara did not efface from Schwarzenberg's consciousness the belief that rigor should be the order of the day. His sovereign, unbending as only a shaken young man can be, detested the relatives who had thrown in with the revolution and was contemptuous of a pope who had discarded, even briefly, the church's neutrality.

Schwarzenberg nevertheless was shrewd enough to realize that the old order was irrevocably compromised. As long as Victor Emmanuel and Azeglio held fast to their *Statuto*, the other Italian states were obliged to provide decent administration and fiscal probity. Beyond the western Alps lay France, where the possessing classes were increasingly willing to accept authoritarianism in return for efficiency and order. Since Louis Napoleon's sympathy for the Italian nationality was no secret, Austria and its Italian allies dared not allow the party of movement to capitalize on ineptness and neglect. The struggle with Prussia over the destinies of Germany and English officiousness in Italy distracted Schwarzenberg, but only his premature death and Francis Joseph's prompt imposition of full ascendancy over his ministers delayed a more conciliatory policy in

Lombardy and Venetia and more positive admonitions to the conservative courts.

The Milanese rising of February 1853 was of no real consequence, but an embarrassed Radetzky and an immature monarch exacted reprisals in the form of sequestration of émigré property. The taunts of the Piedmontese press and that kingdom's solicitation of England and France for protection against Austria excuse Francis Joseph to a degree. No one in Vienna, however, should have credited the emigration with the means and the organization to plot an insurrection. Austria stood condemned as a bully and, as the Mantuan trials proceeded, as a tyrant. Lombards and Venetians suffered death and foul prisons, but their agonies turned opinion in England and France against Habsburg predominance in the peninsula.

Conditions in the satellite states and in the papal and Neapolitan lands added nothing to Austria's image. Florence might be a most pleasant city for tourists and expatriates, but Baldasseroni's competence did not obscure Leopold II's fecklessness. Francis V's dream of an Italian confederation had come to naught, and the intermittent troubles at Massa and Carrara pointed up the artificiality of his dukedom. The regent of Parma trusted not in Austrian advice or soldiery, but her courting of public favor meant more to Victoria and Albert than to her son's subjects. No Austrian diplomat believed that any of the three could survive a crisis without armed Austrian intervention. In Rome, Esterházy would cling to Antonelli as Austria's best friend, but Buol and Colloredo were aghast over the unending infelicity of papal administration. Their suggestions fell on barren ground, and their impotence was compounded by the influence which the French possessed in the curia. Gladstone's philippics against Ferdinand of the Two Sicilies were no revelation to the Ballhausplatz, but, again, the possibility of English and French expeditions discouraged Buol and Francis Joseph from making explicit recommendations for reform. Given the king's character, nothing short of an Austrian invasion would have forced fundamental changes. Such a move was inconceivable, and, by indirection, Austria unfairly won the reputation of being Ferdinand's éminence grise.

The Crimean War and its complications stripped Austria of

reliable friends in the chancelleries of the great powers, while the Congress of Paris in fact arraigned the empire for poor judgment in Lombardy-Venetia and seeming collusion with the papal and Neapolitan regimes. Francis Joseph knew he had to risk his skin by a progress through the kingdom, and he forced Maximilian to take up the direction of civil affairs there. The younger Habsburg's diligence and finesse alarmed Cavour without winning over anything like a commanding part of aristocratic or bourgeois sentiment. Buol and his colleagues directly assaulted his recommendations for a believable representative system and won the emperor to their point of view, possibly because Francis Joseph was already convinced that no change would keep the French out of Lombardy or diminish the hostility of the noble and the well-to-do.

These pages may seem to slight Cavour, but there is no intention to discount his ability to vitalize his country, win the plaudits of the West, and play upon the sensibilities of a man like Napoleon III. Buol's dispatches and Francis Joseph's letters indicate they knew his measure. Almost to the end, Buol assumed that he could stave off an unassisted war with the French. Francis Joseph concluded, however, that honor and duty required the use of cold steel when a neighbor of hostile intent wiggled out of pledges to behave decently. In time he learned greater patience without losing his own standards of value. The war of 1859 compelled him in a very few years to make a reckoning with the Magyars. In the same period he made his peace with constitutionalism, recognized Polish supremacy in Galicia, and acquiesced in the discontinuance of the concordat. With Taaffe in the 1880s, he temporarily appeased the Czechs and introduced social insurance. In his last years he opted for universal manhood suffrage in Austria and threatened momentarily to impose it upon Hungary when his prerogatives as supreme war lord seemed to be encroached upon.

He was only twenty-nine when he decided that Cavour had to knuckle under or be attacked. Buol had misread the diplomatic auspices, and authoritative voices within the highest military circles had warned that a full-scale campaign would be a dubious undertaking. There was no promise whatsoever of Prussian aid and not the slightest likelihood that the armies of Tuscany, Modena, or Parma would be anything but potential foes. Francis Joseph bears the chief blame for the loss of Lombardy and the end of Austrian prestige in Italy in 1859–60.

One man, even three men like Cavour, Napoleon III, and Francis Joseph, cannot encompass great shifts in power independently of social and economic factors. Tuscans, Sicilians, and Romans would learn to despise the carpetbaggers from Piedmont once unity was achieved, but their respect for their own rulers in 1859 was virtually nil. Although most of the world had suffered from economic malaise in the 1850s there was a tendency to contrast Austria's sluggish reactions in the kingdom with Cavour's innovations beyond the Ticino. The victims of Belfiore inspired hundreds of young men to chance a third encounter, and the surety of help from Napoleonic legions made defeat unimaginable. That Italian nationalism has ever triumphed over the sound of the local bell tower or dialect is moot. But a Giuseppe Verdi, who had gratefully accepted a decoration from Marie Louise of Parma before 1848, was the symbol of patriotic fervor in the 1850s. The bulk of the common folk might stand aside from personal involvement in the heroic struggles of 1859–60, but that did not mean they regretted the flight of their princes or the news that Austria had asked for an armistice.

Francis Joseph had experienced his second brush with nationalism. If he had suffered grievous losses in Italy, he also had learned enough to hang on to most of his inheritance until death relieved him of his burdens decades later.

Abbreviations
Notes
Bibliography
Index

Abbreviations

AM	Archiv K. Maximilians von Mexico, Haus-, Hof-, und Staatsarchiv, Vienna.
AMAE	Archive du Ministère des Affaires Etrangères, Paris.
ASR	Archivio di Stato, Ministero degli Affari Esteri, Rome.
ASV, NV	Archivio Segreto Vaticano, Nunziatura di Vienna, Rome.
CL	Copialettere, Archivio di Stato, Ministero degli Affari Esteri, Rome.
DC, AST	Dépêches chiffrées, Archivio di Stato, Turin.
DP, AST	Dispacci politici, Archivio di Stato, Turin.
LM, AST	Lettere ministri, Legazione di Austria, Archivio di Stato, Turin.
MCZ, MKZ, MRZ, RMZ	Die Protokolle des österreichischen Minister-rates, Haus-, Hof-, und Staatsarchiv, Vienna.
PA	Politisches Archiv, Haus-, Hof-, und Staats-archiv, Vienna.
RSR	*Rassegna Storica del Risorgimento.*
Rel. dipl. Aust.-Sard.	*Le relazioni diplomatiche fra l'Austria e il Regno di Sardegna*, Angelo Filipuzzi and Franco Valsecchi, eds.
Rel. dipl. Aust.-SP.	*Le relazioni diplomatiche fra l'Austria e lo Stato Pontificio*, Richard Blaas, ed.
Rel. dipl. Aust.-Tosc.	*Le relazioni diplomatiche fra l'Austria e il Granducato di Toscana*, Angelo Fili-puzzi, ed.
Rel. dipl. Fr.-Tosc.	*Le relazioni diplomatiche fra la Francia e il Granducato di Toscana*, Armando Saitta, ed.
Rel. dipl. GB-Sard.	*Le relazioni diplomatiche fra la Gran Bretagna e il Regno di Sardegna*, Federico Curato and Giuseppe Giarrizzo, eds.

Rel. dipl. Sard.-GB.   *Le relazioni diplomatiche fra il Regno di Sardegna e la Gran Bretagna*, Federico Curato, ed.

Rel. dipl. SP-Fr.   *Le relazioni diplomatiche fra lo Stato Pontificio e la Francia*, Michele Fatica, ed.

Notes

Insurrection, War, and Peace, 1848–1849

1. Gunther E. Rothenberg, *The Army of Francis Joseph* (West Lafayette, Ind., 1976), pp. 17, 19, 25.
2. Count Egon Caesar Corti, *Vom Kind zum Kaiser* (Graz, Salzburg, and Vienna, 1950), pp. 216–17, 241, 274–94.
3. The standard works on Schwarzenberg are Adolph Schwarzenberg, *Prince Felix zu Schwarzenberg* (New York, 1946) and Rudolf Kiszling, *Fürst Felix zu Schwarzenberg* (Graz and Cologne, 1952).
4. For the young Victor Emmanuel, see Antonio Monti, *La giovinezza di Vittorio Emanuele II, 1820–1849* (Milan, 1939).
5. The text of the definitive armistice, Ennio Di Nolfo, *Storia del Risorgimento e dell'unità d'Italia*, 6 (Milan, 1959): 912 and 914 n. 62.
6. *Rel. dipl. Aust.-Sard.*, 1:433–37.
7. Angelo Filipuzzi, *La pace di Milano* (Rome, 1955), pp. 43–49.
8. Howard McGaw Smyth, "The Armistice of Novara: A Legend of a Liberal King," *Journal of Modern History* 7 (1935): 141–82.
9. *Rel. dipl. Aust.-Sard.*, 2:32–34.
10. Ibid., 2:39–41.
11. *Rel. dipl. Sard.-GB*, 2:132–33, 140–42.
12. *Rel. dipl. Aust.-Sard.*, 2:77–78; Monti, pp. 287–88.
13. Filipuzzi, pp. 119–28, 233–36.
14. MRZ 2299, 9 July 1849.
15. *Rel. dipl. Aust.-Sard.*, 2:428–31.
16. Monti, p. 288.
17. Filipuzzi, pp. 345–67.

Schwarzenberg and Azeglio, 1849–1852

1. An excellent portrait is Ronald Marshall, *Massimo d'Azeglio: An Artist in Politics* (London, 1966).
2. *Rel. dipl. Aust.-Sard.*, 3:129–30.
3. Ibid., 3:xii.
4. Eugène de Guichen, *Les grandes questions européennes et de la diplomatie des Puissances sous la seconde république française* (Paris, 1925), 1:479–81.
5. *Rel. dipl. GB-Sard.*, 2:337.
6. Alessandro Aspesi, *I rapporti tra Piemonte e Austria, marzo-novembre 1849* (Turin, 1954), pp. 150–52.

7. *Rel. dipl. GB-Sard.*, 2:335.

8. Brignole to Azeglio, 21 Dec. 1849, DC/83, AST; Brignole to Azeglio, 21 Dec. 1849, LM/54, AST.

9. *Rel. dipl. Aust.-Sard.*, 3:29–33.

10. Ibid., 3:74–76; Brignole to Azeglio, 4 Feb. 1850, LM/90, AST; Azeglio to Brignole, 10 Feb. 1850, DP/64, AST.

11. *Rel. dipl. Aust.-Sard.*, 3:90–103; Brignole to Azeglio, 14 Mar. 1850, LM/119, and 15 Mar. 1850, LM/120, AST; Azeglio to Brignole, 19 Mar. 1850, DP/64, AST.

12. *Rel. dipl. GB-Sard.*, 3:83–93; Azeglio to Brignole, 30 Mar. 1850, DP/64, AST.

13. Revel to Azeglio, conf. E, 18 June 1850, CL/80, ASR.

14. Revel to Azeglio, 1 Aug. 1850, LM/38, AST.

15. *Rel. dipl. Aust.-Sard.*, 3:143–44.

16. Revel to Azeglio, 16 Aug. 1850, LM/48, AST.

17. Azeglio to Revel, 27 Aug. 1850, DP/64, no. 160, AST.

18. *Rel. dipl. Aust.-Sard.*, 3:105 n. 1.

19. Ibid., 3:135–38.

20. Revel to Azeglio, conf. B, 16 Aug., and conf. A, 16 Sept. 1850, LM, AST.

21. *Rel. dipl. Aust.-Sard.*, 3:162–67.

22. Azeglio to Revel, 1 Dec. 1850, DP/64, AST.

23. Revel to Azeglio, 13 Dec. 1850, LM/134, AST.

24. Revel to Azeglio, 28 Feb. 1851, LM/174, AST.

25. *Rel. dipl. Sard.-GB*, 4:32–34.

26. Revel to Azeglio, 13 Mar. 1851, LM/180, AST.

27. *Rel. dipl. Aust.-Sard.*, 3:237–40, 242–43; Revel to Azeglio, conf. 18 Oct. 1851, LM, AST.

28. *Rel. dipl. Aust.-Sard.*, 3:257–58.

29. Di Nolfo, *Risorgimento*, 8 (Milan, 1965): 546–56.

30. *Rel. dipl. GB-Sard.*, 3:346–47.

31. *Rel. dipl. Aust.-Sard.*, 3:189–90, 226–27.

32. Ibid., 3:260–61, 267.

33. Azeglio to Revel, 24, 26, 27 Jan. 1852, DP/78, AST.

34. *Rel. dipl. Aust.-Sard.*, 3:271–72.

35. Ibid., 3:288, 289 n. 1.

36. Ibid., 3:296–98, 305–7, 309–10; Revel to Azeglio, conf. 11 May and conf. 11 June 1852, CL/80, ASR; Azeglio to Revel, 1 June and conf. 1 June 1852, DP/78, AST.

37. Guichen, 2:406.

38. *Rel. dipl. Aust.-Sard.*, 3:345–48.

39. Ibid., 3:351, 354–55.

The Kingdom of Lombardy-Venetia and Trieste, 1849–1856

1. Leopoldo Marchetti, "Il decennio di resistenza," in *Storia di Milano*, 14

(Milan, 1960): 501–2; Carlo Pagani, "Ricordi della dominazione austriaca in Italia: L'ordinamento politico amministrativo della Lombardia dal 1848 al 1859," *Rassegna Storica del Risorgimento* 7 (1920): 553–54.

2. MRZ 4838, 26 Dec. 1849.

3. Bruno Caizzi, *L'economia lombarda durante la Restaurazione, 1814–1859* (Milan, 1972), p. 310.

4. MRZ 1954, 7 May 1850.

5. Nicola Raponi, *Politica e amministrazione in Lombardia agli esordi dell'unità* (Milan, 1967), p. 48.

6. Di Nolfo, *Risorgimento*, 8:67; Raponi, pp. 60–61; Marchetti, p. 502.

7. MKZ 994, 22 Mar. 1851.

8. Pagani, pp. 553–54.

9. MRZ 3571, 5 Oct. 1849; MRZ 3735, 14 Oct. 1849.

10. Raponi, p. 24.

11. MRZ 23, 2 Jan. 1851.

12. The basic sources for administration and justice are Raponi, pp. 23–45, and Pagani, pp. 539–48.

13. Friedrich Walter, *Die österreichische Zentralverwaltung*, Abt. III, Bd. I, *1848–52* (Vienna, 1964), pp. 381–85.

14. Luigi Zini, *Storia d'Italia dal 1850 al 1866*, 2, pt.1 (Milan, 1866), p. 41.

15. *Briefe des Feldmarschalls Radetzky an seine Tochter Friederike, 1847–1857*, ed. Bernhard Duhr (Vienna, 1892), p. 96.

16. Aurelio Bianchi Giovini, *L'Austria in Italia e le sue confische* (Turin, 1853), pp. 320, 324, 329–30.

17. MRZ 2240, 2 July 1851; MKZ 2241, 4 July 1851.

18. César Vidal, "Le royaume Lombardo-Vénetien en 1851–53 d'après les dépêches des consuls de France á Milan et á Venise," *RSR* 42 (1955): 489–90.

19. For the imperial trip, see ibid., 490–92; Count Egon Caesar Corti, *Mensch und Herrscher* (Graz and Vienna, 1952), pp. 80–81; Ausano Labadini, *Milano ed alcuni momenti del Risorgimento italiano* (Milan, 1909), p. 38.

20. Raffaele Fasanari, *Il Risorgimento a Verona, 1797–1866* (Verona, 1958), pp. 206–17; Alberto Maria Ghisalberti, "La seconda Restaurazione (1849–52)," in *Storia d'Italia*, 3 (Turin, 1959): 798.

21. Antonelli to Esterházy, 31 Jul. 1852; Radetzky to Esterházy, 10 Aug. 1852; Buol to Esterházy, 18 Aug. 1852, PA XI/195. See William Roscoe Thayer, *The Life and Times of Cavour* (Boston and New York, 1911), 1:251–62.

22. The best treatment of the rising is Leo Pollini, *La rivolta di Milano del 6 febbraio 1853* (rept., Milan, 1953). See also Franco Catalano, *I Barabba* (Milan, 1953); Piero Pieri, *Storia militare del Risorgimento* (Turin, 1962), pp. 540–52; Marchetti, pp. 531–47.

23. Corti, *Mensch und Herrscher*, pp. 105–10.

24. Marchetti, p. 563.

25. C. A. Macartney, *The Habsburg Empire, 1790–1918* (New York, 1969), pp. 484–85; Marchetti, p. 565.

26. *Briefe des Feldmarschalls Radetzky*, pp. 136–37.

27. MCZ 1752, 9 June 1855; Raponi, pp. 27–30.

28. MCZ 3673, 17 Nov. 1855.

29. MCZ 3873, 4 Dec. 1855.

30. MCZ 362, 29 Jan. 1856.

31. MCZ 3853, 28 Oct. 1856; MCZ 3951, 5 Nov. 1856.

32. For educational affairs, see Raponi, pp. 107–9, 144–48; Pagani, p. 567.

33. Raponi, pp. 113–14, 118–19, 122; Marchetti, p. 643; Raffaello Barbiera, *Il salotto della Contessa Maffei* (Milan, 1940), pp. 143–44.

34. MRZ 4835, 24 Dec. 1849.

35. Viale to Antonelli, 12 Mar. 1856, ASV, NV/326.

36. Giuliano Gaeta, "Il 'Corriere Italiano' di Vienna (1850–57) ed il suo redattore," *RSR* 44 (1957): 691–724.

37. Raponi, pp. 126–33, 143.

38. Excellent treatments of the Lombard economy are Bruno Caizzi, *L'economia lombarda* and his earlier "La crisi economica del Lombardo-Veneto nel decennio 1850–1860," *Nuova Rivista Storica* 42 (1958): 205–22; Ira A. Glazier, "Il commercio estero del Regno Lombardo-Veneto dal 1815 al 1865," *Archivio Economico dell'Unificazione Italiana*, 15, lst ser. (Rome, 1961).

39. The best recent surveys of Lombard society are Franco Della Peruta, *Democrazia e socialismo nel Risorgimento* (Rome, 1965), pp. 37–58, and Raponi, pp. 87–105.

40. Barbiera, pp. 139–77; Giovanni Visconti-Venosta, *Ricordi di gioventù* (2d ed., Milan, 1904), pp. 187–90; Anna Maria Canasi, "Tendenze politiche in Lombardia prima e dopo il 1859," *Archivio Storico Italiano* 101 (1943): 123–54.

41. Giovanni Gambarin, "La delegazione veneziana a Vienna nel settembre 1849," *RSR* 44 (1957): 725–30.

42. MRZ 3476, 29 Sept. 1849.

43. MRZ 4686, 17 Dec. 1849; MRZ 4730, 20 Dec. 1849.

44. Gambarin, pp. 731–33.

45. MKZ 601, 22 Feb. 1851; MKZ 974, 21 Mar. 1851; MKZ 994, 22 Mar. 1851.

46. Gambarin, p. 733.

47. Glazier, p. 38.

48. Giovanni Zalin, *Aspetti e problemi dell'economia veneta dalla caduta della Repubblica all'annessione* (Vicenza, 1969), pp. 173–74.

49. Gino Luzzatto, "L'economia veneziana dal 1797 al 1866," in *La civiltà veneziana nell'età romantica* (Venice, 1961), pp. 106–7.

50. Marino Berengo, *L'agricoltura veneta dalla caduta della Repubblica all'unità* (Milan, 1962), pp. 82–88, 162–72.

51. Ibid., pp. 116–24, 337; Zalin, pp. 176–79.

52. Domenico Demarco, "L'economia degli stati italiani prima dell'unità," *RSR* 44 (1957): 195, 211–12; Caizzi, "La crisi economica," p. 209.

53. Macartney, pp. 460–61, 485–86; Caizzi, *L'economia lombarda*, pp. 186–96.

54. MRZ 3035, 1 Sept. 1849; MRZ 3065, 3 Sept. 1849; MRZ 3106, 4 Sept. 1849; MRZ 3152, 7 Sept. 1849; MRZ 3162, 9 Sept. 1849; MRZ 3264, 12 Sept. 1849.

55. Attilio Tamaro, *Storia di Trieste* (Rome, 1924), 2:395.
56. Giulio Cervani, "Un aspetto della vita economica triestina di cento anni fa, attraverso le carte del Barone P. Revoltella relative al Canale di Suez," *RSR* 39 (1952): 495–96; Giorgio Negrelli, "Dal muncipalismo all'irredentismo: Appunti per una storia dell'idea autonomistica a Trieste," *RSR* 57 (1970): 375–76; Angelo Vivante, *Irredentismo adriatico* (rept., Florence, 1954), pp. 27–28; Carlo Schiffrer, *Le origini dell'irredentismo triestino, 1813–1860* (Udine, 1937), pp. 26, 46.
57. Vivante, p. 60.
58. Antonio de' Bersa, *Il consiglio decennale*, 1 (Trieste, 1887): 1, 62–65, 162, 166.
59. Vivante, p. 62 n. 2.
60. Bersa, 1:68.
61. MKZ 260, 24 Jan. 1851; MRZ 3595, 24 Oct. 1851.
62. MRZ 241, 23 Jan. 1852; Bersa, 2:190–92.
63. Negrelli, "Dal municipalismo," pp. 378–79; Bersa, 1:172–73, 2:204–6.
64. Fulvio Babudieri, ed., "I porti di Trieste e della Regione Giulia dal 1815 al 1918," in *Archivio Economico dell'Unificazione Italiana*, lst ser., 14, fasc. 2 (Rome, 1965), pp. 102–4, 137, 189.
65. Alois Brusatti, ed., *Die Habsburgermonarchie, 1848–1918* (Vienna, 1973), 1:315.
66. Tamaro, 2:407–8.
67. Babudieri, pp. 137, 141 n. 2.
68. Bersa, 2:193, 198, 218.
69. Giulio Cervani, *La borghesia triestina nell'età del Risorgimento* (Udine, 1969), pp. 81–82.

Austria, Parma, and Modena, 1849–1856

1. Schwarzenberg to Charles (III), 19 Apr. 1849, PA XI/17.
2. Charles III to Schwarzenberg, 3 Apr. 1849, ibid.
3. Schwarzenberg to Allegri, 31 Dec. 1849, ibid.
4. Charles III to Ward, 30 Apr. 1849, in Jesse Myers, *Baron Ward and the Dukes of Parma* (London, New York, and Toronto, 1938), p. 174.
5. Francis V to Charles III, 19 Nov. 1849, and Charles III to Ward, 23 Nov. 1849, PA XI/17.
6. Allegri to Schwarzenberg, 11 and 14 Mar. 1850, ibid.
7. Allegri to Schwarzenberg, 17 Mar. and reserved, 31 Mar. 1850, ibid.
8. Schwarzenberg to Allegri, 8 Apr. 1850, ibid.
9. Allegri to Schwarzenberg, reserved, 1 Sept. 1850, ibid.
10. Allegri to Schwarzenberg, 14 Feb., 18 May, 20 Jul., reserved, 22 Oct. 1851, PA XI/18.
11. MRZ 3937, 23 Sept. 1850.
12. MRZ 3507, 13 Oct. 1851.
13. Ward to Charles III, 8 Oct. 1851, in Myers, p. 196.

14. Antonio Archi, *Gli ultimi Asburgo e gli ultimi Borbone in Italia, 1814–1861* (Bologna, 1965), pp. 238–39.
15. Myers, p. 199.
16. Allegri to Schwarzenberg, 6 Mar. 1850, PA XI/17.
17. Schwarzenberg to Allegri, 9 Jul. 1850, ibid.
18. Nicomede Bianchi, *Storia documentata della diplomazia europea in Italia dall'anno 1814 all'anno 1861* (Turin, 1865–72), 7:451–57.
19. Archi, p. 100.
20. Corrado De Biase, *Il problema delle ferrovie nel Risorgimento italiano* (Modena, 1940), pp. 142–43.
21. Bianchi, 7:457–60.
22. Buol to Allegri, 7 Dec. 1853, PA XI/18.
23. Lederer to Buol, 21 and 23 Dec. 1853, ibid., 4 Jan. 1854, PA XI/19.
24. Buol to Martini, secret, 26 Jan. 1854, PA XI/7.
25. Martini to Buol, secret, 13 Feb. 1854, ibid.
26. Buol to Martini, secret, 14 Mar. 1854, ibid.
27. Ward to Charles III, 15 and 16 Feb., 23 Mar. 1854, in Myers, pp. 208–11.
28. Lederer to Buol, 8 Apr. 1854, PA XI/19.
29. Buol to Lederer, 17 Apr. 1854, ibid.
30. Pier Luigi Spaggiari, *Il Ducato di Parma e l'Europa, 1854–1859* (Parma, 1957), pp. 28-32.
31. Buol to Grünne, 11 Aug. 1854; Grünne to Buol, 28 Aug. 1854; Buol's *Vortrag* for Francis Joseph, 6 Oct. 1854, PA XI/19.
32. Buol to Lebzeltern, 14 Mar. 1855; Lebzeltern to Buol, 21 and 24 Mar. 1855, PA XI/20.
33. Lebzeltern to Buol, 2 May 1855, ibid.
34. Buol to Lebzeltern, 4 May 1855, ibid.
35. Spaggiari, pp. 42–50.
36. Buol to Lebzeltern, 22 Jan., 5 and 24 May, 10 June 1856, PA XI/21.
37. The correspondence involving Pallavicino, Crenneville, Radetzky, Louise Marie, and Francis Joseph is found in the *Varia* 1856, ibid. See also Spaggiari, pp. 53–60.
38. Buol to Lebzeltern, 1 Jul. 1856; Lebzeltern to Buol, 4 Jul. 1856, PA XI/21.
39. *Documenti relativi al governo degli Austro-Estensi in Modena* (Modena, 1859–60), pp. 221–22.
40. Buol to Lebzeltern, 19 Dec. 1856; Lebzeltern to Buol, 27 Dec. 1856, PA XI/21.

Austria and Tuscany, 1849–1855

1. Achille Gennarelli, *Le sventure italiane durante il pontificato di Pio Nono* (Florence, 1863), p. 46.
2. Archi, pp. 136–63; Sergio Camerani, "Leopoldo II e l'intervento austriaco in Toscana (1849)," *Archivio Storico Italiano* 107 (1949): 62–71.
3. For the original German text, see Giacomo Lumbroso, "L'intervento austriaco in Toscana e l'opera della Commissione Governativa," *RSR* 18 (1931): 345 n. 29.

4. Licurgo Cappelletti, *Austria e Toscana, 1824–1859* (Turin, 1918), p. 231.

5. Gennarelli, *Le sventure*, pp. 52–55.

6. *Rel. dipl. Aust.-Tosc.*, 1:25–26.

7. Cappelletti, pp. 255–65.

8. Ibid., p. 274; Di Nolfo, *Risorgimento*, 7 (Milan, 1960): 178–79, 182.

9. *Rel. dipl. Aust.-Tosc.*, 1:91, 93–94; Di Nolfo, *Risorgimento*, 7:188–90.

10. *Rel. dipl. Aust.-Tosc.*, 1:116–21.

11. Filipuzzi, pp. 304, 307.

12. *Rel. dipl. Aust.-Tosc.*, 1:132–37; *Rel. dipl. Fr.-Tosc.*, 1:269.

13. Arnaldo D'Addario, "Problemi della politica estera toscana dal maggio 1849 all'aprile 1850," *Rassegna Storica Toscana* 2 (1956): 17–20.

14. *Rel. dipl. Aust.-Tosc.*, 1:175.

15. Achille Gennarelli, *Epistolario politico toscano* (Florence, 1863), pp. 203–10.

16. *Rel. dipl. Aust.-Tosc.*, 1:182–83, 185–88, 191–96.

17. Ibid., 1:234–37.

18. On the initial negotiations, ibid., 1:236, 243, 249–53, 278–79, 312–16, 326, 339–40, 402–6.

19. Ibid., 1:284–86, 331–34, 347–48, 365–66.

20. Ibid., 2:35–40, 70–72, 76–79, 104–5, 131–33; D'Addario, 26–30; Di Nolfo, *Risorgimento*, 8:184–85.

21. *Rel. dipl. Aust.-Tosc.*, 2:137–38, 186–89.

22. Ruggero Moscati, *Austria, Napoli, e gli stati conservatori italiani, 1849–1852* (Naples, 1942), p. 113.

23. Note of 13 Sept. 1849, busta 2467, Ministero degli Affari esteri, Archivio di Stato, Florence.

24. Gennarelli, *Epistolario*, pp. 30–31.

25. Giovanni Baldasseroni, *Memorie, 1833–1859*, ed. Renato Mori (Florence, 1959), pp. 125–33.

26. Moscati, *Austria, Napoli*, pp. 116–17.

27. *Rel. dipl. Aust.-Tosc.*, 2:247–52.

28. Moscati, *Austria, Napoli*, pp. 132–38; Di Nolfo, *Risorgimento*, 8:190–94.

29. Moscati, *Austria, Napoli*, pp. 148–71; *Rel. dipl. Aust.-Tosc.*, 2:484, 486–87, 511–21, 3:58–64, 87–88, 107–9.

30. *Rel. dipl. Aust.-Tosc.*, 3:112–14, 137–42, 186–87, 193–97.

31. Di Nolfo, *Risorgimento*, 8:221–22.

32. *Rel. dipl. Aust.-Tosc.*, 3:274–79, 287–89, 295–96, 433–35, 436–37, 453–55.

33. Ibid., 3:289–91, 293–94, 327, 4:35–37, 40, 156–57, 168–69.

34. Ibid., 4:325–26, 329–31, 333–37, 346–47, 351–53.

35. Ibid., 4:387–97, 399.

Austria and the Papacy, 1849–1856

1. Viale to Antonelli, 26 Dec. 1848, ASV, Archivio della Segreteria di Stato, Sezione Esteri 1814–1850/413. See also *Rel. dipl. Aust.-SP*, 1:49–52.

2. Antonelli to Viale, 16 Jan. 1849, ASV, NV/330.

3. *Rel. dipl. Aust.-SP*, 1:58–67, 73–81, 90.

4. Antonelli to Viale, 14 Feb. and 2 Mar. 1849, ASV, NV/330. Francis Joseph quickly had the fine of 200,000 scudi romani assigned to Pius IX (*Rel. dipl. Aust.-SP*, 1:133–34).

5. *Rel. dipl. SP-Fr.*, 2:59.

6. Ibid. 2:65–68, 89–94.

7. Viale to Antonelli, 12 Apr. 1849, ASV, NV/322.

8. *Rel. dipl. SP-Fr.*, 2:117–21.

9. Antonelli to Viale, 7 and 27 May 1849, ASV, NV/330.

10. Viale to Antonelli, 18 May 1849, ASV, NV/322.

11. Moscati, *Austria, Napoli*, pp. 70–71; *Rel. dipl. Aust.-SP*, 1:226–28, 234–35, 260–66.

12. Facsimile of Wimpffen's *Notificazione* to the Bolognese, Di Nolfo, *Risorgimento*, 7:485.

13. Federico Comandini, *Cospirazioni di Romagna e Bologna* (Bologna, 1899), pp. 216–17.

14. Antonelli to Viale, 23 June 1849, ASV, NV/330.

15. Note from Esterházy, 14 July 1849, ibid.

16. Viale to Antonelli, 19 June, 28 Aug., and 6 Sept. 1849, ASV, NV/322; *Rel. dipl. Aust.-SP*, 1:323–25, 369–80.

17. Viale to Antonelli, 12 Sept. 1849, ASV, NV/322.

18. *Rel. dipl. Aust.-SP*, 1:404–8.

19. Roger Aubert, "Antonelli, Giacomo," *Dizionario biografico degli Italiani*, 3 (Rome, 1961): 484–93; Pietro Pirri, "Il Cardinale Antonelli tra il mito e la storia," *Rivista di Storia della Chiesa in Italia* 12 (1958): 81–102; Friedrich Engel-Jánosi, *Österreich und der Vatikan*, 1 (Graz, Vienna, and Cologne, 1958): 46–47.

20. Macartney, p. 444.

21. Schwarzenberg to Esterházy, 29 Jan. and 15 Feb. 1850, PA XI/194.

22. Viale to Antonelli, July 1850, ASV, NV/322.

23. Antonelli to Viale, 16 and 27 July 1850, ASV, NV/331.

24. Engel-Jánosi, *Österreich und der Vatikan*, 1:64.

25. Schwarzenberg to Esterházy, reserved, 8 Aug. and 5 Sept. 1850, PA XI/194.

26. Antonelli to Viale, 9 June 1851, ASV, NV/332; Viale to Antonelli, 14 July; 25 Aug., and 24 Sept. 1851, ASV, NV/323, and 31 Mar. 1852, ASV, NV/324.

27. German and Italian texts of the protocol of 5 Sept. 1852, ASV, NV/372, pp. 100–115.

28. Viale to Antonelli, 2 and 4 Sept. 1852, ASV, NV/324.

29. Antonelli to Viale, 19 Sept. and 21 Oct. 1852, ASV, NV/333.

30. Viale to Antonelli, 3 Nov. 1852, ASV, NV/324.

31. Friedrich Engel-Jánosi, ed., *Die politische Korrespondenz der Päpste mit den österreichischen Kaisern, 1804–1918* (Vienna and Munich, 1964), pp. 29–30, 242, 244–45, 248–49, 273.

32. Esterházy to Buol, 8 July 1852, PA XI/195.

33. Enrico Bottrigari, *Cronaca di Bologna* (Bologna, 1960–62), 2:204–5.

34. Antonio Mambelli, *La Romagna nel Risorgimento* (Forlì, 1960), pp. 161–64; Mario Natalucci, *Ancona attraverso i secoli* (Città di Castello, 1960), 3:165.

35. Aldo Berselli, "La situazione politica a Bologna e nelle Legazioni dal 1849 al 1856," in *Il 1859–60 a Bologna* (Bologna, 1961), pp. 67–69.

36. Mambelli, pp. 161–62.

37. Esterházy to Buol, 25 Feb. 1853, PA XI/196.

38. Buol to Gozze, 31 Dec. 1853, PA XI/195; Gozze to Buol, 25 Feb. 1854, PA XI/196.

39. Antonelli to Viale, 11 July (encoded) and 7 Oct. 1853, ASV, NV/334; Gozze to Buol, 12 Nov. 1853, PA XI/196; Viale to Antonelli, 16 Nov. 1853, ASV, NV/324, and 24 Jan. 1854, ASV, NV/325.

40. Antonelli to Viale, 25 July (encoded) and 5 Sept. 1853, ASV, NV/334.

41. Antonelli to Viale, 9 and 26 Jan. 1854, ASV, NV/335; Gozze to Buol, 4 Jan. 1854, PA XI/196.

42. Antonelli to Viale, 12 Oct. 1855, ASV, NV/336.

43. MCZ 1146, 2 Apr. 1856.

44. Erika Weinzierl-Fischer, *Die österreichischen Konkordate von 1855 und 1933* (Vienna, 1960), pp. 35–36, 40, 56.

45. Antonelli to Viale, 18 Sept. (encoded) and 26 Oct. 1853, ASV, NV/334.

46. Antonelli to Viale, 1 Apr. 1854, ASV, NV/335.

47. Viale to Antonelli, 8 July 1855, ASV, NV/325.

48. Weinzierl-Fischer, p. 76.

49. Viale to Antonelli, 19 Aug. 1855, ASV, NV/325.

50. Viale to Antonelli, 17 Jan. 1856, ASV, NV/326; Antonelli to Viale, 31 Jan. and 13 Mar. (encoded) 1856, ASV, NV/337.

51. MCZ 1321, 12 Apr. 1856.

52. Viale to Antonelli, 19 Apr. 1856, ASV, NV/326.

53. Engel-Jánosi, *Österreich und der Vatikan*, 1:72.

54. *Rel. dipl. Aust.-Sard.*, 4:310.

55. Zini, 2, pt. 1, pp. 540–51.

56. Buol to Colloredo, 8 May 1856, PA IX/197.

57. Viale to Antonelli, 28 June 1856, ASV, NV/326.

58. Antonelli to Viale, most reserved, 10 July 1856, ASV, NV/337.

Austria and the Two Sicilies, 1849–1856

1. Friedrich Engel-Jánosi, "Österreich und der Untergang des Königreiches Neapel," *Historische Zeitschrift* 194 (1962): 62–63.

2. Martini to Schwarzenberg, 9 Oct. 1849, PA XI/4. Petrulla did not actually leave for Vienna until July 1850.

3. Schwarzenberg to Martini, 31 Oct. 1849, ibid.

4. MRZ 2452, 17 June 1850; MRZ 2503, 21 June 1850.

5. Schwarzenberg to Martini, reserved, 25 June 1850, PA XI/5.

6. Martini to Schwarzenberg, reserved, 13 July 1850, ibid.

7. Martini to Schwarzenberg, reserved, 24 May 1850, ibid.
8. Martini to Schwarzenberg, 24 Dec. 1850, ibid.
9. Martini to Schwarzenberg, reserved, 29 Jan. 1851, PA XI/6.
10. Schwarzenberg to Martini, reserved, 8 July 1851, ibid.
11. Schwarzenberg to Martini, 6 Aug. and 26 Sept. 1851, ibid.
12. Martini to Buol, secret, 8 May 1852, PA XI/7.
13. César Vidal, "Le second empire et Ferdinand II de Naples (1852–59)," *RSR* 39 (1952): 837; Salvo Mastellone, "Le carte della Legazione napoletana a Parigi," *RSR* 42 (1955): 602–3.
14. Buol to Martini, 14 Feb. 1854, PA XI/7.
15. Buol to Martini, 2 Aug. 1854, ibid.; Ruggero Moscati, *Ferdinando II di Borbone nei documenti diplomatici austriaci* (Naples, 1947), pp. 150–53.
16. A. J. P. Taylor, *The Struggle for Mastery in Europe, 1848–1918* (paperback, New York, 1971), pp. 67–70.
17. Buol to Martini, 19 Aug. and 9 Sept. 1855, PA XI/8.
18. Buol to Martini, coded telegram 14 Sept. and dispatch 15 Sept. 1855, ibid.
19. Martini to Buol, 16 Sept. 1855; Buol to Martini, 17 Sept., 17 Oct., coded telegrams 18, 19, 21 Oct. 1855; Martini to Buol, telegram 23 Oct. 1855, ibid.
20. Moscati, *Ferdinando II*, pp. 156–57.
21. The best modern résumé is Ennio Di Nolfo, *Europa e Italia nel 1855–1856* (Rome, 1967), pp. 305–10.
22. Wimpffen to Buol, 13 June 1856, PA XI/8.
23. Buol to Wimpffen, 19 July 1856 (with copy of Walewski's note), ibid.
24. Wimpffen to Buol, coded telegram 29 July 1856, ibid.
25. Di Nolfo, *Europa e Italia*, pp. 429–30.

Buol and Cavour, 1852–1857

1. *Rel. dipl. Aust.-Sard.*, 4:27–28; Revel to Dabormida, conf. 12 Jan. 1853, CL/80, ASR.
2. *Rel. dipl. Aust.-Sard.*, 4:35–38; Revel to Dabormida, 26 Jan. 1853, CL/80, ASR.
3. *Rel. dipl. GB-Sard.*, 4:141; *Rel. dipl. Aust.-Sard.*, 4:39–40.
4. Di Nolfo, *Risorgimento*, 8:644.
5. *Rel. dipl. Aust.-Sard.*, 4:46–48.
6. Dabormida to Revel, 8 Feb. 1853, DP/79, AST.
7. *Rel. dipl. Aust.-Sard.*, 4:49–56.
8. Dabormida to Revel, 11 Feb. 1853, DP/79, AST.
9. *Rel. dipl. Aust.-Sard.*, 4:64–65, 73–74.
10. Text, ibid., 4:83 n. 1.
11. Corti, *Mensch und Herrscher*, pp. 105–11.
12. Revel to Dabormida, 7 Mar. 1853, LM/594, AST.
13. Revel to Dabormida, conf. G, 11 Mar. 1853, CL/80, ASR; *Rel. dipl. Aust.-Sard.*, 4:90.

14. Revel to Dabormida, conf. F, 11 Mar. 1853, CL/80, ASR; *Rel. dipl. Aust.-Sard.*, 4:78–80.
15. Dabormida to Revel, 20 Mar. 1853 (no. 557 and conf. letter), DP/79, AST; Revel to Dabormida, conf. 31 Mar. 1853, CL/80, ASR.
16. Text in Franco Valsecchi, *L'unificazione italiana e la politica europea dalla Guerra di Crimea alla Guerra di Lombardia* (Milan, 1939), pp. 63–74.
17. *Rel. dipl. Aust.-Sard.*, 4:121–22, 130.
18. *Rel. dipl. GB-Sard.*, 4:258–59.
19. Cantono to Dabormida, 19 Dec. 1853, DC/AST; *Rel. dipl. Aust.-Sard.*, 4:153.
20. *Rel. dipl. Aust.-Sard.*, 4:169–170.
21. *Le lettere di Vittorio Emanuele II*, ed. Francesco Cognasso (Turin, 1966) 1:423.
22. Cantono to Dabormida, 10 and 14 Dec. 1854, DC/AST.
23. The classic treatment of Sardinia and the Crimean War is Franco Valsecchi, *L'alleanza di Crimea* (2d ed., Florence, 1968).
24. *Rel. dipl. GB-Sard.*, 4:350–52.
25. The unexcelled account of Piedmontese foreign policy, 1855–56, is Ennio Di Nolfo, *Europa e Italia nel 1855–56* (Rome, 1967). The present analysis of Austro-Sardinian relations during that period follows this study, save for details which will be accounted for in notes.
26. Cantono to Dabormida, 7 Jan. 1855, DC, AST; Cantono to Cavour, 31 Jan. 1855, LM/922, AST.
27. *Rel. dipl. GB-Sard.*, 5:94–95, 97–99.
28. For an able analysis of Austrian policy, see Paul W. Schroeder, *Austria, Great Britain, and the Crimean War* (Ithaca and London, 1972), pp. 256–84.
29. *Rel. dipl. GB-Sard.*, 5:136–38; Cantono to Cibrario, 3 Sept. 1855, DC/AST.
30. *Rel. dipl. GB-Sard.*, 5:198–202.
31. *Rel. dipl. Aust.-Sard.*, 4:236.
32. *Rel. dipl. GB-Sard.*, 5:209, 216.
33. Cantono to Cibrario, 2 Jan. 1856, LM/1, AST.
34. Cibrario to Cantono, conf. 19 Feb. and conf. 27 Feb. 1856, DP/82, AST.
35. *Rel. dipl. Aust.-Sard.*, 4:240–41, 246–47.
36. Denis Mack Smith, "Cavour and Clarendon: English Documents on the Italian Question at the Congress of Paris," in Instituto per la storia del Risorgimento italiano, *Atti del XXXV Congresso, Turin, 1956* (Rome, 1959), pp. 242–43.
37. Cantono to Cavour, conf. 13 May 1856, LM, AST.
38. Serre to Walewski, 14 May 1856, Di Nolfo, *Europa e Italia*, pp. 517–19.
39. *Rel. dipl. Aust.-Sard.*, 4:271–72.
40. Cantono to Cavour, 24 May 1856, LM/63, AST.
41. Mossi to Cantono, 18 Feb. 1856, DP/82, AST; Cantono to Cavour, 6 June 1856, LM/67, AST.
42. De Biase, p. 132.

43. *Rel. dipl. Aust.-Sard.*, 4:275–76.
44. Cantono to Cavour, 8 July 1856, DC/AST, 18 July 1856, LM/85, AST, and conf. A, 25 July 1856, LM, AST.
45. De Fortis to Cavour, 13 Sept. 1856, DC/AST, and 1 Oct. 1856, LM/112, AST.
46. *Rel. dipl. GB-Sard.*, 5:335–36.
47. Cantono to Cavour, 4 Dec. 1856, LM/128, AST.
48. Cantono to Cavour, 20 Jan. 1857, LM/6, AST.
49. Cavour to Cantono, 1 Feb. 1857, DP/83, AST.
50. Cavour to Cantono, cabinet letter 4 Feb. 1857, ibid.
51. *Rel. dipl. Aust.-Sard.*, 4:295–97.
52. Cavour to Cantono, cabinet letter 20 Feb. 1857, DP/83, AST.
53. Cantono to Cavour, 4 and 8 Mar. 1857, DC/AST; Cavour to Cantono, telegram 8 Mar. 1857, DP/83, AST; Cantono to Cavour, 10 Mar. 1857, DC/AST.

The Policy of Conciliation in Lombardy-Venetia, 1856–1859

1. AMAE, Autr. 20, Dépêches politiques de Milan, 11 Aug., 29 Nov., 29 Dec. 1855; 14 Jan., 14 Feb., 14 Apr., 12 May, 14 June 1856.
2. *Franz Joseph I in seinen Briefen* ed. Otto Ernst (Vienna, Leipzig, and Munich, 1924), letter of 1 June, 1856, pp. 86–87.
3. Marchetti, p. 584.
4. *Franz Joseph I in seinen Briefen*, letter of 3 Dec. 1856, pp. 92–93.
5. Ibid., letter of 27 Dec. 1856, pp. 94–96.
6. AMAE, Autr. 20, Dépêches politiques de Milan, 15, 18, 19, 26, 28, 30 Jan. 1857; Marchetti, pp. 591–96.
7. AM, carton 83, folder 1.
8. *Franz Joseph I in seinen Briefen*, letter of 4 Apr. 1857, pp. 98–99.
9. AMAE, Autr. 21, 20 and 30 Apr., 14 May 1857.
10. Lina Gasparini, "Massimiliano d'Austria: Ultimo governatore del Lombardo-Veneto nei suoi ricordi," *Nuova Antologia*, 16 Jan. 1935, p. 363.
11. Pagani, pp. 537–38.
12. AM, carton 84, "Rückblick," pp. 3–4. When pages from this manuscript are cited, the numbers are those at the bottom of the pages.
13. AM, carton 88, letter of 9 Sept., telegram of 22 Sept. 1857.
14. AM, carton 84, "Rückblick," pp. 9–14; Marchetti, pp. 606–9; Gasparini, pp. 371–72.
15. AMAE, Autr. 21, Dépêches politiques de Milan, 10 and 14 Nov., 14 and 29 Dec. 1857, 3 Jan. 1858.
16. AMAE, Autr. 19, Dépêches politiques de Venise, 2 Oct., 2, 7, 30 Dec. 1857.
17. Marchetti, p. 613.
18. AM, carton 88, letter of 10 Mar. 1858.
19. Ibid., telegram of 12 Mar. 1858.
20. AM, carton 84, "Rückblick," pp. 20–25.

21. *Franz Joseph I in seinen Briefen*, letter of 19 Mar. 1858, pp. 103–5.

22. AM, carton 84, "Rückblick," pp. 27–28.

23. MCZ 2533, 12 July 1858.

24. AM, carton 88, letter of 12 Sept. 1858.

25. MCZ 2533, 12 July 1858, Beilage; *Franz Joseph I in seinen Briefen*, draft of 17 July 1858, pp. 107–8.

26. AM, carton 87.

27. AM, carton 88, instructions of 12 Sept. 1858.

28. AM, carton 84, "Rückblick," pp. 42–44.

29. Marchetti, p. 621.

30. AM, carton 88, letter of 1 and 22 Nov. 1858.

31. Heinrich Benedikt, *Kaiseradler über dem Apennin: Die Österreicher in Italien, 1700 bis 1866* (Vienna and Munich, 1964), p. 193.

32. AM, carton 88, letters of 3 and 5 Dec. 1858.

33. Marchetti, p. 623.

34. AMAE, Autr. 21, Dépêches politiques de Milan, 29 Dec. 1858.

35. AM, carton 84, "Rückblick," pp. 55–58; and carton 88, letters of 22 and 26 Dec. 1858.

36. *Franz Joseph in seinen Briefen*, letter of 26 Dec. 1858, pp. 110–13.

37. Gasparini, p. 572.

38. Barbiera, pp. 208–9; Marchetti, p. 625.

39. Marchetti, pp. 631–33; AMAE, Autr. 22, Dépêches politiques de Milan, 22 Feb. and 2 Mar. 1859.

40. AM, carton 88, letter to Francis Joseph, 24 Feb. 1859.

41. AMAE, Autr. 23, Dépêches politiques de Venise, 23 Feb., 6 and 9 Mar. 1859; Autr. 22, Dépêches politiques de Milan, 7, 15, and 22 Mar. 1859.

42. AM, carton 83, sketch of telegram 12 Apr. 1859.

43. AMAE, Autr. 23, Dépêches politiques de Venise, 13 Apr. 1859; AM, carton 84, "Rückblick," pp. 65–66.

44. Gasparini, *Nuova Antologia*, 1 Mar. 1935, p. 104.

45. Visconti-Venosta, p. 392.

Austria and the Conservative Italian States, 1856–1859

1. Umberto Marcelli, *Cavour diplomatico* (Bologna, 1961), pp. 289–302.

2. Buol to Paar, 30 May 1857, PA XI/22.

3. Marcelli, pp. 307–21.

4. *Rel. dipl. Aust.-Tosc.*, 5:34–36.

5. Ibid., 5:382–83; *Rel. dipl. Fr.-Tosc.*, 3:82–83.

6. Engel-Jánosi, *Österreich und der Vatikan*, 1:69–70.

7. Buol to Colloredo, 13 Oct. 1856, PA XI/197.

8. Colloredo to Buol, 14 Nov. and 12 Dec. 1856, ibid.

9. Antonelli to De Luca, 30 Jan. and 26 Mar. 1857, ASV, NV/374.

10. Colloredo to Buol, 13 May 1857, PA XI/198.

11. Antonelli to De Luca, 25 Apr. and 11 May 1857, ASV, NV/374; De Luca to

Antonelli, 9 June 1857, ASV, NV/378.

12. Buol to Colloredo, 3 June 1857, PA XI/198.

13. Pietro Pirri, *Pio IX e Vittorio Emanuele II dal loro carteggio privato*, 2,(*La questione romana, 1856–1864*), pt. 2 (Rome, 1951), pp. 31–32.

14. Colloredo to Buol, 18 June and 14 July 1857, PA XI/198.

15. Pirri, *Questione romana*, pt. 2, p. 104.

16. AM, carton 83, letter of 8 July 1857.

17. Ibid., Colloredo to Buol, 14 July 1857.

18. De Luca to Antonelli, 23 Aug. 1857, ASV, NV/378, 14 Apr., 27 Aug., and 30 Sept. (encoded) 1857, ASV, NV/379.

19. Pirri, *Questione romana*, pt. 2, pp. 104–8.

20. Buol to Martini, 4 and 14 Nov. (reserved) 1856, PA XI/8.

21. Martini to Buol, 28 Nov., 11 Dec. 1856, ibid; Moscati, *Ferdinando II*, pp. 176–77.

22. Moscati, *Ferdinando II*, pp. 180–83.

23. Buol to Martini, letter of 3 June 1857; Martini to Buol, letter of 16 June 1857, PA XI/9.

24. Bolton King, *A History of Italian Unity, 1814–1871* (New York, 1899), 2:38–40; Giuseppe Berti, *Russia e stati italiani nel Risorgimento* (Turin, 1957), p. 699.

25. Moscati, *Ferdinando II*, pp. 184–85.

The Coming of War

1. Berti, pp. 693–94.

2. *Rel. dipl. GB-Sard.*, 6:65 (with note).

3. Alexander von Hübner, *Neuf ans de souvenirs* (Paris, 1904), 2:10, 15, 20.

4. *Rel. dipl. GB-Sard.*, 6:411–21.

5. Ibid., 6:96.

6. *Rel. dipl. Aust.-Tosc.*, 5:227–28.

7. Paul Matter, *Cavour et l'unité italienne* (Paris, 1922–27), 3:63–68.

8. *Rel. dipl. GB-Sard.*, 6:182.

9. AM, carton 83, disp. 22 Feb. 1858.

10. Ibid., disp. 1 Mar. 1858.

11. Ibid., Buol to Hübner, 9 Mar. 1858.

12. Matter, 3:74.

13. Ibid., 3:76–82.

14. Hübner, pp. 161–70.

15. For the post-Plombières maneuvering, see Taylor, pp. 103–8.

16. AM, carton 83, Buol to Hübner, 8 Dec. 1858.

17. Hübner, p. 238.

18. *Franz Joseph in seinen Briefen,* letter of 12 Jan. 1859, pp. 113–14.

19. *Il carteggio Antonelli-Sacconi, 1858–60*, ed. Mariano Gabriele (Rome, 1962), 2:14.

20. Antonelli to De Luca, 22 Jan. 1859, ASV, NV/376; De Luca to Antonelli, 29 Jan. 1859, ASV, NV/379.

21. Buol to Colloredo, 12 Feb. 1859, personal letter of 13 Feb. 1859; Colloredo to Buol, personal letter of 12 Feb. 1859, PA XI/199; Colloredo to Buol, telegram (encoded) 19 Feb. 1859, PA XI/200.

22. *La guerra del 1859 nei rapporti tra la Francia e l'Europa*, ed. Armando Saitta (Rome, 1960–61), 1:132–34.

23. Colloredo to Buol, 26 and 27 Feb. (telegram encoded) 1859, PA XI/200.

24. Zini, 2, pt. 2, pp. 30–33, 35, 37–39.

25. *La guerra del 1859*, 1:126, 147–51 n. 1.

26. Matter, 3:158.

27. Zini, 2, pt. 2, pp. 47–56.

28. *La guerra del 1859*, 1:140–42.

29. Franco Valsecchi, "Le convenzioni austriache coi ducati italiani e la preparazione diplomatica della guerra del 1859," in *Atti del XXIV Congresso di storia del Risorgimento Italiano* (Venice, 1936), pp. 475–79.

30. *Rel. dipl. Aust.-Tosc.*, 5:469–70.

31. Buol to Martini, 23 Mar. 1859, PA XI/11.

32. *Carteggio Antonelli-Sacconi*, 2:44–45, 50.

33. Bianchi, 8:472–73.

34. *Rel. dipl. Aust.-Tosc.*, 5:473.

35. Bianchi, 8:475; *Carteggio Antonelli-Sacconi*, 2:66.

36. *Rel. dipl. Aust.-Tosc.*, 5:473–77, 478 n. 1.

37. Buol to Martini, 3 Apr. 1859, PA XI/11.

38. Paar to Buol, 14 Apr. 1859, PA XI/23.

39. Buol to Paar, 21 Apr. 1859, ibid.; Valsecchi, "Le convenzioni," pp. 480–82.

40. *Rel. dipl. Aust.-Tosc.*, 5:484–85 n. 1, 485, 488–89, 492–94, 497–502.

41. Friedrich Engel-Jánosi, "L'*Ultimatum* austriaco del 1859," *RSR* 24 (1937): 1419–25, 1565–80.

42. *Rel. dipl. Aust.-Tosc.*, 5:521–22.

43. Pirri, *Questione romana*, pt. 1, pp. 93–96; Buol to Colloredo, telegram (encoded) 11 May 1859, PA XI/199; Bianchi, 8:494–95.

44. Pirri, *Questione romana*, pt. 1, pp. 74–75.

45. Bianchi, 8:495–96.

46. Paar to Buol, telegram (encoded) 15 May 1859; Paar to Rechberg, 16 May 1859; Rechberg to Paar, telegram (encoded) 18 May 1859, PA XI/23.

47. Antonelli to De Luca, telegrams (encoded) 4 and 5 June 1859, ASV, NV/376.

48. Rechberg to Colloredo, 9 and 11 June 1859, PA XI/199.

49. Rechberg to Colloredo, 13 June 1859, PA XI/199; Pirri, *Questione romana*, pt. 1, pp. 100–102.

50. Archi, pp. 108, 252.

Bibliography

Primary Sources

Archives

Archive du Ministère des Affaires Etrangères, Paris
  Dépêches politiques de Milan, 1855–1859
  Dépêches politiques de Venise, 1857–1859
Archivio di Stato, Florence
  Ministero degli Affari esteri, 1849
Archivio di Stato, Ministero degli Affari Esteri, Rome
  Copialettere, 1850–1854
Archivio di Stato, Turin
  Legazione di Austria
    Dépêches chiffrées, 1849–1857
    Dispacci politici, 1850–1857
    Lettere Ministri, 1849–1857
Archivio Segreto Vaticano, Rome
  Archivio della Segreteria di Stato, Sezione Esteri, 1814–1850
  Nunziatura di Vienna, 1849–1859
Haus-, Hof-, und Staatsarchiv, Vienna
  Archiv K. Maximilians von Mexico, 1856–1859
  Politisches Archiv XI, 1849–1859
  Die Protokolle des österreichischen Ministerrates, 1849–1858

Printed Documents, Letters, and Memoirs

Antonelli, Giacomo Cardinal, and Sacconi, Nuncio Carlo. *Il carteggio Antonelli-Sacconi, 1858–60*, Vol. 2. Ed. Mariano Gabriele. Rome, 1962.
Baldasseroni, Giovanni. *Memorie, 1833–1859*. Ed. Renato Mori. Florence, 1959.
Bianchi, Nicomede. *Storia documentata della diplomazia europea in Italia dall'anno 1814 all'anno 1861*, vols. 7, 8. Turin, 1870, 1872.

Documenti relativi al governo degli Austro–Estensi in Modena. Modena, 1859–60.

Engel-Jánosi, Friedrich, ed. *Die politische Korrespondenz der Päpste mit den österreichischen Kaisern, 1804–1918*. Vienna and Munich, 1964.

Francis Joseph I, emperor of Austria. *Franz Joseph I in seinen Briefen*. Ed. Otto Ernst. Vienna, Leipzig, and Munich, 1924.

Gennarelli, Achille. *Epistolario politico toscano*. Florence, 1863.

_____. *Le sventure italiane durante il pontificato di Pio Nono*. Florence, 1863.

Hübner, Alexander von. *Neuf ans de souvenirs*, vol. 2. Paris, 1904.

Istituto Storico Italiano per l'Età moderna e contemporanea. *Le relazioni diplomatiche fra l'Austria e il Regno di Sardegna*. 3d series: 1848–1860. Vols. 1–2, ed. Angelo Filipuzzi, vols. 3–4, ed. Franco Valsecchi. Rome, 1961–63.

_____. *Le relazioni diplomatiche fra l'Austria e lo Stato Pontificio*. 3d ser.: 1848–1860. Vol. 1, ed. Richard Blaas. Rome, 1973.

_____. *Le relazioni diplomatiche fra l'Austria e il Granducato di Toscana*. 3d ser.: 1848–1860. Vols. 1–5, ed. Angelo Filipuzzi. Rome, 1966–69.

_____. *Le relazioni diplomatiche fra la Francia e il Granducato di Toscana*. 3d ser.: 1848–1860. Vols. 1, 3, ed. Armando Saitta. Rome, 1959.

_____. *Le relazioni diplomatiche fra la Gran Bretagna e il Regno di Sardegna*. 3d ser.: 1848–1860. Vols. 2-5, ed. Federico Curato, vol. 6, ed. Giuseppe Giarrizzo. Rome, 1961–69.

_____. *Le relazioni diplomatiche fra il Regno di Sardegna e la Gran Bretagna*. 3d ser.: 1848–1860. Vols. 2, 4, ed. Federico Curato. Rome, 1955 and 1964.

_____. *Le relazioni diplomatiche fra lo Stato Pontificio e la Francia*. 3d ser.: 1848–1860. Vol. 2, ed. Michele Fatica. Rome, 1972.

Pius IX, pope, and Victor Emmanuel, king of Sardinia-Piedmont. *Pio IX e Vittorio Emanuele II dal loro carteggio privato*, vol. 2, *La questione romana, 1856–1864*, pt. 2. Ed. Pietro Pirri. Rome, 1951.

Radetzky von Radetz, Feldmarschall Josef Wenzl, Count. *Briefe des Feldmarschalls Radetzky an seine Tochter Friederike, 1847–1857*. Ed. Bernhard Duhr. Vienna, 1892.

Saitta, Armando, ed. *La guerra del 1859 nei rapporti tra la Francia e l'Europa*, vol. 1. Rome, 1961.

Victor Emmanuel II, king of Sardinia-Piedmont. *Le lettere di Vittorio Emanuele II*. Ed. Francesco Cognasso. Turin, 1966.

Visconti-Venosta, Giovanni. *Ricordi di gioventù*. 2d ed. Milan, 1904.

Zini, Luigi. *Storia d'Italia dal 1850 al 1866*, vol. 2, pts. 1 and 2. Milan, 1866.

Secondary Sources

Archi, Antonio. *Gli ultimi Asburgo e gli ultimi Borbone in Italia, 1814–1861.* Bologna, 1965.

Aspesi, Alessandro. *I rapporti tra Piemonte e Austria, marzo-novembre 1849.* Turin, 1954.

Aubert, Roger. "Antonelli, Giacomo," *Dizionario biografico degli Italiani*, 3:484–93. Rome, 1961.

Babudieri, Fulvio, ed. "I porti di Trieste e della Regione Giulia dal 1815 al 1918," in *Archivio Economico dell'Unificazione Italiana*, 1st ser., 14, fasc. 2. Rome, 1965.

Barbiera, Raffaello. *Il salotto della Contessa Maffei.* Milan, 1940.

Benedikt, Heinrich. *Kaiseradler über dem Apennin: Die Österreicher in Italien, 1700 bis 1866.* Vienna and Munich, 1964.

Berengo, Marino. *L'agricoltura veneta dalla caduta della Repubblica all'unità.* Milan, 1962.

Bersa, Antonio de'. *Il consiglio decennale*, 2 vols. Trieste, 1887.

Berselli, Aldo. "La situazione politica a Bologna e nelle Legazioni dal 1849 al 1856," pp. 63–91 in *Il 1859–60 a Bologna*. Bologna, 1961.

Berti, Giuseppe. *Russia e stati italiani nel Risorgimento.* Turin, 1957.

Bianchi Giovini, Aurelio. *L'Austria in Italia e le sue confische.* Turin, 1853.

Bottrigari, Enrico. *Cronaca di Bologna*, vol. 2. Bologna, 1962.

Brusatti, Alois, ed. *Die Habsburgermonarchie, 1848–1918*, vol. 1. Vienna, 1973.

Caizzi, Bruno. "La crisi economica del Lombardo-Veneto nel decennio 1850–1859," *Nuova Rivista Storica* 42 (1958): 205–22.

———. *L'economia lombarda durante la Restaurazione, 1814–1859.* Milan, 1972.

Camerani, Sergio. "Leopoldo II e l'intervento austriaco in Toscana (1849)," *Archivio Storico Italiano* 107 (1949): 62–71.

Canasi, Anna Maria. "Tendenze politiche in Lombardia prima e dopo il 1859," *Archivio Storico Italiano* 101 (1943): 123–54.

Candeloro, Giorgio. *Storia dell'Italia moderna*, vols. 2–4. Milan, 1958–64.

Cappelletti, Licurgo. *Austria e Toscana, 1824–1859.* Turin, 1918.

Catalano, Franco. *I Barabba.* Milan, 1953.

Cervani, Giulio. "Un aspetto della vita economica triestina di cento anni fa, attraverso le carte del Barone P. Revoltella relative al Canale di Suez," *Rassegna Storica del Risorgimento* 39 (1952): 495–507.

———. *La borghesia triestina nell'età del Risorgimento.* Udine, 1969.

Comandini, Alfredo. *L'Italia nel secolo XIX*, vol. 3 (1850–59). Milan, 1908–18.

Comandini, Federico. *Cospirazioni di Romagna e Bologna*. Bologna, 1899.

Corti, Count Egon Caesar. *Vom Kind zum Kaiser*. Graz, Salzburg, Vienna, 1950.

——. *Mensch und Herrscher*. Graz and Vienna, 1952.

D'Addario, Arnaldo. "Problemi della politica estera toscana dal maggio 1849 all'aprile 1850," *Rassegna Storica Toscana* 2 (1956): 5–31.

De Biase, Corrado. *Il problema delle ferrovie nel Risorgimento italiano*. Modena, 1940.

Della Peruta, Franco. *Democrazia e socialismo nel Risorgimento*. Rome, 1965.

Demarco, Domenico. "L'economia degli stati italiani prima dell'unità," *Rassegna Storica del Risorgimento* 44 (1957): 191–258.

Di Nolfo, Ennio. *Europa e Italia nel 1855–1856*. Rome, 1967.

——. *Storia del Risorgimento e dell'unità d'Italia*, vols. 6, 7, 8. Milan, 1959–65.

Engel-Jánosi, Friedrich. "Österreich und der Untergang des Königreiches Neapel," *Historische Zeitschrift* 194 (1962): 62–84.

——. *Österreich und der Vatikan*, vol. 1. Graz, Vienna, and Cologne, 1958.

——. L'*Ultimatum* austriaco del 1859," *Rassegna Storica del Risorgimento* 24 (1937): 1393–1425, 1565–1600.

Fasanari, Raffaele. *Il Risorgimento a Verona, 1797–1866*. Verona, 1958.

Filipuzzi, Angelo. *La pace di Milano*. Rome, 1955.

Gaeta, Giuliano. "Il 'Corriere Italiano' di Vienna (1850–57) ed il suo redattore," *Rassegna Storica del Risorgimento* 44 (1957): 691–724.

Gambarin, Giovanni. "La delegazione veneziana a Vienna nel settembre 1849," *Rassegna Storica del Risorgimento* 44 (1957): 725–30.

Gasparini, Lina. "Massimiliano d'Austria: Ultimo governatore del Lombardo-Veneto nei suoi ricordi," *Nuova Antologia* 377 and 378 (1935): 249–68, 353–87, 550–79, 105–31.

Ghisalberti, Alberto Maria. "La seconda Restaurazione (1849–52)," in *Storia d'Italia*, vol. 3. Turin, 1959.

Glazier, Ira A. "Il commercio estero del Regno Lombardo-Veneto dal 1815 al 1865," *Archivio Economico dell'Unificazione Italiana*, vol. 15, 1st. ser. Rome, 1961.

Guichen, Eugène de. *Les grandes questions européennes et de la diplomatie des Puissances sous la seconde république française*, vols. 1, 2. Paris, 1925.

King, Bolton. *A History of Italian Unity, 1814–1871*, vol. 2. New York, 1899.

Kiszling, Rudolf. *Fürst Felix zu Schwarzenberg*. Graz and Cologne, 1952.

Labadini, Ausano. *Milano ed alcuni momenti del Risorgimento italiano*. Milan, 1909.

Lumbroso, Giacomo. "L'intervento austriaco in Toscana e l'opera della Commissione Governativa," *Rassegna Storica del Risorgimento* 18 (1931): 329–48.

Luzzatto, Gino. "L'economia veneziana dal 1797 al 1866," in *La civiltà veneziana nell'età romantica*. Venice, 1961.

Macartney, C. A. *The Habsburg Empire, 1790–1918*. New York, 1969.

Mack Smith, Denis. "Cavour and Clarendon: English Documents on the Italian Question at the Congress of Paris," pp. 235–49 in Istituto per la storia del Risorgimento italiano. *Atti del XXXV Congresso, Turin, 1956*. Rome, 1959.

Mambelli, Antonio. *La Romagna nel Risorgimento*. Forlì, 1960.

Marcelli, Umberto. *Cavour diplomatico*. Bologna, 1961.

Marchetti, Leopoldo. "Il decennio di resistenza," in *Storia di Milano*, vol. 14. Milan, 1960.

Marshall, Ronald. *Massimo d'Azeglio: An Artist in Politics*. London and New York, 1966.

Mastellone, Salvo. "Le carte della Legazione napoletana a Parigi," *Rassegna Storica del Risorgimento* 42 (1955): 602–7.

Matter, Paul. *Cavour et l'unité italienne*, vol. 3. Paris, 1927.

Monti, Antonio. *La giovinezza di Vittorio Emanuele II, 1820–1849*. Milan, 1939.

Moscati, Ruggero. *Austria, Napoli, e gli stati conservatori italiani, 1849–1852*. Naples, 1942.

——. *Ferdinando II di Borbone nei documenti diplomatici austriaci*. Naples, 1947.

Myers, Jesse. *Baron Ward and the Dukes of Parma*. London, New York, Toronto, 1938.

Natalucci, Mario. *Ancona attraverso i secoli*. Città di Castello, 1960.

Negrelli, Giorgio. "Dal municipalismo all'irredentismo: Appunti per una storia dell'idea autonomistica a Trieste," *Rassegna Storica del Risorgimento* 57 (1970): 347–416.

Pagani, Carlo. "Ricordi della dominazione austriaca in Italia: L'ordinamento politico amministrativo della Lombardia dal 1848 al 1859," *Rassegna Storica del Risorgimento* 7 (1920): 533–75.

Pieri, Piero. *Storia militare del Risorgimento*. Turin, 1962.

Pirri, Pietro. "Il Cardinale Antonelli tra il mito e la storia," *Rivista di*

Storia della Chiesa in Italia 12 (1958): 81–102.

_____ . *Pio IX e Vittorio Emanuele II dal loro carteggio privato*, vol. 2: *La questione romana, 1856–1864*, pt. 1. Rome, 1951.

Pollini, Leo. *La rivolta di Milano del 6 febbraio 1853*. Rept., Milan, 1953.

Raponi, Nicola. *Politica e amministrazione in Lombardia agli esordi dell'unità*. Milan, 1967.

Rothenberg, Gunther E. *The Army of Francis Joseph*. West Lafayette, Ind., 1976.

Schiffrer, Carlo. *Le origini dell'irredentismo triestino, 1813–1860*. Udine, 1937.

Schroeder, Paul W. *Austria, Great Britain, and the Crimean War*. Ithaca and London, 1972.

Schwarzenberg, Adolph. *Prince Felix zu Schwarzenberg*. New York, 1946.

Smyth, Howard McGaw. "The Armistice of Novara: A Legend of a Liberal King," *Journal of Modern History* 7 (1935): 141–82.

Spaggiari, Pier Luigi. *Il Ducato di Parma e l'Europa, 1854–1859*. Parma, 1957.

Spellanzon, Cesare. *Storia del Risorgimento e dell'unità d'Italia*, vols. 2, 3, 5. Milan, 1934–50.

Tamaro, Attilio. *Storia di Trieste*, vol. 2. Rome, 1924.

Taylor, A. J. P. *The Struggle for Mastery in Europe, 1848–1918*. Paperback. New York, 1971.

Thayer, William Roscoe. *The Life and Times of Cavour*, vol. 1. Boston and New York, 1911.

Valsecchi, Franco. *L'alleanza di Crimea*. 2d ed. Florence, 1968.

_____ . "Le convenzioni austriache coi ducati italiani e la preparazione diplomatica della guerra del 1859," pp. 475–82 in *Atti del XXIV Congresso di storia del Risorgimento italiano*. Venice, 1936.

_____ . *L'unificazione italiana e la politica europea dalla Guerra di Crimea alla Guerra di Lombardia*. Milan, 1939.

Vidal, César. "Le royaume Lombardo-Vénetien en 1851–53 d'après les dépêches des consuls de France á Milan et á Venise," *Rassegna Storica del Risorgimento* 42 (1955): 489–97.

_____ . "Le second empire et Ferdinand II de Naples (1852–59)," *Rassegna Storica del Risorgimento* 39 (1952): 837–44.

Vivante, Angelo, *Irredentismo adriatico*. Rept., Florence, 1954.

Walter, Friedrich, *Die österreichische Zentralverwaltung*, Abt. 3, Bd. 1, *1848–52*. Vienna, 1964.

Weinzierl-Fischer, Erika. *Die österreichischen Konkordate von 1855 und 1933*. Vienna, 1960.

Zalin, Giovanni. *Aspetti e problemi dell'economia veneta dalla caduta della Repubblica all'annessione*. Vicenza, 1969.

Index